DATE DUE

MY 15 '03			
DE 2 '04			

DEMCO 38-296

GLOBALIZATION, GROWTH, AND GOVERNANCE

GLOBALIZATION, GROWTH, AND GOVERNANCE

Creating an Innovative Economy

Edited by
JONATHAN MICHIE
and
JOHN GRIEVE SMITH

OXFORD UNIVERSITY PRESS
1998

ıt Clarendon Street, Oxford OX2 6DP
rd New York
ok Bogotá Buenos Aires Calcutta
Cape Town Chennai Dar es Salaam Delhi Florence Hong Kong Istanbul
Karachi Kuala Lumpur Madrid Melbourne Mexico City Mumbai
Nairobi Paris São Paolo Singapore Taipei Tokyo Toronto Warsaw
and associated companies in
Berlin Ibadan

Oxford is a registered trade mark of Oxford University Press

Published in the United States
by Oxford University Press Inc., New York

© the Various Contributors 1998

The moral rights of the authors have been asserted

First published 1998

British Library Cataloguing in Publication Data
Data available

Library of Congress Cataloging in Publication Data
Data available
ISBN 0–19–829345–3
ISBN 0–19–829344–5

1 3 5 7 9 10 8 6 4 2

Typeset by Hope Services (Abingdon) Ltd.
Printed in Great Britain
on acid-free paper by
Biddles Ltd,
Guildford and King's Lynn

PREFACE AND ACKNOWLEDGEMENTS

All the following chapters were commissioned specifically for this book and draft versions were discussed at a working conference in June 1997 at Robinson College, Cambridge. We are grateful to the authors for travelling to Cambridge to participate in these discussions, and in particular to Michael Best for travelling from the USA, Bill Lazonick and Mary O'Sullivan for travelling from France, and Mario Pianta for travelling from Italy.

We are grateful to Robinson College for hosting this event. We are also grateful to the contributors to our earlier books *Unemployment in Europe* (Academic Press, 1994), *Managing the Global Economy* (Oxford University Press, 1995), *Creating Industrial Capacity: Towards Full Employment* (Oxford University Press, 1996), and *Employment and Economic Performance* (Oxford University Press, 1997) who kindly agreed that their royalty payments would go to the Robinson College Economic Research Fund which met the remainder of the expenses, and to the contributors to this book for similarly donating their royalties to help fund future such events. We are grateful for their participation to David Connell, David Cormier, Simon Deakin, Charlotte Denny, Ciaran Driver, Vivien Fleck, Geoffrey Gardiner, Elizabeth Garnsey, Laurence Harris, Robyn May, David Musson, Renée Prendergast, Angelo Reati, Brian Reddaway, Andy Robinson, Maura Sheehan, Aubrey Silberston, Giles Slinger, John Smithin, and Romesh Vaitilingam.

Our thanks as editors go to all the authors for the speedy incorporation of points made on their draft chapters; Sandra Dawson, Jane Humphries, and Frank Wilkinson for chairing the sessions at the June 1997 conference; David Musson and Leonie Hayler of Oxford University Press for the speedy turnround of the manuscript; Lesley Haird for typing and other help; and Robyn May for gathering in virus-free disks and other assistance. Our personal thanks for putting up with weekend editing go respectively to Carolyn, eight-year-old Alex, and two-year-old Duncan, and to Jean.

JONATHAN MICHIE
JOHN GRIEVE SMITH

CONTENTS

Part III. GOVERNANCE, BUSINESS PERFORMANCE, AND PUBLIC POLICY

FIGURES

TABLES

CONTRIBUTORS

MICHAEL H. BEST is Co-Director, Center for Industrial Competitiveness, and University Professor, University of Massachusetts, Lowell.

MICHELLE BLAKEBOROUGH was at the Judge Institute of Management Studies, University of Cambridge, and is now with the Personal Investments Authority, London.

KEITH COWLING is Professor of Economics, University of Warwick.

RONALD DORE is at the Centre for Economic Performance at the LSE.

JOHN GRIEVE SMITH is Fellow of Robinson College, University of Cambridge.

JEREMY HOWELLS is at the CRIC ESRC Centre and PREST, Manchester Federal School of Business and Management, University of Manchester/UMIST.

MICHAEL KITSON is Fellow of St Catharine's College and Research Associate, ESRC Centre for Business Research, University of Cambridge.

WILLIAM LAZONICK is Co-Director, Center for Industrial Competitiveness, and University Professor, University of Massachusetts, Lowell, and also at INSEAD.

JONATHAN MICHIE is Professor of Management, Birkbeck College, University of London.

MARY O'SULLIVAN is Assistant Professor, INSEAD.

NICK OLIVER is Reader in Management Studies, University of Cambridge.

MARIO PIANTA is at ISRDS-CNR in Rome and at the University of Urbin.

AJIT SINGH is Professor of Economics, University of Cambridge.

ROGER SUGDEN is Professor of Economics, University of Birmingham.

PETER SWANN is Professor of Economics of Innovation, Manchester Business School and PREST, University of Manchester.

ERIC WOOD is Research Fellow, ESRC Centre for Business Research, University of Cambridge.

ANN ZAMMIT is at the South Centre, Geneva.

INTRODUCTION

The development of new products and processes has always been a major factor in competition between firms. Recently, however, it has increasingly been seen as a key weapon in a competitive struggle between countries or regional blocs. Indeed the rapid spread of technology has been in danger of receiving more attention for its supposed adverse effect on employment in industrialized countries than for its beneficial effects in raising living standards in developing countries. We therefore commissioned chapters for this book which would aim to describe, analyse, and explain these processes, and would also consider what policy responses could and should be being developed.

As with our previous books in this series, *Unemployment in Europe* (Academic Press, 1994), *Managing the Global Economy* (Oxford University Press, 1995), *Creating Industrial Capacity: Towards Full Employment* (Oxford University Press, 1996), and *Employment and Economic Performance* (Oxford University Press, 1997), we are particularly concerned with the implications of the topic for restoring full employment. As long as there is heavy unemployment, advances in process technology are increasingly seen as a spur to downsizing and a threat to jobs. We need to consider afresh how to make innovation more benign and less threatening. A higher level of demand for labour in the industrialized countries is one essential. But from a global point of view, we want on the one hand to speed up the development and spread of technology; on the other hand, we need (a) to pinpoint and tackle the problems of transition in individual firms, industries and areas, and (b) to devise an effective world strategy for trade and payments which will avoid intolerable surpluses or deficits in either industrialized or developing countries. The problem of harnessing technological development to economic progress cannot be separated from national and international macroeconomic policies governing levels of demand, exchange rates, and so on.

This is an ambitious and challenging project, and the present book does not aim to tackle the whole range of these issues. Rather it focuses on how firms can be made more innovative in the sense of seeking to introduce new products and services, opening up new markets and developing new industries.

GLOBALIZATION AND TECHNOLOGY

In his opening chapter on 'Production Principles, Organizational Capabilities, and Technology Management', Michael Best argues that technological change is central to explaining industrial leadership and that by tapping the world's pool of technology, technology-following nations can achieve much faster growth rates than the technology trailblazers, but that economics as an academic discipline has little to offer on these important concerns. For Best, the disjuncture between technology and economic theory is caused, in part, by the failure of economics to get a grip on production and business organization, and the chapter illustrates this idea through a series of case-studies. The central claim of this opening chapter is that technology management is a powerful tool for the growth of firms, regions, and nations at every level of industrial development. Success, however, depends upon certain key principles of production and organization being in place. Otherwise, no amount of investment in R&D or technology transfer or commitment to technology policy will impact on growth.

In Chapter 2, 'Foreign Direct Investment: Towards Co-operative Institutional Arrangements Between the North and the South?', Ajit Singh and Ann Zammit start with the orthodox view that the liberalization of trade and capital movements, and the associated phenomena of the globalization of markets and production, lead to a more efficient allocation of the world's resources and faster world growth rates. Specifically in relation to Northern multinational investment in the South, both the North and the South are thought to gain from it. Developing countries are supposed to benefit in a number of different ways, including notably the transfer of technology from the North to the South. The shareholders of multinationals in the advanced countries ostensibly gain from the higher returns in developing countries than they otherwise might earn. The North's workers, it is suggested, benefit from the export of capital goods which investment by multinationals invariably involves. To consolidate these supposed benefits of liberalization and globalization, the OECD countries are currently negotiating a binding multilateral agreement on investment (MAI) which would remove most of the remaining constraints on the free flow of FDI. Developing countries are being invited to accede to the final negotiated agreement—an agreement in whose formulation they will have had no say—and it is possible that some Latin American countries will be early joiners. It is expected that this will generate an irresistible momentum with other low-income countries feeling impelled to join also. The OECD's objective is that the MAI should become a global policy framework, based on high standards with regard to the rights and treatment of FDI. However, Singh and Zammit argue that, on balance, the proposed OECD treaty will not be helpful either to countries in the South or in the North. It is suggested that the question of FDI needs to be considered instead in relation to the overall growth of the world economy.

In Chapter 3, on 'Innovation and Technology Transfer Within Multinational Firms', Jeremy Howells analyses the issue of international innovation and technology transfer specifically on an intrafirm basis, and considers how the organizational and locational context of this affects both corporate and national performance. Within the whole issue of international technology flows, intrafirm cross-border technology flows has remained a neglected issue for analysis and discussion. This is despite being long recognized as a major element in international technology transfer. Even in the late 1970s technological balance of payments analysis revealed that intrafirm payments accounted for between two-thirds and three-quarters of total cross-border technology flows for the USA, UK, and Germany and that this figure had increased in all three countries over the late 1960s and 1970s. Howells argues that internal technology and knowledge flows do have a significant and indeed increasing impact on the organization and location of firms. Specifically, in the more strategic and tacit areas of communication where trust and shared learning are involved, face-to-face contact is still important and thus proximity continues to have a strong influence on organizational shape.

In Chapter 4, on 'New Technology and Jobs', Mario Pianta notes that the growing literature on innovation has only recently addressed the issue of the employment impact of technological change—but with unemployment reaching 18 million in the European Union and 35 million in OECD countries, this is a much needed development. Pianta presents new evidence showing that the employment impact of technological change varies widely across countries, sectors, and between manufacturing and services, but that generally in the 1990s there is evidence of widespread negative consequences of innovation in Europe, marked by unprecedented unemployment levels and a new pattern of 'jobless growth'. Technological change in the 1980s accompanied the process of structural change, favouring the emergence of new activities which offered new employment, but such growth opportunities were captured by countries after a strongly competitive process, where national specializations and technological advantages are crucial, and European countries are less present in the most dynamic sectors at the world level. They therefore found it harder to benefit from the 'virtuous circle' between technology, growth, and employment which operated at the global level. Conversely, negative effects of technological change emerged more clearly. More detailed indicators drawn from the Community innovation surveys show evidence of a generally negative impact of technology on employment in the 1990s. This appears to be the result of the labour-saving bias of the innovation strategies carried out by European firms and of a macroeconomic context marked by slower growth and sluggish demand. While technology and industrial policies have spurred innovation and competitiveness on the supply side, the importance of demand factors has been neglected. Technological and structural change—and employment growth—cannot be achieved without a combination of supply-push and demand-pull effects, and without a coherence between technological change and macroeconomic conditions, including the pace of growth and the distribution patterns. The current constraints on the expansion of demand, set by the convergence criteria for the European

Economic and Monetary Union, and the increasingly uneven distribution of income may turn out to be equally important factors preventing the evolution of economic structures towards a direction more consistent with the potential offered by technological change.

INNOVATION AND GROWTH

Chapter 5 by Michael Kitson and Jonathan Michie on 'Markets, Competition, and Innovation' draws on the surveys conducted by Cambridge University's ESRC Centre for Business Research (CBR) to suggest first that the notion that firms compete in markets where the norm is a large number of customers and competitors misrepresents the competitive process; secondly, that most firms do not compete mainly in terms of prices and costs but rather that other factors such as personal attention to client needs, reputation, and product quality are more important; and thirdly that both innovation and co-operation appear to play important roles in the success or otherwise of firms. An important ingredient for achieving competitive success is shown to be the establishment of effective collaboration with others—customers, suppliers, higher education establishments, and so on. Such collaboration allows firms to expand their range of expertise, develop specialist products, and achieve other corporate objectives. Collaboration is also one of the most important means of fostering innovation and effective competition in international markets. It may be, then, that those who interpret the labour and product market reforms of the Thatcher era as having been good for economic performance have overestimated the beneficial effects of the increased ability which has been provided to firms to variously cut costs and shed labour, hence boosting competitiveness; there are many other facets to the competitiveness picture which are ignored by such a focus. Indeed, the chapter argues that progress along these other avenues of upgrading product and process quality may be stymied by the low road of cost cutting. Similarly, a Hayeckian focus on the benefits of competition may be to the detriment of productive co-operation.

In Chapter 6 on 'The Determinants of Innovation in Small and Medium-Sized Enterprises', Eric Wood reports an analysis of the CBR data according to different clusters of firms, divided according to their responses to questions asked about their innovative performance, finding for example that by comparison with firms reporting negligible innovation output, those with substantial innovation output are significantly more likely to have any staff engaged in R&D, to be engaged in R&D on a continuous as opposed to an occasional basis and to enter into collaborative agreements. While fewer than 20 per cent of firms with negligible innovation output report staff engaged in R&D, over 70 per cent of other firms have staff engaged in R&D activity. And while 50 per cent of firms with substantial innovation output engage in R&D

on a continuous basis, only 8 per cent of other firms do so. Innovative firms also tend to have a higher proportion of staff who are technically skilled. Finally, it appears that non-innovating firms are significantly less likely than innovative firms to make use of information from outside sources including universities as well as suppliers and customers for the purposes of innovation. While this may simply reflect the fact that these firms are less likely to be engaged in innovation activity at all, and hence that they are not seeking information for innovation, it could also mean that attempts to innovate in these firms are less likely to succeed due to the fact that they do not consult widely enough amongst external organizations. These results all point towards the conclusion that the innovation output reported by the firms in the innovating clusters is not simply the result of 'a look in the suggestion box', but is rather the result of a considerable depth of costly innovative activity involving both internal and external searches for new technologies.

In Chapter 7, 'Innovation Networks: The View from the Inside', Nick Oliver and Michelle Blakeborough argue that although interfirm collaborations and partnerships are increasingly advocated as routes to superior innovative performance, remarkably little attention has been paid to multifirm new-product development projects. Their chapter examines the dynamics of seven such projects, each involving between five and thirteen firms. The normal challenges of product development are found to be exacerbated when several firms are involved in a project, with issues of intellectual property rights, authority, ownership, and geographical dispersion providing additional complications. Contradictions on the part of some players in terms of the desire for project 'ownership' on the one hand and 'risk minimization' on the other were also apparent.

In Chapter 8 on 'Innovation in Consumption and Economic Growth', G. M. Peter Swann points out that for the most part, analysis of the effects of innovation on economic growth has focused on the supply side, with the literature examining the effects of innovative activity by producers, whether in the form of process innovations or product innovations. But Swann argues that the consumer is also an innovator. While the traditional literature looks at the effect of innovation on the production function, this chapter looks at the effect of innovation on the utility function. The implications of innovation in consumption for growth and inflation are also discussed.

GOVERNANCE, BUSINESS PERFORMANCE, AND PUBLIC POLICY

In a short note on 'Innovation and Corporate Structures: USA and Japan', Ronald Dore relates how in the 1980s, studies on 'who's ahead' in a number of fields of science and technology, concluded—in Japan with glee, and in the

USA with alarm—that Japan was catching up fast and destined in many fields soon to overtake the USA. Particularly disturbing for Americans was the fact that some of their smartest weaponry depended on bought-in Japanese components. The effect of the technological news was magnified by the economic news. The Japanese economy was booming in the second half of the 1980s; the USA was a byword for productivity stagnation and the triple deficit. However, in the 1990s the situation is very different: it is now America which has the dynamic economy; the solidity of Japan's recovery from its post-bubble stagnation seems still uncertain. Dore discusses this change in terms of business structures, and whether Silicon Valley is what America has and Japan lacks.

In Chapter 10 on 'Sustainable Prosperity, Corporate Governance, and Innovation in Europe', Mary O'Sullivan argues that the Anglo-American debates on corporate governance neglect the integral role that enterprises and institutions have played in the process of innovation and development in the advanced industrial economies. These debates have been dominated by what she calls the 'shareholder-control' perspective on governance. The proponents of this perspective view shareholders as the 'owners' or 'principals' in whose interests the corporation should be run. They recognize, however, that in the actual running of the corporation, shareholders must rely on managers to perform certain functions. The shareholder control perspective combines traditional notions of property rights with deep-seated beliefs in the economic efficacy of the market mechanism that find expression in neoclassical economic theory and represent a distinctively 'Anglo-American' economic ideology. Yet, since the 1920s, if not before, the very existence of the corporation as a central and enduring entity in the advanced economies has prompted a number of economists to question the relevance of these beliefs. As they should, according to O'Sullivan, for the realities of successful industrial development in the United States as well as in Europe and Asia during this century flatly contradict the basic assumptions of the shareholder-control perspective. Public shareholders have not exercised strategic control in the US industrial corporation during this century; this in no way implies that shareholders have either the incentives or abilities to perform that function. Rather the problem for corporate governance is to understand why the corporate managers who currently occupy positions of strategic control in major industrial corporations lack the incentives and abilities to allocate resources to innovative investment strategies.

In Chapter 11 on 'Organizational Learning and International Competition', William Lazonick argues that since the 1970s a persistent feature of the US economy has been increasing income inequality, to the point where the United States now has the most unequal distribution of income among the advanced industrial economies, and that sustainable prosperity—the spreading of the benefits of economic growth to more and more people over a prolonged period of time—appears to have become an elusive objective. At the same time, in the late 1990s, after more than two decades of intense competitive challenges, the United States retains international leadership in a range of science-based industries such as computer electronics and pharmaceuticals as well as in service sectors related to such things as finance and food. The US economy appears capable of innovation, but incapable of sustainable prosperity. In previous work Lazonick and O'Sullivan hypothesized that the coexistence of innovation and inequality in the US economy in the 1980s and 1990s reflects a systematic bias of major US corporations against making innovative investments in broad and deep skill bases, and that instead these corporations, which exercise inordinate control over the allocation of resources and returns in the economy, are choosing to invest, and are best able to innovate, in the production of goods and services that use narrow and concentrated skill bases to develop and utilize technology. This hypothesis is embedded in a theory of innovation and economic development in which the impacts of international competition and technology on income distribution are not independent of either corporate investment strategy or the national institutions that influence corporate strategy. This skill-base hypothesis implies that, by investing in broad and deep skill bases, corporations can generate innovation and contribute to sustainable prosperity. The key supply-side policy issue then is how to influence corporate strategy to innovate in technologies that demand investments in broad and deep skill bases.

Finally in Chapter 12, on 'Technology Policy: Strategic Failures and the Need for a New Direction', Keith Cowling and Roger Sugden argue that something is amiss with the process of technological development within the industrial economy and that a new direction in technology policy is required to sustain a new direction for the economy. Initiatives to foster and stimulate technological change should be designed as part of a wider concern with developing a democratic economy, necessitated by the strategic failure associated with the concentrated decision structures embedded within the free market system. But different regions and different countries have very different starting positions, witness the stark contrast between the established advanced capitalist economies, the transition economies and the various groups of developing economies. Building diffuse, deconcentrated economies from this contrasting patchwork implies the need for a bottom-up and varied approach rooted in local communities, with these communities encouraged to pursue their common interests at national and indeed multinational level.

Part I
Globalization and Technology

1. Production Principles, Organizational Capabilities, and Technology Management*

Michael H. Best

INTRODUCTION: THE IDEA OF TECHNOLOGY MANAGEMENT

Technology fits uneasily in economic theory.[1] Growth theory and trade theory, for example, do not control for technology. But everyone knows both that technological change is central to explaining industrial leadership and that technology-following nations can achieve much faster growth rates than the technology trailblazers by tapping the world's pool of technology.[2]

Government 'technology policy', planned and inadvertent, has had a major impact on technological development. Historically, technological breakthroughs have been bound up in wars, hot and cold. United States government R&D funding and defence procurement during the cold war were catalysts for a range of new technologies and high-tech industries important to American growth and trade.[3] More recently, high-tech 'hot spots' in the United States have engendered regional growth and become models for policy-makers around the world. Governments in the rapidly growing East Asian economies, following Japan, have pursued activist technology policies. Their goal has been to move up the export product ladder to more technologically advanced products.

* Thanks to Jane Humphries, Sukant Tripathy, Jonathan West, Karel Williams, and CIC colleagues Robert Forrant, William Lazonick, and William Mass.

¹ For a survey see G. N. von Tunzelmann (1995), *Technology and Industrial Progress*: *The Foundations of Economic Growth*, Brookfield, Vt.: Edward Elgar.

² The transfer of technology has not been so simple. At the same time, the high growth East Asian success stories all suggest that rapid rates of growth are associated with high rates of technology adoption and diffusion. This is not inconsistent with either neoclassical or new growth theory. In Robert Solow's 1957 article, roughly 80 per cent of US growth was explained by 'technology' ('Technical Change and the Aggregate Production Function', *Review of Economics and Statistics*, 39: 312–20). However, technology was neither defined nor made endogenous to the growth model and innovation. The New Growth Theory is equally sympathetic to 'technology' in the form of new ideas. Recent studies in international trade have, likewise, brought in technology and organization through the backdoor to explain high rates of unemployment (Paul Krugman and Robert Z. Lawrence, 'Trade, Jobs, and Wages', *Scientific American*, Apr. 1994, 22–7).

³ In this sense America had an inadvertent industrial policy.

Technological leadership has long been an object of business strategy as well. AT&T, DuPont, GE, and IBM, decades ago, established in-house laboratories to conduct fundamental scientific research which, it was anticipated, would identify future technologies and engender market-place success.

At the same time, the relations between scientific research, industrial innovation, and competitiveness are controversial. Noting the cutbacks in federal funding for research and corporate long-range fundamental research, pessimists argue that America is failing to maintain the research foundation that has supported America's competitive advantage in new technologies and high-tech industries. But optimists hold that America's industrial resurgence is due, in part, to the emergence of new models of technology management enabled by and reinforcing new models of business and industrial organization.

Economics has little to offer on these important concerns. The disjuncture between technology and economic theory is caused, in part, by the failure of economics to get a grip on production and business organization. A linear process has been taken for granted which proceeds across autonomous spheres of science, technology, and economic growth. The beauty of the model is its simplicity for policy prescription: growth can be enhanced by funding science which leads to technological breakthroughs followed by new products. Such a model ignores the overlap of, and space between, science and technology, technology and product development, product development and production. The associated range of mediating activities, institutions, capabilities, and purposes are ignored but at a cost in understanding how economies actually function. To the extent, then, that technology is important to understanding economies it should have a place in economics.

The technology-economic growth process can be divided into two sub-processes. The first puts fundamental scientific research and technological innovation at centre stage. Government technology policy and economic research on technological change tend to focus here. The second targets relations between production, new product development, technology choice, and applied R&D within and across business enterprises. This is the domain of technology management and the concern of this chapter.

Five heuristic case-studies are presented to explore the idea of technology management from a production perspective. The cases highlight the interfaces of production and technology. The method is to explore technology management from the context of major innovations in production principles and associated organizational capabilities.

The central claim is that technology management is a powerful tool for growth of firms, regions, and nations at every level of industrial development. Success, however, depends upon certain key principles of production and organization being in place. Otherwise, no amount of investment in R&D or technology transfer or commitment to technology policy will impact on growth.

The challenge of technology management in leading industrial enterprises today is to develop the organizational capability to combine and recombine new and existing technologies with production in the pursuit of rapid new product development. The challenge to technology-follower firms and regions is to develop technology management capabilities that enhance competitive advantage specific to time and place. This does not mean a one-off introduction of a new technology or 'turnkey' plants. Nor does it mean that a company or country can continue to thrive on the basis of a specific technology management capability. The five case-studies suggest that sustained industrial growth depends upon making a series of transitions to more advanced technology management capabilities. These transitions, however, depend upon the requisite production principles and organizational capabilities being in place.

TM 1: THE AMERICAN SYSTEM AND INTERCHANGEABILITY

Surprisingly, the timeless principles of mass production are not widely understood in many parts of the world either by academics or practitioners. The first principle, interchangeability of parts, was established nearly a century before mass production became a hallmark of industrialization. The American System of Manufactures, as the British labelled it, was based on interchangeability. Applied first at the Springfield Armory in Springfield, Massachusetts in 1817, interchangeability revolutionized production. The concept of interchangeability is as relevant today as ever. Before interchangeability each drawer in a desk was hand-sanded and hand-fitted, each firing-pin on a rifle was hand-filed. Without interchangeabilty armies would still need to include a regiment of hand-fitters to repair arms and furniture manufacturers a department of hand-sanders to individually fit pieces. The idea is simple but it is rarely deployed in Third-World factories today.[4]

Designing a production system around the principle of interchangeability was, at the same time, the origins of technology management. A range of specialist machines had to be designed and built to convert the principle into practice. Product engineering emerged as a set of standard procedures, an organizational capability, and an occupational category to specify, identify, design, make, set up, modify, adopt, refine, and operate efficiently the requisite machines. The rudiments of process engineering also appeared as methods were established to lay out, interface, standardize, measure, operate, and trouble-shoot machining activities along a production line. The elements of a production management system were taking shape. Technology

---

[4] For examples see Michael Best and Robert Forrant, 'Production in Jamaica: Transforming Industrial Enterprises', in Patsy Lewis (1994) (ed.), *Preparing for the Twenty-First Century: Jamaica 30th Anniversary Symposium*, Kingston, Jamaica: Ian Randle Publishers, 53–97.

management was no longer a one-off affair in which a machine with superior performance capacity was introduced; instead, it was becoming an ongoing organizational capability of industrial enterprises.

Product engineering means, first, deconstructing a product into its constituent pieces; second, reorganizing the flow of material according to the logical sequence of operational activities for manufacturing the piece; third, analysing each operation for simplification by identifying, modifying, and designing machinery; and fourth, networking with machine tool companies to make, modify, and maintain machines, tools, and streamline processes.

The stock of a gun at the Springfield Armory was subjected to a product engineering exercise. To eliminate hand-sanding, and the need for craft-skilled woodworkers, a bank of fourteen specialist lathes were designed, built, and integrated into a production line. The performance of each machining operation, tended by a machine operator, was measured by precision gauges and compared with formal specifications. Failure meant adjustments to the machine and/or operator tasks.

In early industrial New England, an interfirm technology management dynamic was set in motion between specialist machine users and makers. Incremental and radical innovations in the machine tool industry were both induced by machine users and fed back to increase productivity.[5] The system was not centrally managed; it was self-organizing with a powerful, timely, boost from orders and services provided by the Springfield Armory.[6] But without the development of a set of (informal) management practices known as 'product engineering' for guiding the design and development of machines, it likely would not have been self-sustaining.

Inadvertently, New England became the site of a regional technology management capability. The world's first machine tool industry, created in the wake of applying interchangeability, facilitated the integration and mutual development of production and technology. But it also diffused the new principle to the whole region and other parts of the country and, by so doing, created a vehicle for transferring technology across sectors.[7]

---

[5] For examples of both types of innovation and references to original sources see Michael Best and Robert Forrant, 'Community-based Careers and Economic Virtue: Arming, Disarming, and Rearming the Springfield Armory', in Michael Arthur and Denise Rousseau (1996) (eds), *The Boundaryless Career*, Oxford: Oxford University Press, 314–30; and Robert Forrant (1994), 'Skill Was Never Enough: American Bosch, Local 206, and the Decline of Metalworking in Springfield, Massachusetts 1900–1970', University of Massachusetts doctoral diss., Amherst, Mass.

[6] The district model of industrial organization is associated with networking as distinct from pure market or hierarchy as a mode of co-ordination of economic activity (see Michael Best (1990), *The New Competition*, Cambridge, Mass.: Harvard University Press). Networking suggests long term, consultative relationships which facilitate investment in design and R&D. The process involved technology policy by the Federal government.

[7] Nathan Rosenberg (1996), *Perspectives on Technology*, Cambridge University Press: Cambridge, 9–31.

While the makers and users of the specialist machines were independent firms, they were fuelled by a regional innovation process which, in turn, was anchored in a community of workers and practical engineers skilled in the development, use, and improvement of the new technologies. While the idea of product engineering was not always formalized into standard operating procedures, without the emergence of a set of tools and skills associated with blueprint reading, metallurgy, geometry, and trigonometry the machine-making sector would not have flourished. It did and with it the management of technology became an organizational capability. Often as not, technology management as a capability was embedded in the tacit knowledge and skills of workers who learned product engineering without knowing it was an organizational accomplishment that introduced a whole new world of production potential over its craft predecessor.

The centrality of networking and technology diffusion to the growth process was also established in early industrial New England. The practice of technology management was not found in textbooks or management training courses; instead, it was embedded in the dynamic relationships between machine-makers and users and in the skills of the labour force. The elements of product engineering, a machine tool sector, and a skilled labour force provided the method and means for the region to make the transition from an industry organized according to the principle of craft to one organized according to interchangeability.[8]

Application of the production principle of interchangeability led to the redefinition of a whole range of products and created new industrial sectors.[9] In its wake, New England enjoyed a rapid rate of industrial growth. It also demonstrates that an organizational capability can be the source of competitive advantage.

TM 2: HENRY FORD AND SINGLE PRODUCT FLOW

Henry Ford wrote: 'In mass production there are no fitters.'[10] The implied emphasis on interchangeability does not describe what was novel about Ford's plants. Henry Ford's plants were organized according to the principle of flow. The point is captured by one of Ford's most successful students, Taiichi Ohno, creator of the Toyota 'just-in-time' system:[11]

---

[8] The lack of a craft tradition meant less resistance to the new principle of production than in gun-making regions of England.

[9] See Best, *The New Competition*, ch. 1.

[10] H. Ford (1926), *Today and Tomorrow*, 40; repr. in 1988 by Cambridge, Mass.: Productivity Press.

[11] Taiichi Ohno (1988), *Toyota Production System: Beyond Large-Scale Production*, Cambridge, Mass.: Productivity Press.

By tracing the conception and evolution of work flow by Ford and his associates, I think their true intention was to extend a work [read material: MB] flow from the final assembly line to all other processes . . . By setting up a flow connecting not only the final assembly line but all the processes, one reduces production lead time. Perhaps Ford envisioned such a situation when he used the word 'synchronization'. (Ohno, 1988: 100)

Ohno identifies the single term that captures the revolution at Ford Motor company even though it does not, I believe, appear in Ford's published writings. It was not interchangeability, as stated by Ford, the moving assembly line, or economies of size, but synchronization. It is captured in the words of Charles Sorensen, Ford's chief engineer: 'It was . . . complete *synchronization* which accounted for the difference between an ordinary assembly line and a mass production one.'[12]

Sorensen uses the term in a more expansive description of the Model T where all the 'links in the chain' were first connected at the Highland Park plant in August 1913:

Each part was attached to the moving chassis in order, from axles at the beginning to bodies at the end of the line. Some parts took longer to attach than others; so, to keep an even pull on the towrope, there must be differently spaced intervals between the delivery of the parts along the line. This called for patient *timing* and rearrangement until the flow of parts and the speed and intervals along the assembly line meshed into a perfectly *synchronized* operation throughout all stages of production. (Sorensen, 1957: 130–1, my emphasis)

Sorensen finishes the paragraph with the phrase: 'a new era in industrial history had begun.' Few would deny this conclusion. But, ironically, most explanations do not capture the fundamental challenge that ushered in the new vision of production and thereby the real difference between the old and the new approach to production as articulated by Sorensen.

The production organizing concept for Ford and his engineers was timing. The challenge was to regulate material flow so that just the right amount of each part would arrive at just the right time. In Ford's words:

The traffic and production departments must work closely together to see that all the proper parts reach the branches at the *same time*—the shortage of a single kind of bolt would hold up the whole assembly at a branch. (Ford, 1926: 117, my emphasis)

Making one part too few slowed the flow; making one part too many produced waste in the form of inventory and Ford was vigilant against the 'danger of becoming overstocked' (Ford, 1926: 117).

Sorensen referred to the process as 'progressive mechanical work' which reached its pinnacle with the introduction of the V-8 engine at the Rouge plant in 1932:

---

[12] C. E. Sorensen (1957), *Forty Years with Ford*, London: Cape.

All materials entering the Ford plant went into operation and stayed there. They never came to rest until they had become part of a unit like an engine, an axle, or a body. Then they moved on to final assembly or into a freight car for branch assembly, and finally to the customer. It was a glorious period; a production man's dream come true. (Sorensen, 1957: 231)

The vision of a flow line concentrated the attention of engineers on barriers to throughput. A barrier, or bottleneck, occurred wherever a machining operation could not process material at the same pace as the previous operation. The bottleneck machine was the activity that constrained not only the throughput at that machine but of the production system as a whole. Increasing the pace of work on any other machining activity could not increase output, only inventory.

Henry Ford's assembly lines can be seen in this light. It was not the speed of the line that was revolutionary in *concept*, it was the idea of synchronizing production activities so that bottlenecks did not constrain the whole production system. Unfortunately, all too often the basis of mass production was mistakenly defined in terms of economies of size when it was really synchronized production that drove the rate of throughput up and the per unit costs down.[13] Flow requires synchronization which, in turn, requires system integration.

Sorensen's assistant superintendent on the first assembly line was Clarence Avery. Avery spent a total of 8 months working in every production department. In Sorensen's words: 'Beginning at the bottom in each department, he did all the physical work necessary to understand its operations, then moved on to the next' (p. 130). Avery then moved into Sorensen's office and elaborated the whole system:

With firsthand familiarity with each step in each parts department, Avery worked out the *timing* schedules necessary before installation of conveyor assembly systems to motors, fenders, magnetos, and transmissions. One by one these operations were *revamped* and continuously moving conveyers delivered the assembled parts to the final assembly floor.   (Sorensen, 1957: 130; my emphasis)

Linking up an assembly line was a final step and one which, by itself, had no direct impact on throughput time.[14] A conveyor line is a physical linkage system that integrates all of the requisite machining and other operations required to convert material into finished product. Before a conveyor can be

---

[13] A prime example is Lenin's admiration of Henry Ford and Frederick Taylor which, based on the mistaken view that mass production was about economies of size, figured in the identification of modernism with giant factories throughout the Soviet Union and Eastern Europe. Unpub. paper by Robin Murray, Sussex University.

[14] The rate of material flow was not determined by the pace of the conveyor line; rather the speed of the conveyor line was adjusted to the pace of material flow. The pace of material flow depends upon the slowest cycle-time in the whole production process. Otherwise timing would be thrown off.

connected operations must be 'revamped' one by one to equalize the cycle-time for each constituent operation. A cycle-time is the time it takes to complete a single operation, usually on a single piece-part. Ohno argues that Ford's engineers did not go the whole way: they did not equalize cycle-times for *one-piece flow* (see next section). But they did balance material flow so that the right parts would arrive at the right place at the right time.[15]

The principle of flow yields a simple rule to concentrate the attention of engineers: equalize cycle-times. Optimally, every operation on every part would match the standardized cycle-time, the regulator of the pace of production flow. Failure to synchronize appears as inventory build-up in front of the slower operation. Any activity that takes more time does not meet the condition and requires engineering attention. The way to increase the flow of material is not to speed the pace of the conveyor belt but to identify the bottleneck, or slowest cycle-time, and develop an action plan to eliminate it.

Ford's assembly line, from the perspective of flow, was primarily a signalling device or a visual information system for continuous advance in throughput performance. It established a standard cycle-time. The engineering task was to revamp each operation into conformity with the standard cycle-time.[16] Every time a bottleneck was removed, productivity and throughput advanced.

The visual signalling feature of inventory in the system was not obvious or perhaps even understood before it was implemented. Ford attacked inventory because it was waste and waste added to costs. But without a near-zero inventory system the signalling function of the conveyor line would be knocked out. With the near-zero inventory system, the work assignments of engineers were signalled by material build-up on the line. They were prioritized without central direction. Ford approved; this meant less indirect labour which, for Ford, was another form of waste.

Scheduling, too, was decentralized in Ford's system. The idea that Ford's system could indeed operate without chaos would have seemed, understandably, far-fetched. At an output rate of 8,000 cars per day, production of the Model A, with 6,000 distinct parts, involved 48 million parts in motion. A huge planning and scheduling department would seem to be necessary. But instead of chaos, Ford's plants were orderly. Schedules were met and order was achieved by the application of the synchronization rule: equalize cycle-times. Once the system was in sync, more cars could not be produced by

---

[15] Some of Ford's heavy machinery stamped in lot sizes of greater than one. This meant that inventory crept into the system as piece-parts were pulled into assembly one at a time. The output of all machines were regulated by the standard cycle-time but cycle-time was not equated for the fabrication of each piece-part. In this, Ford's plants were single-product but not single-piece flow. This point is elaborated in the next section.

[16] Equal cycle-times does not mean each machine is operating at the same pace but that just the right amount of parts for each car are made in each time-cycle.

increasing the speed of the line, the operational efficiency of individual machines, or the intensity of work.

Production rates could be increased in two ways: reduce the cycle-time of the slowest operation (successive elimination of bottlenecks) and driving down the standardized cycle-time. To this day production managers would not believe that the Ford system would work if, in the meantime, the Japanese had not demonstrated it. This is why it is known by the Japanese term: 'kanban'. A failure to understand Ford's assembly line as a visual scheduling device, backed by standardized cycle-times, is what led American volume producers to build huge, centralized planning and scheduling departments. Their efforts have demonstrated that no amount of information technology can avoid bottlenecks in such systems.[17]

Like interchangeability, the principle of flow is simple but implementation demanded a revolution in the organization of production and the management of technology. Ford simplified the organizational challenge, including co-ordination, by constraining the production system to one product.[18] The technological challenge was considerable. Equalizing cycle-times for even a single product was a monumental achievement. Equalizing cycle-time for more than one product was inconceivable without organizational innovations that go well beyond Ford's system. In fact, the conveyor line itself precludes multi-product flow (see next section).

Synchronization and the equal cycle-time concept necessitate two technology-management activities both for Ford and today. First, adjustments are required in operational activities to meet the synchronization constraint. Ford could not simply purchase machines 'in the market' even if a market existed for high-volume machines. Achieving the narrow time and timing specifications required by the principle of flow involved Ford engineers in continuously 'revamping', searching for new technologies, adjusting, regearing, retooling, fitting new jigs and fixtures, and redesigning machines and plant layout. This was a never-ending process for Ford as it is for practitioners of the management philosophy of continuous improvement today.

Second, the pursuit of new technologies is to reduce the standard cycle-time. Ford attacked the standard cycle-time by addressing generic

[17] Ironically, the Ford production system was self-regulating much like a perfectly competitive market system in economic theory. Instead of prices as the adjustment mechanism, surpluses and shortages of inventory set in motion corrective forces; instead of the 'invisible hand' the reaction agent was the engineer re-establishing equal cycle-times.

[18] Ford seemed to worship his original product design. Sorensen writes: 'In all the years with Model T no one worried or bothered Mr. Ford with design changes, and it was hard to be told he should adopt something else for Model A' (p. 224). Ford adamantly refused to modify even the brakes when the Model T was banned in Germany and at risk from emerging state safety boards in the United States. See Karel Williams, Colin Haslam and John Williams, 'What Henry did, or the relevance of Highland Park', in Keith Cowling and Roger Sugden (1992) (eds.), *Current Issues in Industrial Economic Strategy*, Manchester: Manchester University Press, 90–105.

technologies that impacted on all machines. One example is power. Before Ford, most manufacturing plants were powered by centralized power systems and machines were linked to the source of power by lines and shafts.[19] The synchronization rule would have no meaning in such a system. Ford innovated. He substituted wires.[20] And he built his own power system.

The River Rouge plant was fuelled by powdered and gasified coal which powered steam turbines designed and built by Ford and his team. Immediately obvious was the impressive 90 per cent efficiency rate in conversion of heat to water. Thermal efficiencies of purchased electricity from centralized power stations were restricted by the Rankine (Carnot efficiency) barrier from surpassing 35 per cent. Ford's generators included a number of innovations: they were a third less in size than turbines then available, the first to use all-mica insulation, and relied upon a 'radically' different system of ventilation.[21]

Why did Ford pursue innovation in electric-power generation? Part of the answer is that the cost of power determined the location of plant (Ford, 1926: 116). More important, implementation of the principle of flow depended upon and was intertwined with technological innovations in electric power. Flow applied to car production is impossible without the electric motor: the (unit-drive) electric motor meant that plant layout and machine location could be freed from the dictates of a central power system and the associated shafts and belts. Power, for the first time, could be distributed to individual machines and machinery could be arranged on the factory floor according to the logic of product engineering and the material conversion process.

Ford's innovation in electricity supply enabled his engineers to organize the plant according to the logic of material flow; competitors departmentalized factories according to machining activity. For Ford, the independently powered machines went to the material; for his competitors, material went to the machine and the machine was located by the power system.

Flow meant redesigning machines to incorporate unit-drive motors. While electrical power had become commonplace in factories in the first decades of the twentieth century its delivery system was unchanged. A 1928 textbook indicates only a 'trend toward incorporating the motor as an integral part of the machine tool' even though the concept had been understood since the turn of the century (Devine, 1983: 369).

[19] See Warren D. Devine, Jr. (1983), 'From Shafts to Wires: Historical Perspective on Electrification', *Journal of Economic History*, 43/2 (June), 347–72. I have drawn heavily on Devine's work in this section.

[20] Belts and shafts cluttered the factory and precluded machine layout according to the logic of the process. In theory, cycle-times could be equalized in such a plant but the challenge of adjusting gearing ratios and machine speeds would have created gridlock with the clutter of power transmission devices.

[21] Ford gives an insight into an important secret to his success and a key aspect of technology management in reference to his coal-gasification system. 'The processes are well known—most of our processes are well known. It is the combination of processes that counts' (Ford, 1926, 172).

Why the slow growth in distributed electrical drive systems? Answer: the limited diffusion of the principle of flow. The fusion of the electric motor with machines offered enormous potential to expand productivity but only with a prior commitment to a radical reorganization of the factory. Ford systematically pursued innovations in processes, procedures, machines, and factory layout to exploit the productivity potential of the principle of flow. The electric motor was a tool in the process.[22] Technological change in electric power awaited organizational change. Unit drive, in turn, created unforeseen opportunities in advancing productivity when integrated with production redesign.[23]

In short, technology management for Ford meant integrating technology and production in pursuit of the principle of single-product flow. While followers of Ford could take advantage of innovations developed by technological leaders, the synchronization requirement will always demand a technology-management capability.

With hindsight, Ford, from the perspective of technology management, is a story of both productivity leaps and limits. The challenge of high throughput forced Ford's engineers to integrate a range of technologies, apply new ones, and continuously adapt others to facilitate flow. At the same time the organizational practices associated with single-product flow place limits on other forms of technological advance and erect constraints to the introduction of new technologies. Toyota, not General Motors, exposed the limits of single-product flow.[24]

Like interchangeability, the concept of synchronization is simple but implementation demanded a revolution in the organization of production and the management of technology. This was so even though Ford simplified the co-ordination problem by constraining the production system to one basic product and even though Ford's engineers did not go the whole way (the cycle times were not equalized for all fabrication activities).

Ford's revolution was practical; the principle of flow was not conceptualized into a theory of production. Cycle times on the final assembly line regulated flow and established timing targets. But the Ford system was not pure 'just-in-time' (JIT) system for reasons explored in the next section.[25] The

[22] Ford's earlier experience as chief of engineering at Detroit Illuminating served him well.
[23] For a more extensive treatment of the relationships between energy and manufacturing processes see Michael Best and Denise Martucci (1997), *Power to Compete*, Lowell, Mass.: University of Massachusetts, Center for Industrial Competitiveness.
[24] General Motors moved from the organizing concept of material flow, developed by Ford, to that of functional departmentalization and the concept of 'economic order quantity'. In terms of throughput efficiency, GM was a step backwards; they did multiple products without multiple-product flow (see Best, *The New Competition*, 151).
[25] For example, some of Ford's machines processed more than one piece-part at a time which meant that inventory crept into the system and all material was not kept in motion. The point is not that such inventories were uneconomic, but that they were not deemed a challenge to be addressed as in the Toyota Production System.

completion of Ford's system was limited by the failure to conceptualize the principle of flow.

Again, as in interchangeability, the refinement in both concept and application was a multi-decade affair. The concept of flow penetrated into management thought and, less often, practice, in the early 1990s masquerading as 're-engineering' and 'lean production'.

A final word. Ford, unlike American industrial followers, had no interest in measuring labour productivity, conducting time-and-motion studies, or devising piece-rate systems. The rate of production depended on throughput efficiency and associated cycle-times. Ford increased the rate of production by technology management: bottlenecks were eliminated and standardized cycle-times were driven down. Unfortunately, the principle of flow was not written into industrial engineering manuals which, instead, adopted the 'scientific management' paradigm. Less surprising was the complementary practice in economic research of focusing on capital and labour to the exclusion of production and organizational issues. Both obscured the sources of productivity gains in America's most celebrated production system for roughly half a century after Ford's engineers first applied the principle of flow. Toyota forced the issue back onto the manufacturing agenda by extending the principle of flow to multiple products.[26]

TM 3: TOYOTA AND MULTI-PRODUCT FLOW

When Toyota developed JIT, engineers were not aware that they were triggering a sequence of organizational innovations in production that would create the conditions for a new trajectory of industrial growth.[27] They were just in time.

Japan had wrung the growth out of the early post-war trajectory driven by labour-intensive and raw material-intensive products, processes, and sectors. The high growth rate of the old trajectory had undermined its own preconditions: wages were driven up and imported raw material inputs were

[26] As noted, neither the principle of flow nor system were widely diffused in American business until the 1990s. Deming often stated that what he took to Japan was the 'theory of the system'. He meant, in part, that much of American business enterprise was organized into profit centres and the associated logic of local optimization; the Japanese management system came to embody the idea of managing interrelationships or interfaces across business activities, hence the idea of process integration or global optimization.

[27] In the final section, links among technology platform, production capability, and growth trajectory are suggested. The idea, in brief, is that for any set of production capabilities the rate of growth depends upon the wage rate relative to other nations at the same level of development of production capabilities. Japan's rising wage rates were choking growth potential for low-skilled, labour-intensive products and processes. But, relative to countries with complex production process capabilities Japan enjoyed a cost and, equally important, quality advantage. Hence the idea of a new production capability platform and associated growth trajectory.

constraining critical industries such as steel. Equally important, Japanese success was not lost on business enterprises in nearby nations with lower wages and indigenous raw materials and aspirations to develop the same industries. Sustained growth, for Japan, depended upon the establishment of more complex production products, processes, and sectors.

The new production system known variously as 'just-in-time', the 'Toyota Production System' and 'lean production' was not the consequence of large investments in capital. Nor was it about the introduction of new hardware-related technologies or lower-cost production methods. But it was an organizational prerequisite to both. The new system was based on the development, application, and diffusion of new principles of production and organizational capabilities that enabled Japanese manufacturing enterprises to compete on more comprehensive performance standards combining cost, quality, time, and flexibility. The new performance standards put industrial enterprises and regions throughout the world on notice, much as Henry Ford had done half a century before: failure to adapt to, or counter, the new production system would lead to industrial decline.

The central organizing concept of Toyota can be described as multi-product flow. The major difference with Ford—and it is a major one—is that Toyota was not constrained to one product. Toyota applied the principle of flow to a range of products: different models go down the same line. For Henry Ford, this idea was an anathema: the timing task would have been overwhelming as the product range proliferated. It would have implied an unacceptable compromise to the production goals of minimal throughput time and of low inventory targets. Finally, it would have meant delinking the conveyor lines and all this implied for labour discipline.

Nevertheless, Toyota, the JIT standard setter, achieved an inventory turn (ratio of sales divided by work-in-process) approaching 300. It is unlikely that Ford ever achieved above 200 and was probably considerably below. When General Motors began to measure work-in-progress turns the rate was in the neighbourhood of 6 to 8.[28]

Toyota took Ford's challenge of synchronization two steps beyond Ford. The first step, as noted, was to introduce multi-product flow. The second was more fundamental: equalization of the cycle-times for every part. Taiichi Ohno, who is to JIT what Ford was to mass production, describes the difference between Ford and Toyota in the following words:

---

[28] The low inventory turn ratio for GM is because GM did not take on board the challenge of equalizing cycle times. Product flow was deeply congested by the mass-batch system in which plant layout was organized by machine function. Instead of sequencing machines in the order dictated by the sequence of operations required to make a part, they were grouped by machining function. Material moved back and forth from department to department in large 'optimized' batches. Inventory adjustments were used in lieu of synchronization even at the final assembly line.

where the Ford system sticks to the idea of making a quantity of the same item at one time, the Toyota system synchronizes production of each unit . . . Even at the stage of making parts, production is carried out one piece at a time.   (Ohno, 1988: 96)

Thus Ford did not achieve complete synchronization.[29] This would require one-piece flow or transfer-lot sizes of one throughout the production system. But in certain fabrication stages, Ford's shops produced in large lot sizes. Lot sizes of more than one entail inventory if a single car absorbs less than the lot size. In these cases the process was fragmented into separated operations with the resulting interruption in flow and throughput inefficiencies.

The reasons that Ford did not produce each of the 6,000 distinct parts in the same cycle-time are not hard to understand. The practice of equalizing cycle times can be directed by engineers but it is best accomplished by a management system in which workers take on a quasi-technology management role. This necessitated a revolution in management philosophy. Consideration of such a move was completely alien to Ford.

The work organization ideally suited to the challenge of multi-product flow is cellular manufacturing. The idea harks back to the concept of group technology in which work 'cells' are organized by the logic of the product. The reason? Multi-product flow requires equalizing cycle-times and the flexibility to have different, but equal cycle-times. This enables the product mix to be varied in response to demand shifts. While cycle-times vary according to the product, they are the same for each individual product.

Flexibility comes from, first, being able to adjust the number of workers in a cell, second, quick set-up and changeover design of the machines, and. third, multi-skilled workers. Each worker must operate not one machine, but three or four machines, and also do set-ups (and maintenance activities) on the machines. What was revolutionary at Toyota was not just-in-time production but the idea of single-minute-exchange-of-die (SMED). To produce multiple products on the same line it is necessary to make the machines capable of being programmable (mechanically or electronically) for different products. The challenge at Toyota was to go beyond multiple products on the same line to the idea of multiple products on the same line in batch sizes of one. This meant the worker had to be able to set-up the machine and, in certain circumstances, set-up several machines.

By establishing cellular production, Toyota was able to achieve the same high performance standards in terms of equal cycle-time as Henry Ford, but with multiple products.[30] Machines, as along Ford's assembly line, are laid

---

[29] As noted, Ford's engineers aggressively attacked inventory waste and clearly saw it as an interruption to flow. But they did not make the next step to equalize cycle-times for every single piece-part. A stamping machine, for example, may stamp 100 pieces at a time. This meant that all pieces would not be in motion; some would be waiting.

[30] The benefits of the Toyota production system do not stop with shorter production lead times. Mass-batch production methods are extremely costly in finance because of low working

out and reconfigured according to the dictates of the routing sheet or flow chart but in U-cells and without a conveyor line.[31]

The new management paradigm makes possible the organizational capability of continuous, incremental innovation in the form of an accumulation of thousands of tiny improvements and an unrivalled persistence in production detail built into the organization of production. The plan-do-check-act management paradigm of W. Edwards Deming was an organizational corollary to the principle of multi-product flow. While Deming's focus was not on innovation but on continuous improvement of product and process, his approach to integrating thinking and doing on the shop floor introduced a new dimension to the management of technology.

For Deming, the discovery of knowledge is not the preserve of science just as thinking is not the preserve of management; the business challenge became to build the discovery process into every level and activity of the organization. For example, knowledge can be discovered about the causes of product defects by the workers involved if the organization is properly designed. The purpose of statistical process control was not only to distinguish systemic from special causes of defects, but to focus attention on improvement of the organization as the means to advance quality and productivity. The idea was to design quality into the system, not inspect it into the product. This required innovation capability on the shop-floor. It created whole new possibilities for decentralized technology management which will take us beyond Toyota.

Multi-product flow is the mirror image of a new organizational principle which appears in a range of variants and goes under the popular names of 'continuous improvement', 'TQM' (total quality management), 'kaizen', 'small group activity', and 'self-directed work teams'.[32] Deming considered each of these management practices to be aspects of the 'theory of system' which, for him, meant replacing the hierarchical, up/down, vertical information flows and functional departmentalization with cross-functional

capital productivity. JIT plants require much less inventory and indirect labour per car. See Abegglen and Stalk, and Cusumano for comparative measures of indirect to direct labour and inventory per car.

[31] Group technology developed in England in the 1950s by, among others, John Burbidge was a forerunner of cellular manufacturing. Ironically, the concept was probably developed first in the Soviet Union in the 1930s even though it was never used in the Soviet Union to achieve high throughput efficiency (probably because it reeked of capital productivity, an oxymoron to Marxian ideology and Soviet thinking). Burbidge believes that group technology was applied successfully in at least eleven UK engineering plants in the 1950s and 1960s. Preliminary research, based primarily on conversations with Burbidge, suggests that the experiments were successful but did not survive the transition to finance-dominated management and the merger activities of the 1970s. Burbidge himself, a brilliant engineer who has written several books on production, did not integrate the principles of production with those of organization. Here we have to wait for Taiichi Ohno and the Toyota Production System for the first systematic treatment.

[32] Each of these management orientations are secondary to the fundamental principle of system integration (see below).

relations, and horizontal, interactive information flows of process integration.[33]

The new principles of production (multi-product flow) and corollary organizational capability (kaizen) are interdependent and self-reinforcing; neither can be successfully applied without the other. Successful implementation, however, depended upon a prior or simultaneous development of specific organizational capabilities and investments in the skills required to convert the new production principle into production capabilities and pursue the new technological opportunities. Equalizing cycle-times in production and driving down throughput times had an even more powerful, however unintentional, side effect: it created the possibility for driving down new-product development cycle-times and introduced a new form of product-led competition. And, to yet a new model of technology management.

TM 4: CANON AND NEW PRODUCT DEVELOPMENT

Driving down manufacturing process times (increasing throughput efficiency) lowers costs, improves quality, and shortens delivery times. But the logic of reduced process times is not limited to the transformation of material in production. It can be extended to, and linked into, other business processes such as new-product development (NPD). The implications for technology management are profound.

While the Toyota Production System laid the foundation, consumer electronics companies applied and extended it to develop a new dimension to technology management and source of competitive advantage. Canon, for example, uses the same multi-product flow platform to institutionalize dynamic feedbacks between production and R&D. The result gives new force to product-led competition. Technology is put in the service of continuous product redefinition as never before.

Reducing new product development process time means redesigning and integrating every activity in the product development process which includes:

  product concept
  • conceptual design
  • product architecture
  • technology search and analysis
  • target market

---

[33] Deming inspired enterprises to focus on the management of interrelationships as well as the plan-do-check-act (PDCA) paradigm of total quality management. The idea of system or process integration spread from the material conversion process in the factory to the business enterprise which became understood, not as a collection of profit centres but as an integrated set of interrelated processes such as material flow, order fulfilment, new-product development.

product planning
- model building
- structural testing
- technology design viability testing
- technology R&D and integration
- investment/financial projections

product/process engineering
- detailed design of product
- tooling/equipment design and specification
- building/testing prototypes
- master technology and engineering interfaces
- setting standards
- supplier tie-ins

pilot project/scale-up
- initial production runs
- establish work skills and activities
- volume production tests

production
- factory start-up
- volume ramp-up
- establish performance standards (cost, quality, time)
- maintain standards
- master engineering and work team interfaces for continuous improvement

Shorter new-product development cycles means more product introductions. But it has a secondary, powerful benefit: integration of NPD and new-technology introduction cycles. For any given product, life-cycle, product, and process architecture are locked into place. To change any part requires new tooling, supplier specifications, testing, work-task definitions, etc. Each new product introduction, however, is an opportunity for the adoption of new technologies and technology ideas (Gomory, 1992).[34]

The shorter the NPD cycle, the greater the opportunity and organizational capability to introduce both discontinuous or radical technological innovations and new combinations of existing technologies into production. A company that is capable of reducing the NPD cycle to half that of a competitor can introduce technological innovations at twice the rate. Being first to

[34] Ralph Gomory makes this point in distinguishing 'the cyclic process' from a 'ladder' type of innovation. 'Ladder' refers to the step-by-step process by which an innovation descends from science downward 'step-by-step' into practice. The 'cyclic process' refers to 'repeated, continuous, incremental improvement' built into a series of dynamic design/manufacturing cycles. (See R. Gomory (1992), 'The Technology–Product Relationship: Early and Late Stages', in N. Rosenberg, R. Landau, and D. Mowery (eds.), *Technology and the Wealth of Nations*, Stanford, Calif.: Stanford University Press, 383–94.)

market with a new technology is important, but having the shortest NPD process time is also important in that technology adoption and adaptations can be introduced more rapidly.[35]

The potential for rapid technological introduction induced a complementary organizational change: the shift of laboratory technicians from the laboratory onto the shop-floor. New technological knowledge is discovered by laboratory technicians conducting research on the shopfloor. What can appear as the elimination of R&D may be the development of cross-functional product development teams integrated into the production process.

In another application of the organizational principle of system integration, the Deming critique of the functional division of labour can be applied to the science-push model of innovation. The science-push model is one of central laboratories doing R&D and pushing it on to design engineer departments and on to production managers. In the interactive model responsibility for discovering new technological knowledge is spread from the central corporate laboratory to functionally integrated production groups. The chain-linked metaphor for technology innovation has been elaborated by Stephen Kline to capture the interaction and feedback loops common to many revolutionary new products and industries including, for example, the jet engine.[36]

The NPD-pull, interactive model seeks to permeate R&D throughout the organization in a way that draws the customer/user into the definition of the problem and the solution. The concept of customer here is not only the final customer, but the chain of customers in which each producing link treats the next link as the customer. Decentralizing technology management for purposes of NPD mirrors the displacement of the responsibility for quality control from a central department into the operating activities of work teams on the shop-floor.

Teruo Yamanouchi, an ex-Canon Director of the Corporate Technical Planning and Operations Center, distinguishes a range of technology categories.[37] Discovery-driven knowledge and pre-competitive knowledge are at the base of a technology pyramid and overlap with the domain of science. Yamanouchi argues that technology management with the Japanese business enterprise has not made contributions to these areas of technological knowledge. Rather, the pool of scientific knowledge is tapped by Japanese enter-

---

[35] The engineering change orders and other changes required to implement rapid new product development are not conceivable under the Scientific Management paradigm.

[36] See S. Kline (1985), 'Innovation is not a Linear Process', *Research Management*, 28 (July–Aug.), 36–45; id. (1991), 'Styles of Innovation and Their Cultural Basis', *ChemTech*, 21/8: 472–80.

[37] See T. Yamanouchi (1995), *A New Study of Technology Management*, Tokyo: Asian Productivity Center (distributed in North America and Western Europe by Quality Resources, New York).

prises for purposes of identifying a third layer of generic technologies to institutionalize a Schumpeterian innovation process. Here is where the Japanese technology management system has made significant contributions. Generic technologies form the foundation for ensuing layers described as core technology, product technology, engineering technology, and environmental technology.

Technology management at Canon is not a linear process beginning with generic technology. The process begins with developmental research for purposes of product innovation on technological categories near or at the top of the technology pyramid. This research is conducted on or next to the shopfloor. Findings at this level feed into applied research in design centers or business level labs which, in turn, leads to modifications in core technology; where applied research is not enough, fundamental research in corporate laboratories is conducted at the generic technology level. Contributions here lead to technological advance which can feed back into scientific knowledge. The Japanese technology management system has been particularly strong at recombining generic technologies and integrating these with process technologies. But, to date, most of the Japanese contributions to fundamental knowledge has been at the generic technology level as distinct from the more narrowly defined levels of scientific knowledge at the bottom two layers of the pyramid.

The technology management model is consistent with Deming's underlying concept of system and, as in production, led to the replacement of a push for a pull analogy.[38] However, such a small conceptual step represents a paradigm shift in the power relationships within an existing business enterprise. In the process of creating a knowledge-discovering business organization, the activities of work, management, and R&D are profoundly redefined.[39] The new business model connects Deming's focus on continuous redesign of the product to Kline's chain-linked model of technological innovation.

The new model of the business enterprise, the 'entrepreneurial firm', is one that not only achieves continuous innovation built on Deming-inspired organizational methods but one that combines continuous innovation with technology management and thereby develops the capability to manage technology transitions. Canon, for example, redefined the camera by rethinking the camera as a computer with a lens. The means was to combine the electronics and optical technology (generic technologies) with precision-machinery technology and component-assembly technology (engineering technologies).

[38] Combining the concepts of chain-of-customers and interactive or chain-linked R&D results in an organization in which each production link is also a customer to central R&D units. The resulting NPD-pull is analogous to 'kanban' or pull-scheduling in which decisions to produce are governed not by a centralized scheduling department but by the demand of succeeding units.

[39] The Wagner Act was not set up to deal with quality, productivity, or innovation. The plan-do-check-act model of work organization is a prerequisite as is the development of a quality system.

Canon didn't simply combine generic technologies. It adopted, adapted, and refined generic technologies and combined them in unique ways. The result was the emergence of specialized, proprietary-product technologies which were not easily imitated. Firms without the Deming type organizational capabilities could not meet the time and quality standards; companies without the expertise across the range of technologies could not match the production-performance standards.

Canon did not stop here. The emergent technological capabilities gave the company sophisticated resources to target on technologically related areas. Canon moved first into the electronic office-equipment business by developing electronic calculators which, in turn, led to the development of digital-technology capabilities. The big hit came in the photocopier business in which Canon established a unique cartridge-product technology by combined technologies transferred from the camera and office-equipment businesses with new technologies such as electrophotographic-process technology, photosensitive-materials technology, and toner technology.

Combining Deming and Schumpeter in the same business enterprise has led to the development of an organizational chart that is unique in that two organizations function side by side within the same company: one accomodates the cost, quality, and delivery-time performance standards associated with Deming; the other accommodates technological management to drive innovation and competitive strategies based on ever-shorter product life-cycles.[40]

The organizational structure is designed to establish layers in the R&D process to target product development at the business-unit level and the development of long-term core technologies at the company level. The concept of the company is defined in terms of the core technologies and associated organizational capabilities. Separating the organizations enables the company to engage in both incremental and breakthrough innovation. The company has relatively open channels for internal technology transfer to new business units and core technologies are revitalized as new products and business units are developed.

To summarize: product-led competition has engendered new organizational capabilities which involve the redefinition and integration of four processes:

1. *manufacturing*: the cell is the building block of the whole edifice; without cellular manufacturing the rest of the business system cannot drive product-led competition and continuous improvement.

---

[40] The chief technologist of each centre or laboratory does not report along the business system chain of command; instead, he/she reports to a technology-strategy committee with the vice-president of R&D as chair. The central labs, in turn, are hubs which network with the product-specific research centres with responsibility to their respective business groups.

2. *design/manufacturing cycle*: companies need to compete on the basis of rapid new product development or they will fall behind in technology adoption.
3. *technology adoption*: technologies are pulled by the first two processes as distinct from being pushed by autonomous R&D activities.
4. *technology R&D*: increased technology knowledge is generated by developmental research, applied research, and generic technological research.

TM 5: INTEL AND SYSTEM INTEGRATION

America's semiconductor industry looked dead in 1990. Massachusetts, the home of Route 128, lost one-third of its manufacturing jobs between 1986 and 1992. The loss in industrial leadership was not expected in high-tech industries. Scientific research in the great laboratories of corporations like AT&T, DuPont, GE, IBM, and Xerox were seemingly unable either to develop new commercially successful products or to stem the loss of technological leadership as Japanese and South Korean companies developed manufacturing capabilities in high-tech industries.[41] Many warned of a 'hollowing out' of American industry given the capability of the Japanese model to engage in rapid new product development, diffuse technological innovations, and achieve new comprehensive production-performance standards.

But by 1996 the USA had established dominant position in microprocessor chips (the most technologically complex semiconductor) and a strong leadership position in personal computers, telecommunications including internet related activities, and software. Sales in information and communication technology (ICT) related industries grew from $340 billion in 1990 to $570 billion in 1995, a period during which Japanese ICT related industries grew less than one-quarter as much, from $450 billion to $500 billion (*The Economist*, 29 Mar. 1997). Both Silicon Valley and Route 128 were booming again.

Why the resurgence? The resurgence can be explained, in part, by the development and diffusion of a new technology-management model which builds on American strengths in fundamental research and software. In addition, the source of American industrial weakness, the lack of system integration, has been reincarnated and become its strength.

At the core of system integration, in American success stories, is the integration of hardware and software which, in turn, creates new potential for

---

[41] Seven Nobel prizes were awarded for science breakthroughs at Bell labs. Most of the major labs were associated with breakthrough innovations that had redefined whole industries such as the transistor at Bell labs or nylon at DuPont. Nevertheless all have suffered loss of support.

product design and process integration in both production and non-production processes. Put differently, the new technology-management model combines system integration and information technology with new product development. It goes beyond the Canon new-product development organizational capability to include the capability to reconstitute the product or service as an application of information technology. The new capability is perhaps less alien to the machining-shop that has always produced custom designs but in limited volume. The new model of technology management expands the possibility of custom design without violating the principle of flow.

Flow production has evolved from Ford's application to a single product to multiple products at Toyota and to new-product development with multiple technologies as in the Canon model; but it has always been based on set designs. Removal of the design constraint is new; the integration of software and hardware is creating new opportunities to custom-design products and processes in high-volume industries.

Custom design is the competitive advantage of the fashion industries of the industrial districts of the Third Italy. Intra- and interfirm flexibility in production combine with great design to produce leadership in a range of light industries. The idea of integrating custom design with flow in industries which combine complex technologies is not yet a completed project but a destination point on a map in which the organizational pathways are taking shape.[42]

The destination point is one-piece flow applied to product design. Mass production at Ford and Toyota held design constant; Canon demonstrated the potential of combining technologies to strategically redefine products and markets. But the integration of software and hardware, both within the chip and across chips and control devices, opens the new frontier as surely as the compass did to navigation. Product engineering is as crucial to the new frontier as it was to mass production, but it is software engineering that opens 'heavy' industry to the design imagination.

New and old firms alike, in a range of industries, have seized opportunities offered by information technology to radically redefine products and processes. They do not, in leading cases, simply add information technology to pre-existing products and processes. Instead, they integrate software and hardware to invent new products, or radically redesign old ones much as Henry Ford used unit-drive electric motors to redesign the production system according to the principle of flow.

The idea of integrating custom design with flow is not simple in industries which combine complex technologies. But the principle can be operative even

---

[42] Route 128 is particularly strong on system integration but relatively weak on volume production and associated engineering technologies. Success stories such as air defence and air traffic control systems are strong on custom design and system integration but weak on production. Silicon Valley's competitive advantage is in the integration of all three.

though its application may be incomplete. In fact, the goal may not be achieved for decades, much as one-piece flow took decades after Ford successfully applied the concept of synchronization to single products.

Intel may be a similar example. The microprocessor is as fundamental to the new model of technology management as the machine tool was to interchangeability and as distinctive to the new era as the car was to mass production. In addition, Intel's production challenge is to combine the design flexibility of machine-shops with the throughput efficiency of the car producers in a technologically complex industry. Intel's distinctive competence is not custom-designed microprocessors but leadership in volume chip production of technologically complex chips with ever-greater performance characteristics. This involves combining fast changing technologies with leadership in chip design.

Intel's production line is reminiscent of Ford's mass production lines without individual machine operators. But whereas Ford pursued process integration and synchronized a range of machines, Intel pursues system integration and integrates over 600 activities embodying an array of technologies with deep roots in various science research programmes being conducted outside the company.[43]

What distinguishes Intel's production system is the construction of full-scale experimentation plants which are replicas of the production line.[44] The idea is that the new-product development process cannot be carried out without experimentation in full-scale, actual operating conditions. Pilot plants which are small scale or which use dated technology will not do. The production line itself, however, can not be subject to experiments; the opportunity costs of shutting down the line are too high.

The experimentation plants are enormously expensive. But instead of a production team driving high throughput, the experiment plants are operated by technology-integration teams. The teams are not conducting fundamental research but collectively team members are familiar with a whole range of technology domains each with deep roots in fundamental science.[45] The experiments may involve an entirely new chip in which case many of the

---

[43] It is no secret that most of the world's chip-making plants are not organized according to the principle of flow, even Intel's. This is changing. Ford and Ohno would have understood the following quote in *Business Week* (4 July 1994): 'Rethinking the plant floor and grouping equipment in clusters should cut the time required for wafers to jump through some 200 processing hoops from the present 60–90 days to just 7. That's because wafers wouldn't spend 90% or more of their shop-floor time being shuffled between operations and sitting in queues.'

[44] This section draws heavily from Marco Iansiti and Jonathan West (1997), 'Technology Integration: Turning Great Research into Great Products', *Harvard Business Review* (May–June) 69–79 and 'Silicon Valley: The Valley of Money's Delight', *The Economist*, 29 Mar. 1997. Intel's basic research budget is a minuscule $10 million annually but Intel funds work at universities and national laboratories (*Business Week*, 26 May 1997, 170).

[45] Iansiti and West point out that a number of the technology-integration team members will be recent graduates who have done dissertations on fundamental science.

technologies will be novel applications, some of which will have never been used before (Iansiti and West, 1997: 70). Or a team may be developing a new version of an existing chip. Intel, for example, produces some thirty different kinds of the 486 chip (*The Economist*, 23 March 1996, 21). Here, too, experiments will be conducted on novel applications and combinations.

The experimentation activities are as much about the complexities of integrating technologies and ramping up production as they are about refining individual technologies. Henry Ford and his chief engineer, Charles Sorensen, would have understood the challenge, and rewards, of system integration. Applying the principle of system entails redesigning the product from inside-out and outside-in to enhance flow. Popularly known as concurrent engineering, new products (inside) are designed simultaneously with production (outside). Intel's cross-functional teams, however, would not have appealed to Henry Ford. Effective management of the experiments depends upon real participation from a range of individuals with technological expertise as well as individuals with experience in design, product and process engineering, and production.

Technology management for both Henry Ford and Intel involves a second concurrent or double redesign challenge: redesign of technologies to fit production and redesign of production to fit the new technologies and technology combinations. Ford, as noted above, redesigned the production system to take advantage of new electric-power technologies, particularly distributed or fractionated power designed into each machine. Ford's engineers revamped machines to fit the cycle-time standard by adjusting, for example, tooling and material speeds. Ford and Intel do not simply add new technologies to the existing system, the idea is to redesign the system to take full advantage of the new technology to make a leap in production performance.

For Ford, technology referred to machines, whereas for Intel technology refers to distinctive science-technology domains with unique science lineage and physical characteristics.[46] Intel has redefined the production system to take advantage of the opportunity for integrating software and hardware. Equally fundamental, Intel combines technologies in both production and rapid new-product development. Like Ford, Intel carries out R&D primarily on combining operations (machines for Ford, technologies for Intel) as distinct from focusing on radical technological breakthroughs. Both treat technology management as the challenge of redesigning and reconfiguring machines, technologies, and processes to improve production performance.

Intel's technology-management process breaks with Henry Ford, Canon, and Toyota in a second way: it is embedded in virtual laboratories in the form

---

[46] In this conception of technology, Intel's application is closer to the Japanese tendency to conflate science and technology into the single term science-technology. Kline, Rosenberg, and others offer many examples of technology assisting in the development of science. Astronomy, for one, depended upon advances in optical instruments.

of broad and deep networks of researchers at the frontiers of scientific and technological research in Silicon Valley. Integration team members are also members of research communities anchored in the research universities. In fact, Silicon Valley project teams are continuously combining and recombining within a population of 6,000 high-tech firms.[47] Silicon Valley is an unparalleled information and communication technology industrial district.

The research networks in districts like Silicon Valley extend beyond the firm enabling project teams to participate in a highly innovative milieu for technology management. The principles of flow and system integration which Japan applied to integrate production and new-product development are present and reinforced at the district level to anchor a new model of regional technology management particularly appropriate to 'knowledge-intensive' industries. It would not work without ties to a strong and growing knowledge base in fundamental research and the associated human-resource development of research universities. It is estimated that 1,000 companies have spun out of both Stanford and MIT.[48]

The Intel/Silicon Valley model of technology management is not a fundamental break in principles but an extension in their application. System integration is being applied at five interactive levels: hardware and software; multiple technologies; production and non-production processes; industrial district or cluster; and custom design and production.

NATIONAL TECHNOLOGY MANAGEMENT AND RAPID GROWTH: A BRIEF NOTE

Successful technology management enhances growth potential. The East Asian economies that have achieved high rates of growth have a critical mass of industrial enterprises with the capability to adopt, adapt, and diffuse technologies that originated in the most technologically advanced nations. Japan, South Korea, and Taiwan-China have developed the capability to develop new products and processes based on refining, fusing, and advancing generic technologies. Together these are attributes of a national system of production and technology management.[49] Sustained high growth rates depend upon

---

[47] The 6,000 high-tech firms of Silicon Valley have sales of approximately $200bn. Intel is not the only driver of new products. One in 5 of the Silicon Valley public companies are gazelles which means they have grown at least 20 per cent in each of the last 4 years (the number for the USA is 1 in 35).

[48] According to a study by the BankBoston Economics Department, MIT graduates have started 4,000 companies nationwide. The study claims that in Massachusetts, the 1065 MIT-related companies account for 25 per cent of sales of all manufacturing firms and 33 per cent of all software sales in the state (See MIT: 'The Impact of Innovation', web page at <http://web.mit.edu/newsoffice/founders>.)

[49] Slow-growth followers, on the other hand, lack the capabilities to tap the world's pool of technologies. This is not surprising. Successful technology management itself requires the

Table 1.1. Five cases of technology management

	Case	Production principle	Application	Performance breakthrough	Organizational capability
TM 1	Armory	Inter-changeability	Replace handfitters	Product performance	Product engineering, special machines and tooling
TM 2	Ford	Flow	Single product	Cost	Process engineering, synchronization
TM 3	Toyota	Flow	Multiple products	Cost, quality, lead time	GT, cellular manufacturing, kaizen
TM 4	Canon	Flow, system integration	New-product development, generic technology integration	Product innovation	Applied R&D, proprietary technology development
TM 5	Intel	Flow, system integration	New-product concept, new-system design	Smart products	Software engineering, science and technology integration and networking, system transitions

making the transition along the technology management spectrum summarized in Table 1.1.

Making such transitions is not easy. The rapid pace of introduction of technologies in the success stories is a consequence of the prior or simultaneous development of a specific set of production capabilities. The high performers started with the idea of cutting-edge technologies, not with the idea of a rapid pace of absorption of technologies. The latter was a consequence of driving down cycle-times first in production and second in new-product development. Other East Asian nations have followed Japan, particularly in driving down production throughput times. But making the transition to multi-product flow requires development of corollary organizational capabilities variously named 'kaizen', 'continuous improvement', 'high performance work organization', 'total quality management', 'self-directed work teams', and

development of three distinct but interrelated capabilities: strategic, organizational, and production. Successful technology management, like the establishment of price for Alfred Marshall, depends upon both blades of a pair of scissors; supply must be matched by effective demand. While demand in price theory is mediated by income, demand in technology management is mediated by production capabilities.

'plan-do-check-act'. This means considerable investment in human capital to achieve the requisite performance standards.

Articulating a technology management strategy is central to economic policy-making for a developmental state. Distinctive technology-management strategies in each of the high-growth East Asian countries can be identified. In fact, the idea of national technology management is to the theory of the developmental state what demand management was to Keynesian economics or money-supply management is to monetarism.

2. Foreign Direct Investment: Towards Co-operative Institutional Arrangements between the North and the South?

Ajit Singh and Ann Zammit

1. THE CONTEXT

The last decade has witnessed a very fast growth of foreign direct investment (FDI)—this both reflects and extends the globalization of production. Although the greater part of FDI is still carried out by multinationals of one advanced country investing in another, a significant and perhaps increasing proportion of multinationals' foreign investment is now taking place in developing countries (the South).

In the orthodox view, the liberalization of trade and capital movements, and the associated phenomena of the globalization of markets and production, lead to a more efficient allocation of the world's resources and faster world growth rates.[1] Specifically, in relation to Northern multinational investment in the South, both the North and the South are thought to gain. Developing countries are supposed to benefit in a number of different ways, including notably through the transfer of technology as well as the augmentation of their investment resources. The shareholders of multinationals in the advanced countries ostensibly gain from the higher returns in developing countries than they might otherwise earn. The North's workers, it is suggested, benefit from the export of capital goods which investment by multinationals invariably involves.

To consolidate the benefits of liberalization and globalization, the OECD countries are currently negotiating a binding multilateral agreement on investment (MAI) which would remove most of the remaining constraints on the free flow of FDI. It is intended that developing countries will be invited to accede (without any special concessions to accommodate their underdevelopment) to the final negotiated agreement—an agreement in whose formulation

---

[1] See for example IMF (1997).

they will have had no say. It is possible that some Latin American countries will be early joiners. It is expected that this will generate an irresistible momentum with other low-income countries feeling impelled to join also. The OECD's objective is that the MAI should become a global policy framework, based on high standards with regard to the rights and treatment of FDI.

The orthodox thesis on FDI has in the past been challenged by developing countries who, while fully recognizing certain advantages to be gained from multinational investment, have been concerned among other things by the enormous economic and political power of multinationals, their potential for monopolistic abuse, and practices such as transfer pricing which reduce the net benefits to the country. However, in the current era of liberalization and globalization, under the guidance and advice of the multilateral financial institutions, there has been a sea change in the attitude of developing countries towards FDI. Today these countries are competing strongly with one another to offer incentives to attract such investment.

The main criticism of multinational investment nowadays comes from workers and the general public in developed countries, who attribute their high unemployment levels to the relocation of enterprises in low-wage developing countries and increasing competition from such countries. This criticism has been given academic expression by some economists who identify increased competition from the South, due in part to investment there by multinationals, as being a main cause of (a) deindustrialization (specifically, in the sense of a reduction either in the absolute numbers or the proportion of workers employed in manufacturing industry); (b) growing inequality in income distribution; and (c) unemployment in many Northern economies.

In this overall context, this chapter has the following objectives:

(a) to discuss, specifically in the light of the experience of the highly successful East Asian economies, the question of technology transfer by the multinationals to developing countries, and to explore the conditions under which it is most likely to occur;
(b) to examine the theses which attribute recent observed unfavourable labour-market outcomes in the North—namely de-industrialization, unemployment, and growing dispersion—largely to multinational investment and to the consequent competition from low-wage countries; and
(c) to examine how the OECD-proposed MAI, or a similar treaty, would affect technology transfer to the South or aid/hinder the South's development effort in other ways, and how it would affect overall welfare in the North.

It will be argued in this chapter that, on balance, the proposed OECD treaty will not in itself be helpful either to countries in the South or in the North. It is suggested that the question of FDI needs to be considered in relation to the overall growth of the world economy.

2. FDI: RECENT TRENDS

1(a) There has been a very rapid growth of FDI during the last ten years or so. Average annual FDI inflows rose from US$77.5bn. during 1983–7 to US$177.3bn. in 1988–92, and to US$315bn. in 1995. This represents an increase over the period 1985–1995 of about 400 per cent in nominal US dollar terms; the increase was just under 200 per cent in real terms (adjusted by the deflator for OECD gross fixed investment) (UN, 1996; WTO, 1996).

1(b) The growth of FDI has also been quite fast in comparison with other relevant variables. Between 1980 and 1994, the ratio of FDI flows to world gross domestic capital formation doubled. The world gross product of foreign affiliates (a value measure of their output produced abroad) accounted for 6 per cent of world GDP in 1991 (the latest year for which data are available), compared with 2 per cent in 1982.

1(c) In absolute terms, as at 1993, multinational companies are estimated to have employed 73 million people worldwide. The global sales of multinational affiliates, again worldwide, in that year was US$6 trillion. This compares with the value of US$4.7 trillion of goods and non-factor services delivered through exports. More significantly, of the latter figure, about a quarter represented intrafirm exports. The bulk of FDI[2] originates in OECD countries and goes to other OECD economies: in recent years the approximate magnitudes are 85 per cent of all outflows and 65 per cent of all inflows, the USA being the major host as well as home (source) country.

2. As Table 2.1 indicates, FDI flows to developing countries nearly doubled between 1981 and 1985 and between 1986 and 1990 from US$13bn. a year to US$ 25 billion. The inflows more than doubled again over the next four years to over US$ 63.4 billion a year between 1991 and 1994. Although there are significant fluctuations, there has been a trend increase in the 1990s in the developing country share in total FDI inflows. The share more than doubled between 1986 and 1990 and below 1991 and 1994, from 16 to 33.3 per cent. However, between 1981 and 1985, the developing country share was 25.9 per cent.

3. Most FDI flows to developing countries have been concentrated in a small number of developing countries. In 1993, 81 per cent of FDI inflows went to ten countries: China, Singapore, Argentina, Mexico, Malaysia, Indonesia, Thailand, Hong Kong, Taiwan, and Nigeria, in descending order of magnitude. Over the past decade, these ten countries have consistently

---

[2] 95 per cent of FDI consists of transactions between multinationals and their subsidiaries. For the purposes of this chapter, FDI and multinational investments are synonymous.

Table 2.1. FDI inflows and stock in developing countries, 1981–1995

	Average annual inflow			Inflow			Stock, 1994
	1981–5	1986–90	1991–4	1993	1994	1995	
Value ($ billion)	13.1	25.3	63.4	73.4	87.0	99.7	584.0
Share of world total (%)	25.9	16.0	33.3	35.2	39.0	32.0	25.2

Source: UN (1996) and UNIDO (1996).

attracted between two-thirds and four-fifths of developing country inward investment (see UNIDO, 1996).

4. Developing countries, during the last ten years, have also become important in FDI outflows. Between 1983 and 1987, these outflows accounted for about 5 per cent of the total world outflows. The corresponding average figure for 1993–5 is about 16 per cent, i.e. more than three times larger.

5. Not only has there been a large trend increase in FDI flows to developing countries during the last ten to fifteen years, but these flows have also been subject to considerable fluctuations. The fluctuations can have significant consequences for macroeconomic management in these countries.

3. MULTINATIONALS, TECHNOLOGY TRANSFER, AND ECONOMIC DEVELOPMENT: ANALYTICAL ISSUES AND EVIDENCE

Analytical issues

In considering the issue of technology transfer, it is useful to bear in mind the following analytical points:

(a) By saving time and resources otherwise devoted to re-inventing known technology, the transfer of technology from advanced industrial economies can speed up the industrialization of developing countries.

(b) Investment by multinationals is only one way for a late-industrializing country to obtain technology: other methods include the import of capital goods, licensing, and reverse engineering. The choice by the government or the private sector as to which method is adopted in any particular case depends on the specific country circumstances and the relative cost of each method.

(c) FDI can be a relatively expensive method of obtaining technology. This is due to the fact that, compared with other sources of capital such as portfolio investment and long-term loans, FDI, other things being equal, is likely to be relatively more risky from the perspective of the investor. Of the three, the form of investment which has the most certain return is long-term loans, because the return is fixed. This would be subject to a greater or smaller default risk, depending on the kind of investment which is selected. Portfolio investment and FDI have more uncertain returns. Portfolio investment may normally be regarded as relatively more liquid than FDI, but the distinction between the two is getting blurred as a result of the enormous development of financial markets which has occurred in the last ten to fifteen years. In the context of such markets, the more significant point is that it is easier and therefore less expensive to hedge against the risks involved in portfolio investment than in FDI. This is largely because the latter risks are less standard and therefore more difficult to express in terms of uniform financial products.[3]

Consequently, investors would expect to receive a higher return on FDI. So if the same technology could be obtained through FDI, the purchase of capital goods, or through licensing, the latter two may be less expensive. However, if the technology is not the same, in that to make it fully operational it requires organizational and management skills which are provided by the multinationals and which can have important spillover effects, this argument may well not apply. To the extent that the multinational has a 'monopoly' of knowledge over such skills, it may be able to gain 'monopoly' rents. Whether or not the latter can be whittled away depends on the degree of competition from enterprises with more or less substitutable products also requiring similar specialized knowledge. It will also be a function of the bargaining power of the host country, which in turn will depend among other things on the country's level of development and the quality of its human capital resources.

Empirical evidence

With respect to empirical evidence, we concentrate here on the experience of the fast-growing East and South East Asian NICs. This is for the following reasons:

(i) many of these countries have been major recipients of FDI;
(ii) they display a variety of experience with respect to their treatment of FDI;
(iii) notwithstanding these varying basic approaches to FDI in different countries, each country has so far been economically highly successful; and
(iv) the international financial institutions ascribe their economic success to their openness to the world economy and to their 'deep integration' with it through FDI.

---

[3] See further Kregel's (1996) excellent discussion of this issue.

Table 2.2. Share of inward FDI flows in gross fixed-capital formation, developed, and Asian economies (percentage)

Region/Economy	1984–9 (annual average)	1990	1991	1992	1993	1994	1990–4 (annual average)
Developed countries	3.9	4.9	3.3	3.1	3.5	3.3	3.6
Canada	5.4	6.5	2.4	4.2	5.0	5.9	4.8
France	3.5	5.2	5.9	8.2	8.9	7.1	7.1
Germany	1.0	0.9	1.2	0.6	0.1	-0.9	0.4
Japan	—a	0.2	0.2	0.3	—a	0.1	0.2
Netherlands	9.9	20.8	10.7	11.9	10.8	6.8	12.2
United Kingdom	11.5	17.0	9.4	9.1	10.2	6.6	10.5
United States	5.8	6.0	3.0	2.2	4.7	4.8	4.1
Developing countries	2.8	3.2	4.0	4.8	6.3	7.5	5.2
China	1.8	2.6	3.3	7.8	20.0	24.5	11.6
Hong Kong	12.2	8.5	2.3	7.7	7.1	8.2	6.8
India	0.2	0.2	0.3	0.3	0.5	1.1	0.5
Indonesia	1.6	2.8	3.6	3.9	3.8	3.6	3.5
Korea	1.4	0.8	1.0	0.6	0.5	0.6	0.7
Malaysia	8.8	23.8	23.8	26.0	22.5	16.1	22.4
Singapore	28.3	47.1	33.5	13.3	24.6	23.5	28.4
Taiwan	3.3	3.8	3.0	2.4	2.4	3.5	3.0
Thailand	4.4	7.1	4.9	4.8	3.5	1.1	4.3

a value zero or negligible.

Source: UN (1996), *World Investment Report: Investment, Trade and International Policy Arrangements.*

Japan and the first tier NICs

We consider first the case of Japan and Korea. A striking fact about these two countries in relation to FDI is that, as Table 2.2 indicates, FDI has not been significant in quantitative terms—its share in gross domestic capital formation has been and continues to be very small. In order to upgrade their technological level, these countries have relied largely on imported purchases of capital goods and on licensing arrangements. These were regarded as a more efficient means of importing technology than FDI in the context of these countries national priorities and institutions, as explained below (Okimoto, 1989; Chang, 1996).

As importantly, these countries built up a national system of technological development as part of their industrial policy, in order to enhance their own capacity to adapt and develop technology.[4] Freeman (1989) has described in detail the main components of this integrated system of national technological development in Japan and Korea. He notes, among other things, that during its high growth phase (1950–73) Japan was producing relatively more engineers than the United States in the same period. More recently, Korea and Taiwan have been outdoing Japan in this respect. Freeman suggests that one reason Korea and Japan discouraged FDI was that foreign multinationals would not have been so readily amenable to the system of administrative guidance in these countries, which was central to the implementation of their industrial policies. Furthermore, using the non-FDI route to achieving technology placed full responsibility for assimilating imported technology on domestic enterprises. This, he argues, is far more likely to lead to 'total system improvements than the turnkey plant mode of import or the foreign subsidiary mode'.

With respect to Korea, UN (1993) suggests that there is a link between the national ownership of large firms ('chaebols') and the level of investment in research and development. Korea has in relative terms by far the largest expenditure on R&D among developing countries—1.9 per cent of GDP in 1988, compared with 0.5 per cent for Argentina (1988), 0.6 per cent for Mexico (1984), and 0.4 per cent for Brazil (1985). Korea outperformed even many developed countries in this sphere (Belgium 1.7 per cent in 1987, Denmark 1.5 per cent in 1987, and Italy 1.2 per cent in 1987). Korea's expenditure on R&D was, of course, still below that of industrial superpowers: Japan 2.8 per cent in 1987 and Germany also 2.8 per cent in 1987.

Nevertheless, despite its relatively small magnitude, in qualitative terms, FDI has been important in Korean economic development. It was used to develop certain key industries regarded by the authorities as critical to their development efforts, when this was seen to be the only means of obtaining the

---

[4] Frederick List had advocated such a system for Germany in the nineteenth century in order to improve its capacity to compete with the UK. Many of his insights remain relevant today.

required technology.[5] FDI projects were therefore carefully screened to achieve national industrial policy objectives.

Turning to Taiwan, Table 2.2 suggests that as a proportion of gross domestic capital formation Taiwan has used relatively more FDI than Korea and Japan. But it will be noted that Taiwan's resort to FDI was well below the developing country average. More importantly, in Taiwan's case too, FDI has been used purposefully under government guidance as part of a conscious effort to upgrade the technological level of the country's production and export structure (Wade, 1990).

The highly successful economic development of the other two countries among the first tier Asian NICs—Singapore and Hong Kong—is of limited general relevance because they are small city states. Nevertheless, it is significant that these two countries followed very different policies with respect to FDI. In the case of Singapore, there has been a high level of FDI, but this has been an integral part of the government's long-term programme of industrial and technological upgrading. Hong Kong, on the other hand, attracted a large amount of FDI but this was essentially on a *laissez-faire* basis. Lall (1995) has argued that the lack of an industrial policy has disadvantaged Hong Kong's industrial development. It has suffered massive de-industrialization over the last ten years, to a much greater extent than would be expected at the colony's level of per capita income. Between 1986 and 1992, Hong Kong's manufacturing employment fell by a colossal 35 per cent. Lall reports that there are now influential voices in Hong Kong calling for an industrial policy in order to reverse this detrimental trend. The city has so far been able to cope with this situation by its development of a high productivity financial services sector. Whether or not this would be adequate to meet Hong Kong's long-term needs is a moot point; such a strategy, however, is not generally feasible for larger economies since this sector is unlikely to generate sufficient foreign exchange to pay for imported manufactured goods for which income elasticity of demand tends to be very high. (See further Singh, 1987, Rowthorn and Wells, 1987.)

Second-tier NICs: Indonesia, Malaysia, and Thailand

It is widely believed that these three countries have relied on large amounts of FDI for their development as compared with the first-tier NICs. But, as Chang (1996) has pointed out (see also figures in Table 2.2) Thailand and Indonesia, though resorting to more FDI than the first-tier NICs in relation to gross domestic capital formation, used about the same or less than the average for developing countries. Only in the case of Malaysia has FDI been relatively much more important.

[5] See further Chang (1996).

Significantly, in all three countries FDI has been used as part of an industrial policy and has involved, among other things, the use of performance requirements. As Jomo and his colleagues (1997) note, however, the effectiveness of industrial policy as an instrument of national development has been diluted in these countries at times by its use for political and rent-seeking ends.

Although these second-tier NICs have been very successful over the last fifteen years in terms of GDP growth, there are questions about the sustainability of their growth record. There are weaknesses in their national technological systems, such that their domestic firms do not yet have a strong capacity to assimilate and develop technology. This renders the countries heavily dependent for their technological development on continuing large inflows of FDI. In addition, Thailand and Malaysia currently have huge current account deficits which are relatively larger than even that of Mexico prior to the crisis in 1994. This also makes them vulnerable to any sudden large reversals of net FDI flows. In this context, it is important to bear in mind the fact that a considerable proportion of FDI normally consists of reinvested profits. Increased profit repatriation by multinationals fearing a currency devaluation because of market doubts about the sustainability of their large current account deficits makes the financial position of countries like Malaysia and Thailand particularly fragile.

China

China has been by far the largest developing country recipient of FDI in the recent period. Although in the 1980s in relative terms FDI inflows into China were quite small, there has been a sharp quantum leap in the 1990s. Table 2.2 shows that in 1994 and 1995 FDI amounted to almost 20 per cent of China's gross domestic capital formation. This figure may somewhat overestimate true FDI because of 'round-tripping' that is, counting in FDI statistics domestic investment routed via a foreign country in order to seek fiscal advantages. More significantly, FDI in China differs in an important way from that in other developing countries. It consists largely of capital investment by overseas Chinese from Hong Kong, Macao, Taiwan, and Singapore. It is estimated that between 1979 and 1993 Hong Kong alone accounted for nearly 70 per cent and Hong Kong and Taiwan together nearly 80 per cent of the total cumulative FDI flows to China during that period. The corresponding figures for the USA and Japan were by comparison, 5.4 per cent and 4.8 per cent respectively.

Case-studies suggest that much the larger part of overseas Chinese investment is directed towards technological upgrading and development.[6] This is

---

[6] As Dhanin Chearavanont, the overseas Chinese chairman of Charoen Pokphand observes:

achieved either by the overseas Chinese establishing their own subsidiaries in China or more frequently by means of them establishing joint ventures in China with other foreign firms whose technology is sought after. To some extent, therefore, the overseas Chinese act as a bridge and/or intermediary with non-Chinese multinationals and technology providers.

To sum up, the high-performing North-East and South-East Asian NICs have used different approaches to FDI in relation to their technological and economic development. Korea and Taiwan accepted only relatively small amounts of FDI, but used it strategically for technological advance. On the other hand, countries like Malaysia, Singapore, and to a degree even China have aggressively sought FDI but encouraged it to enter priority areas of development through fiscal and other incentives. Other than Hong Kong, none of the leading East Asian NICs have had a *laissez-faire* approach to FDI. They have all used industrial policy and imposed performance goals on multinationals to maximize the spillover benefits to the national economy. The experience of East and South-East Asian countries suggests that, in order for FDI to be most effectively used for technological and economic progress, there are three important lessons.[7] First, the governments need to be selective with respect to the choice of products and industries in which FDI is to play a role. Second the government must pay attention to the timing and phasing-in of foreign investment. Thirdly and importantly, the best use is made of FDI when governments have a national technology system of the kind implemented in Japan, Korea, and other countries.

4. MULTINATIONALS, OUTSOURCING, AND COMPETITION FOR THE NORTH FROM THE SOUTH[8]

As mentioned in the introduction, fears have been expressed in the North that technology transfer and shifting of production to the South by the North's multinationals have harmful consequences for workers in advanced countries. Wood (1994) in an important but contentious contribution has argued that most of the recent unfavourable developments in the labour market in the North referred to earlier are caused largely by competition from the

'if you want to invest in China you must bring technology China needs. The Chinese government is not stupid. If they suspect that we are only there to make a profit, they would not be very happy' (Vatikiotis, 1997).

[7] In Latin American and Caribbean countries there is a long held view that FDI doest not lead to substantial technological spillover and that often its main benefit has been to generate employment, as in the case of the *maquiladora* industries on the Mexican border with the USA. Recent evidence comparing multinational investment in Mexico, Venezuela, and the United states confirms this view and suggests that very low spillovers occur in the former two countries. There is much greater incidence in the United States because of the availability of the necessary human capital and infrastructure facilities. See further Aitken, Harrison and Lipsey (1995).

[8] The analysis of this section is in part based on Singh (1995).

South. Manufactured imports from the South into Northern markets increased at a very fast rate in the 1980s and 1990s, a period during which there was also a faster pace of deindustrialization, a large rise in unemployment, and increasing inequality in the wages of skilled and unskilled workers. Wood regards these latter events as being mainly caused by the former.

Wood himself does not deal with the question of Northern FDI in the South in great detail. It is however widely believed in industrial countries that multinational investment and outsourcing in developing countries has been an important factor in contributing to the rapidly increasing competitive capacity of the South and is detrimental to the interests of the North's workers. Thus Bluestone and Harrison (1982) in their influential contribution on US deindustrialization:

In seeking to escape a 'pro-union' or 'anti-business' climate inside the United States, large corporations . . . can build, expand, or acquire facilities outside the country altogether. In fact, all the strategic innovations devised by multi-plant companies for playing off one group of workers against another . . . have become standard operating procedure in the global economy.

Similarly in a special report in the mid-1980s *Business Week* bemoaned the 'hollowing' of US corporations:

By shifting production overseas, US companies are whittling away at the critical mass essential to a strong industrial base. If globalization of industry means that US manufacturers will wind up simply licking the labels and sticking them on products that are made abroad, the nation can look forward to a declining standard of living.[9]

More recently there has been great concern in Germany with the phenomenon of 'standortwettbewerb' (locational competition) under which German firms have been increasingly outsourcing production especially to Eastern European countries.

Wood's thesis is challenged by a number of economists on several points. The main criticism levelled against his conclusions is that they are implausible because imports from the South account for only a small proportion of domestic demand in the North (see Table 2.3). Wood however uses the same data to suggest that although the import penetration has been small overall, there has been a very rapid increase since 1978, particularly in products produced by low-skill labour. His estimates suggest that imports from the South have led to a net reduction of 12 per cent in manufacturing employment in the North. Further, to the extent that Southern competition induces labour-saving technical progress in the North, Wood suggests that this may have resulted in additional job losses of equal magnitude. Thus for Wood the fast growth of imports from the South is a main cause of both deindustrialization and overall unemployment in industrial countries. He also assembles consid-

    [9] 'The Hollow Corporation', *Business Week*, 3 Mar. 1986, 60.

Table 2.3. Share of manufactured imports from developing countries in total manufacturing output in the United States, European Union, and Japan, 1975–1990 (percentage)

Country	1975	1980	1985	1990
United States	2.4	5.0	8.1	10.6
European Union	1.9	3.4	4.3	6.1
Japan	1.3	1.8	1.9	3.2

Source: UNCTAD (1995), *Trade and Development Report*, 133.

erable evidence to suggest that the rising inequality between skilled and unskilled workers in the North is due largely to Southern competition rather than technical change.

However, in overall macroeconomic terms the attribution of the large observed variations in manufacturing employment experienced by industrial countries during the last two decades to changes in manufacturing trade with the South is problematical. Table 2.4 indicates that from 1970 to 1993 manufacturing employment in the G7 countries fell by 15 per cent, whilst there was only a very small decline in the North–South manufacturing trade balance. Moreover, as UNCTAD (1995) notes, the timing of these losses did not systematically coincide with either a decline in the North's overall trade

Table 2.4. Employment and net trade in manufactures in the G7 countries, 1970–1993

Country	Employment (thousands)				Change 1970–93	
	1970	1980	1990	1993	Employment (percent)	Net exports of manufactures to developing countries (percent of GDP)
Canada	1,638	1,853	1,867	1,697	3.6	−1.4
France	5,196	5,103	4,352	3,991	−23.2	−0.5
Germany	8,203	7,229	7,120	7,056	−14.0	−0.9
Italy	3,289	3,333	2,757	2,697	−18.0	0.1
Japan	10,880	10,213	11,173	10,924	0.4	0.7
United Kingdom	7,951	6,462	4,798	4,314	−45.7	−1.9
United States	18,213	19,210	17,502	16,402	−9.9	−0.7
TOTAL G7	55,351	53,403	49,569	47,081	−15.0	−0.3

Source: UNCTAD (1995), *Trade and Development Report*, 137.

Note: For Germany and the United Kingdom the last available figures are for 1992.

surplus with the South or in the rise in imports from developing countries. Manufactured imports from developing countries into the North in fact grew more rapidly in the 1970s than in the 1980s—but the job losses occurred mostly in the latter decade. Moreover, the main reason for the decline in the North's manufacturing trade balance with the South in the 1980s was the fall in the North's exports due to the debt crisis in the South.

In contrast to the above macroeconomic considerations, the important part of Wood's empirical analysis is based on a modified Hecksher-Ohlin model and is carried out in microeconomic terms. He uses factor-content methodology to argue that, even with balanced trade between the North and the South, there would be huge job losses in the North because of the differing factor intensities of the North's exports and imports.

On the question of wage dispersion, the mainstream view is that Wood is wrong to ascribe most of the increased inequality in wages to trade with the South. Wood's critics concede that such trade has led to increased wage dispersion but suggest that no more than 10 to 20 per cent of it can be attributed to competition from developing countries, the rest being due to the nature of technical change. In relation to the effects of multinationals and their outsourcing of inputs to developing countries, the IMF summarizes the available evidence as indicating that workers in the home ('parent') country and workers employed in foreign subsidiaries:

either are only weak substitutes for one another in the production process or might even be complements, so that employment tends to rise or fall together in the parent and subsidiaries. In either case, although there may be some adverse effects in some industries, it does not appear that firms have substituted foreign for domestic workers on a large scale.   (IMF, 1997)

In a significant contribution Feenstra and Hanson (1996) provide a model in which outsourcing by multinationals leads to increased intra-industry wage dispersion. In this model Northern firms respond to import competition from low-wage countries by moving to them non-skill-intensive activities. This results in a relative increase in demand for skilled labour *within* Northern industries. Feenstra and Hanson's analysis undermines the technology hypothesis for increased wage dispersion since the latter is normally invoked as a 'residual' explanation after eliminating other possible theories. In the mainstream contribution it has been argued that since trade can only explain inter-industry but not intra-industry wage dispersion, the latter must be due to other factors such as technology. By linking the observed increase in the intra-industry wage dispersion in the North to multinational investment and southern competition, Feenstra and Hanson's research weakens the technology hypothesis.

It is not the purpose of the present chapter to contribute to the debate on methodology and the details of the empirical analysis between Wood and the mainstream economists[10] but rather to make a different kind of point. This is that the supposed negative effects of competition from the South are in fact due, in part, to the fact that overall economic growth in advanced industrial countries has been much slower than previously. UNCTAD (1995) provides evidence to show that in the 1950s and 1960s there was a fast increase in import penetration of the USA and other advanced country markets by products of the then newly industrializing economies, namely Italy and Japan. This rise in import penetration was as fast as that achieved by the late industrializers in the advanced country markets in the 1980s. Yet, in this earlier period, Northern countries attained very fast rates of growth of real aggregate demand and output; they also sustained full employment, rising real wages, and falling inequality in wages. In addition, during this boom period the percentage of overseas workers in the labour force was increasing.[11]

An important limitation of Wood's analysis is that it is based on the traditional Hecksher-Ohlin model, which abstracts from aggregate demand and capital accumulation. If a rise in real global demand (as a result, for instance, of better policy co-ordination among industrial countries) leads to a higher trend rate of growth of output, the negative impact of Southern competition on unskilled workers in the North may be more than outweighed by what Bhagwati calls the 'lift-all-boats' effect of faster overall growth. In this scenario unskilled labour shifts from manufacturing to non-traded services (Singh, 1995). Therefore, even if Wood is wholly correct in his argument and all the underlying economic processes to which he refers operate in the way he describes, faster economic growth in the North could override their negative impact.

5. THE OECD'S MULTILATERAL AGREEMENT ON INVESTMENT (MAI)

The OECD countries—the major host and home countries for FDI—are working to establish a comprehensive investment agreement among themselves. Briefly, the aim is to establish a binding treaty outside of the WTO framework. This will subject foreign investment to a regime which removes all or most of the remaining restrictions on FDI. It will also ensure that FDI is treated by national authorities no differently from domestic investment. In brief, the proposed regime would be based on the following:

- the right of establishment for foreign investors;
- the principle of 'most-favoured nation' (mfn) treatment;

[10] There is a voluminous literature on this subject. Significant contributions include Lawrence and Slaughter (1993); Sachs and Shutz (1994); Neven and Wyplosz (1996); Leamer (1996).
[11] The reasons for this sustained fast growth in industrial economies during the Golden Age of 1950 to 1973 are examined in detail in Glyn et al. (1990). See also Singh (1995).

- the principle of 'national treatment';
- investment protection, including matters relating to expropriation and the transfer of capital;
- additional disciplines relating to, among other matters, entry, stay, and work of key personnel;
- prohibition of performance requirements on foreign investors in order to secure economic benefits for the country as a whole;
- rules on investment incentives;
- binding rules for settling disputes.

There is consensus within the OECD on a single broad definition of investment, which goes 'beyond the traditional notion of FDI to cover virtually all tangible and intangible assets, and which applies to both pre-establishment and post-establishment' (OECD, 1997). The definition therefore embraces intellectual property and portfolio investment. As noted in the introduction, the OECD's evident intention is to make the MAI eventually into a universal treaty with 'high standards' (for the rights of the investors). If this were to happen, what would be its impact on developing and developed countries? We briefly examine these topics in turn below.

MAI and developing countries

It is clear from the discussion in Section 3 that, to gain the maximum benefit from FDI, it is important for countries to be selective with respect to FDI and for them to have an integrated industrial and technology development policy. Therefore from the perspective of achieving technological development in developing countries a regime of free capital flows would be a retrograde step. It would prevent these countries from being selective with respect to either projects or phasing. Furthermore, the OECD's MAI proposes to proscribe a number of national industrial policy measures such as performance requirements. Indeed the intention is to make the rules in this respect even more stringent than those agreed in the Uruguay Round Agreement on Trade-Related Investment Measures.

Moreover, unfettered FDI inflows may also pose other special hazards for developing countries, such as increasing their long-term financial fragility. The main reason for this is that FDI creates obligations for the payment of dividends and profits in foreign exchange in the future. Unless FDI goes towards exporting activities or a large proportion of multinational profits are always reinvested, it may become difficult for a developing country to meet its payments obligations in the long term, thus reducing its growth potential. Kregel (1996) notes that:

. . . while portfolio flows may have a more direct impact on short-term reserve management and exchange rate policy, FDI may have both a short and a longer-term structural influence on the composition of a country's external payment flows. While financial innovation allows FDI to have an impact in the short run which is increasingly similar in terms of volatility to portfolio flows, the more important aspect is the way it may mask the true position of a country's balance of payments and the sustainability of any particular combination of policies . . . accumulated foreign claims in the form of accumulated FDI stocks may create a potentially disruptive force that can offset any domestic or external policy goals.   (Kregel, 1996)

It has nevertheless been suggested that although unrestricted FDI may have some undesirable consequences for developing countries, these may be more than compensated for by a much greater amount of FDI which may accrue to developing countries if an OECD-type MAI was universally adopted. Several points may be made in response.

First, the large trend increase in FDI to developing countries in the recent period has occurred without any such treaty. Apparently, the existing bilateral treaties between developed and developing countries are regarded as providing adequate protection by multinational investors—for those countries where there are good economic reasons for FDI in any case. Secondly, there are many countries, particularly in Africa, which have attracted little multinational investment even though they have introduced on the whole extremely liberal regimes with respect to FDI. Thirdly, to the extent that FDI inflows may occur in surges which, under a global MAI, developing countries will not be able to regulate, there will be greater instability in the host country economy which is likely to make it less attractive to FDI. Fourthly and importantly, there is considerable evidence to suggest that FDI inflows are much more a function of a country's per capita income and its rate of growth than its FDI regime. Moreover, Granger-causality tests suggest that the causation is from economic growth to FDI rather than the other way around.

MAI and developed countries

Turning to advanced countries, will these countries benefit from unfettered FDI? There are important considerations which suggest that the net impact on advanced countries may also be negative rather than positive. As noted earlier, the first best solution to the North's labour market problems, including those arising from actual or potential competition from the South lies in achieving a large trend increase in the rate of economic growth such as prevailed in these countries in the 1950s and 1960s. Singh (1997a, b) provides detailed analysis and evidence to suggest that the present liberal global regime of more or less free trade and capital movements is unlikely to be successful in such an endeavour. Very briefly,[12] the essential arguments of these papers can be summarized as follows:

[12] These are extremely complex issues. For a fuller analysis and all the nuances and qualifications, the reader must refer to the cited papers.

1. That leading advanced economies have basically operated under such a regime for about the last fifteen years. Their performance in terms of either output or productivity growth has been less than impressive. The trend rate of OECD GDP growth during this period has been approximately half of what it was during the illiberal 1950s and 1960s. The most important failure of the current market supremacist regime lies of course in the existence of mass unemployment in many industrial countries today, whereas there was more or less full employment in the earlier period.

2. That the failures of the current regime are not due to exogenous factors but are intrinsic to the regime itself. Free capital movements and the supremacy of the financial markets in a variety of ways make it difficult to attain a high rate of growth of real demand and output in the world economy.

3. The central constraint on fast economic growth in industrial countries does not lie on the supply side. Not only are there unutilized human resources, but also, significantly, there is a huge backlog of technology. The information and technological communications revolution is regarded by leading scholars on the subject as equivalent in its potential to that of steam engines and electricity. But its full potential has not as yet been realized because of insufficient growth of aggregate demand. Therefore, to the extent that the chief constraint on higher economic growth is the failure on the demand side rather than on the supply side, it is a self-inflicted wound arising from the inefficiency or absence of co-ordinating economic mechanisms.

In so far as the MAI will in effect accentuate such a regime, the prospects are of continuing slow growth of the OECD economies. With slow growth, the negative aspects of Southern competition on the North's labour markets will become progressively more pronounced, particularly as countries like China and India fully enter the global market place.

The North's workers, particularly the unskilled, will be the real losers. Apart from the effects of slow growth they will also be disadvantaged through another channel. Workers will be obliged to bear the full burden of terms of trade shocks to an economy to the extent that mobility of capital will promote a risk-adjusted world rate of return and therefore narrow the range of variations of returns to capital within a country. With greater inflexibility in rates of return, skilled and unskilled workers will have to absorb more of the impact of any product price changes. This will either be reflected in greater volatility and dispersion of workers' earnings or greater unemployment, depending on the country's labour-market institutions.[13]

In conclusion, an essential argument of this chapter is that in order to permit developing countries to reap the full benefits of FDI for their techno-

[13] It may be argued that FDI flows are also relatively immobile because they represent bricks and mortar. This is, as noted earlier, less and less valid in a world of derivatives and ever-increasing ingenuity of financial markets. The MAI, by covering FDI as well as portfolio flows, will make all investment more liquid and all would be hedged to some extent.

logical development as well as to avoid long-term financial fragility, it is necessary for them to retain their current options of selectivity in determining the form and composition of capital flows. Restrictions on FDI of this kind, while benefiting the South, are unlikely to be harmful to the North's workers. Such restraints on footloose FDI may indeed be beneficial to the Northern economies as a whole, to the extent that they make possible greater co-operation between labour and capital in instituting, for example, incomes policies in these countries.

However, from the perspective of workers in advanced countries, what is required is not restrictions on FDI *per se*, but rather faster rates of economic growth. The salient question is whether a faster growth of real demand, output, and productivity is feasible in the world economy today under any reasonable set of policies. Or is it simply the case that there is no viable alternative to liberalization and globalization as the Bretton Woods Institutions insist? It was suggested in Singh (1995) that there does exist an alternative policy programme, but this would involve a decisive move away from the present market supremacist model towards one based on social consensus between as well as within countries. There is considerable analysis and evidence to indicate that such a consensual model played a key role in making possible the high rates of economic growth in the Golden Age period.[14] However, in the situation today, in order to obtain a trend increase in the rate of growth of real demand (rather than simply money demand) and output in the OECD countries, new institutions and institutional mechanisms would be necessary both at the national and international levels. These are required to achieve international macroeconomic policy co-ordination and to maintain wage–price restraint during the growth process.[15]

REFERENCES

Aitken, B., Harrison, A., and Lipsey, R. E. (1995), 'Wages and Foreign Ownership: A Comparative Study of Mexico, Venezuela, and the United States', *Journal of International Economics*, 40: 345–71.

[14] See the references mentioned earlier, in n. 11.

[15] These institutional changes were analysed and examined at length in Singh (1995). Very briefly (and the caveat in n. 12 above is fully applicable here as well), what is required at the international level is for governments to agree to (a) give chief priority to the employment problem; (b) symmetrical, rather than asymmetrical, adjustment in deficit and surplus countries; and (c) macroeconomic policy co-ordination, particularly between industrial countries via a multilateral mechanism. Originally this was the intended role of the IMF, instead of which it has mostly been used to discipline the South. Parallel to these external co-ordinating mechanisms, it is also necessary to have appropriate national pay co-ordinating mechanisms in industrial countries, rather than policies of labour-market flexibility and deregulation. Such incomes policies only work, however, if they are not seen simply as a mechanism to reduce workers' real wages but are regarded as fair and redistributive in a progressive direction. Indeed, James Meade regarded these internal mechanisms in leading industrial countries to be more important than external ones in achieving internal and external balance.

Blueston, B. and Harrison, B. (1982), *The Deindustrialization of America: Plant Closings, Community, Abandonment, and the Dismantling of Basic Industry*, New York: Basic Books.

Chang, H. J. (1996), 'Globalization, Transnational Corporations, and Economic Development', mimeo, Faculty of Economics and Politics, University of Cambridge.

Feenstra, R. C. and Hanson, G. H. (1996), 'Globalization, Outsourcing, and Wage Inequality', *American Economic Review*, 86: 240–6.

Freeman, C. (1989), 'New Technology and Catching Up', *European Journal of Development Research*, 1/1.

Glyn, A., Hughes, A., Lipietz, A., and Singh, A. (1990), 'The Rise and Fall of the Golden Age', in S. Marglin and J. Schor (eds.), *The Golden Age of Capitalism*, Oxford: Clarendon Press.

IMF (1997), *World Economic Outlook*, Washington, DC.

Jomo, K. S. (1997), *Southeast Asia's Misunderstood Miracle*, Boulder, Colo.: Westview Press.

Kregel, J. A. (1996), 'Some Risks and Implications of Financial Globalization for National Policy Autonomy', *Unctad Review*, 55–62.

Lall, S. (1995), 'The Creation of Comparative Advantage: Country Experiences', in Irfan ul Haque (ed.), *Trade, Technology, and International Competitiveness*, Washington, DC: World Bank.

Lawrence, R. Z. and Slaughter, M. J. (1993), 'International Trade and American Wages in the 1980s: Giant Sucking Sound or Small Hiccup?', *Brookings Papers on Economic Activity: Microeconomics*, 2: 161–226.

Leamer, E. E. (1996), 'In Search of Stolper-Samuelson Effects on U.S. Wages', NBER Working Paper, No. 5427.

Neven, D. and Wyplosz, C. (1996), 'Relative Prices, Trade and Restructuring in European Industry', Centre for Economic Policy Research, Working Paper, No. 1451.

OECD (1997), *Symposium on the Multilateral Agreement on Investment*, Seoul, South Korea.

Okimoto, D. I. (1989), *Between the MITI and the Market*, Berkeley: Stanford University Press.

Rowthorn, R. E. and Wells, J. R. (1987), *Deindustrialization and Foreign Trade*, Cambridge: Cambridge University Press.

Sachs, J. D. and Shutz, H. J. (1994), 'Trade and Jobs in U.S. Manufacturing', *Brookings Papers on Economic Activity*, 2: 1–84.

Singh, A. (1987), 'Manufacturing and Deindustrialization', in J. Eatwell, M. Milgate, and P. Newman (eds.), *The New Palgrave*, London: Macmillan.

—— (1995), 'Institutional Requirements for Full Employment in Advanced Economies', *International Labour Review*, 134: 471–95.

—— (1997a), Global Unemployment, Long Run Economic Growth and Labour Market Rigidities: A Commentary, mimeo, Faculty of Economics, University of Cambridge.

—— (1997b), 'Liberalization and Globalization: An Unhealthy Euphoria', in J. Michie and J. Grieve Smith (eds.), *Employment and Economic Performance: Jobs, Inflation, and Growth*, Oxford: Oxford University Press.

UN (1993), *World Investment Report: Transnational Corporations and Integrated International Production*, Geneva/New York: UN.
—— (1996), *World Investment Report: Investment, Trade and International Policy Arrangements*, Geneva/New York: UN.
UNCTAD (1995), *Trade and Development Report*, Geneva: UN, Table 31.
UNIDO (1996), *The Globalization of Industry: Implications for Developing Countries Beyond 2000*, Vienna: UNIDO, 51, 89.
Vatikiotis, M. (1997), 'From Chickens to Microchips', *Far Eastern Review*, 42
Wade, R. (1990), *Governing the Market*, Princeton: Princeton University Press.
Wood, A. (1994), *North-South Trade, Employment and Inequality: Changing Fortunes in a Skill-Driven World*, Oxford: Clarendon Press.
WTO (1996), *Trade and Foreign Direct Investment*, Annual Report, i, Geneva: WTO.

3. Innovation and Technology Transfer within Multinational Firms

Jeremy Howells

This chapter analyses the issue of international innovation and technology transfer within multinational firms. It considers how the organizational and locational context of this affects both firm and national performance. Within the whole issue of international technology flows, intrafirm cross-border technology flows has remained a neglected issue for analysis and discussion. This is despite being long recognized as a major element in international technology transfer. Even in the late 1970s technological balance of payments analysis revealed that intrafirm payments accounted for between two-thirds and three-quarters of total payments in the USA, UK, and Germany and that this figure had increased in all three countries over the late 1960s and 1970s (Madeuf, 1984: 135). Despite these general estimates, however, the scale and process of such transfers has been difficult to measure and quantify and therefore has been resistant to analysis. In part this is bound up with the sensitive nature of such transactions, since it is a key element in transfer pricing and profit flows between subsidiary operations (Chudnovsky, 1981). However, even in relation to a management perspective, the process of intrafirm technology flows has remained relatively neglected.

This neglect from an academic standpoint is surprising given that the key economic model of multinational expansion rests upon two central assumptions surrounding the corporate transfer of technology to competitive advantage (Flaherty, 1986: 88). First, that technology-intensive companies possess competitive advantages based on intangible (technology) assets that can be transferred within a firm with relative ease, but outside a firm only with difficulty. The second is that a company by using its own technology in foreign production allows a company to earn a larger return on its assets (specifically its technology assets) than would be possible through an arm's-length sale of the technology (Caves, 1982). The multinational enterprise largely arises from the advantages of internalizing technology transfers and knowledge flows (Hymer, 1972; Teece, 1976).

FLOWS OF TECHNOLOGY AND KNOWLEDGE

A key element in analysing how technology is transferred internally within the firm is to consider the wider issue of knowledge and information flows. Technology can be transferred in terms of tangible assets, such as new products, plant, and equipment, and in intangible form through formal mechanisms, such as patents and licenses, and informally through information and knowledge flows. Indeed there is an important distinction between knowledge and information flows; information flows relate to individual bits of data or data strands, whilst knowledge involves a much wider process that can assimilate information and put it into a wider context, allowing actions to be undertaken from it. Knowledge in turn combines the process of learning; the take-up of learned behaviour and procedures is a critical element within knowledge acquisition, both in terms of capturing and moving it from the individual to the organizational level (Kim, 1993) but also in more widely diffusing competence throughout the whole organization (Urlich et al., 1993).

There are crucially two main types of knowledge (Polanyi, 1967): explicit and tacit. Explicit or codified knowledge involves know-how that is transmittable in formal, systematic language and does not require direct experience of the knowledge that is being acquired and it can be transferred in such formats as a blueprint or operating manual (in what may be described as 'articulated knowledge'). By contrast tacit knowledge cannot be communicated in any direct or codified way. As such tacit knowledge concerns direct experience and is not codifiable via artefacts. It is hard to conceive of situations where tacit knowledge can be acquired indirectly as this would involve some kind of codification and lack of direct experience (Howells, 1996: 95).

These differences in the nature and type of technology and knowledge are important, particularly in relation to the distinctions between those types of technology and knowledge that are embodied in tangible assets or articulated in formal and codified forms on the one hand, and those that can only be transferred and acquired through informal and tacit channels on the other.

These two different types of technology formats are important in that the former can generally be accessed remotely and transferred indirectly, whilst the latter require direct and close and often ongoing contact. Although the transfer process is affected by geographical distance, in the case of tacit and informal technology flows, distance is much more important; increasing distance limits the likelihood, volume, and effectiveness of such transfers. In short, codified knowledge is seen as being more easily transferable (Antonelli, 1995). As with scientific and technical communication generally there is a pronounced distance–decay effect in terms of links and contact patterns (Allen, 1977). Moreover in the case of the learning aspect of tacit knowledge flow, much of it involves 'situated' learning where information that is being transferred or where the problems to be overcome depend on being present in the same physical location (Lave and Wenger, 1991; see also von Hippel and Tyre, 1993; Arcangeli, 1993; Fleck, 1994).

This effect of distance and proximity on scientific communication and knowledge flows has been noted on a number of different scales covering the macro level, in terms of innovation clusters (between firms and industries) within particular localities or regions, to the micro, intra-firm level in terms of how companies seek to concentrate research, technical, and design facilities together and in turn co-locate them with relevant manufacturing facilities (Malecki, 1979, 1980). Indeed it can even be seen in the individual design and building of research laboratories in terms of where particular groups of individuals are located (Allen and Cohen, 1969). In communications the historic trend has clearly been towards decreased 'friction of distance' in relation to information and knowledge flows (Abler, 1971) and this has gained particular momentum in the late 1980s and early 1990s with the decline in telecommunication costs and the introduction and spread of new information and communication technologies (ICTs) around the world. However, there have been conflicting views on whether the 'tyranny of distance' in respect of research flows and innovation location is coming to an end or becoming more pronounced. These arguments are presented in Table 3.1.

Table 3.1. Technology and knowledge flows: does distance still matter?

Factors inhibiting locational dispersion in innovation and technology transfer	Factors encouraging locational dispersion in innovation and technology transfer
1. Tacit knowledge seen as increasing in importance in relation to successful innovation.	1. Increasing codification of knowledge and science.
2. Tacitness having become more important in competitive advantage under 'new' management and organization strategies.	2. New forms of ICT in research, design, and technical activity allowing decentralization of research and technical activity.
3. Wider organizational change, such as closer supply chains and JIT, encouraging spatial proximity.	3. Increasing dispersion of R&D, design, engineering, and technical support both nationally and internationally.
4. Increasing importance of customers— 'market pull'—necessitating innovation co-location.	4. Move towards 'flatter' organizations necessitates better communication mechanisms.
5. Increased stress on external technical contacts and information sources; such 'first time' and external contacts necessitates more face-to-face informal contact.	5. Increased managerial experience and learning associated with more decentralized forms of research, design, and technical operations.

In relation to the former argument, scientists and engineers through the ages have tried to make their results and applications more widely available to their respective communities and this has been dependent on making their tacit knowledge and skills more formal and codifiable (in Nonaka's model of 'knowledge conversion' this involves the third mode of knowledge conversion from tacit knowledge to explicit knowledge (Nonaka, 1994)). Indeed Arora and Gambardella (1994) argue that technological information is already cast in frameworks and categories that are universal allowing a clear division (and dispersion) of innovative labour. Moreover, codification and formalization of knowledge and skills has been applied widely to the manufacturing and research environment. The 1950s and 1960s witnessed the increasing use of automation as an attempt to capture tacit skills and codify them for replication by machine. This was most marked in the rise of early programmable machine tools which reproduced the skills (if not the knowledge) of the machinist by recording key actions on magnetic tape so that replaying the tape would reproduce the machines' motions under the control of the machinist.

More recently, towards the end of the 1970s, major corporations sought to improve transborder knowledge and information flows in the research and design process through the use of new ICTs. A number of multinational companies have integrated their global R&D units via the use of such ICTs and have reduced the need for face-to-face contacts and spatial proximity (Howells, 1995). Although there was some substitution of tacit for more codified forms of knowledge transfer, the new communication tools also involved a greater ability to combine tacit elements and were 'packaged' in a more sophisticated communication profile.

By contrast, there have been wider organizational and managerial changes which have emphasized the role and competitive advantage of competences in 'soft technologies' often seen to be displayed by Japanese firms, and in the continued and growing importance of tacit knowledge and skills (Howells, 1996). Above all many of the advances in knowledge and techniques still tend to be associated with new tacit knowledge (Senker, 1995: 106). Many of these advances and developed competences are contingent on local conditions and much of the learning and transferring associated with them is highly constrained by spatial distance. Moreover, although this analysis focuses on intrafirm technology transfers, the ability to tap into key external loci of scientific and technical expertise has grown in importance (see, for example, Creamer, 1976; Pearce and Papnastassiou, 1996).

These differing views regarding the changing nature of knowledge and information, its transfer and the need for spatial proximity, are finely balanced and their impact will be expected to vary by firm, industry, and nationality. Those firms surveyed in a study in the early 1990s were increasingly confident of the application of ICTs integrating their international R&D

operations and overcoming the problems of distance (Howells, 1995). However, these firms largely came from high-technology sectors, with a long history of international R&D activity and also had considerable expertise in the use and application of ICTs. Undoubtedly there has been a clear widening and deepening of the use of new forms of communication in R&D (De Meyer, 1993) but it is still likely to be restricted to a comparatively small, but growing, group of multinational firms.

THE CHANGING NATURE OF INTERNATIONAL INTRAFIRM TECHNOLOGY TRANSFER

Under what may be termed the traditional, top-down, centralized model of the product life-cycle model, firms were presented with the issue of transferring *existing* technologies from the 'home base' to overseas subsidiaries. Thus whilst overseas subsidiaries transferred products and processes which were already well established, the parent company reserved the most advanced and profitable lines for its home market (Taylor, 1994: 127). The focus of such transfers were in the form of embodied technologies, such as plant and equipment, or in existing codified knowledge available in blueprints, technical drawings, and manuals. These transfers were therefore essentially an issue about moving the 'results' of innovation, rather than the delivery of a mechanism which would allow understanding and learning about the innovation process itself. At this level, therefore, such transfers involve little in the way of building long-term technological competencies in overseas subsidiaries. The barriers associated with the transfers of existing technologies should not however be underestimated, as although such technologies may not have been 'new' to the firm as a whole, they are new to that particular overseas operation. Even embodied or codified technologies, which are relatively mature, involve the development of new organizational and technical skills which allows the assimilation and adaption of imported technology. Indeed Grant and Gregory (1997) go further and argue that mature technologies may indeed be *harder* to assimilate than newer ones. This is because as a technology matures, improvements are made which are harder to capture in codified and transferable forms. Trying to transfer a mature technology successfully may therefore be harder as accumulated experiential knowledge about a mature technology is rarely recorded and much of the knowledge is tacit in nature.

Regardless of what type of technology is being transferred, there is clearly a learning process involved here for subsidiary operations as they become more skilled at adopting and developing new technologies (Young, Hood, and Dunlop, 1988; Young, Hood, and Peters, 1994; Fleetwood and Mölleryd, 1992). This learning process helps to drive down the costs of technology transfer through the increasing experience and knowledge gained of the transfer process (Teece, 1977; 259).

Over time, as the pace of technological change and diffusion has speeded up and as the number and age of subsidiary operations has matured, multinationals have been increasingly faced with transferring 'softer' forms of technology and knowledge as the shift of competitive advance towards these more disembodied forms of technological change has become more prominent. The 'absorptive capacity' of overseas operations must be considerably strengthened if such subsidiaries are to progress from merely *receptors* of standardized technologies to *adapters* and indeed, over time, *developers* of new technologies. The organizational strategy has shifted away from transferring existing technologies and the codified information about how to operate it, towards transferring knowledge and establishing learning capabilities and competences about such knowledge in different parts of the organization (Ruggles, 1997).

The role and capability of overseas subsidiaries has been associated with such changes, although it has not been necessarily a rapid or recent process (often going back to the inter-war period, if not earlier (Taylor, 1994)). Subsidiaries have gained more autonomy in terms of research and technology and in some cases World Product Mandates (WPMs) or Continental Product Mandates (CPMs) (Roth and Morrison, 1996).

In addition to the shift from transferring hard and more formal technologies towards softer and tacit forms has been a move away from the more centralized and hierarchical organizational structures of multinational companies towards a more decentralized pattern of relationships. Although technology flows have never been simply one-way forward vertical flows from the domestic base to overseas periphery (with reverse flows being in evidence) (Mansfield and Romeo, 1984) they have become more horizontal, two-way flows between all the firms' domestic and subsidiary operations (Bartlett, 1986). Firms have sought to implement structures to allow more autonomy and flexibility throughout their organization; horizontal structures of information have become more efficient than vertical ones (Aoki, 1986). There has been a shift, at least in some firms, from what Kogut (1990: 58) terms 'a dyadic relationship between headquarters and each subsidiary to the profile management of an international network'. Hedlund (1986) similarly sees the internal hierarchy of the corporation being replaced by balanced interdependence or what he calls a 'heterarchy'. Bartlett (1986) views the multinational corporation moving from a position of hierarchical control to a more cooperative and reciprocal relationship between headquarters and subsidiaries (Prahalad and Doz, 1987). All this has therefore meant that for most companies there has been a gradual shift away from hierarchical, top-down flows of command and information from the parent to the subsidiaries, towards a more open two-way flow between subsidiaries, and between subsidiaries and the parent organization. In such an 'integrated network' organization communication patterns become much more complex with considerable lateral contacts between subsidiaries (Håkanson 1990: 270).

In one way more subsidiary operations now have an improved capacity to receive and utilize technology and knowledge transfers from the home base and the rest of the firm so that the *individual* international technology transfer process within the firm has become easier. On the other hand, the *collective* situation of intrafirm technology transfer has become much more complex and fragmented, and hence difficult to manage and organize.

Indeed the discussion so far (given the focus of this chapter) has considered international intrafirm technology flows; and this issue becomes even more complex when external knowledge and technology flows are examined. Firms are increasingly having to gain information from outside parties and enter into research and technological collaborations with other firms and organizations. There has been a sustained growth in global interorganisational research and technical links by firms during the 1980s, which requires effective co-ordination and maintenance on an international scale. Multinationals are having to consider external as well as internal technology and knowledge flows in their overall organizational structure. An increasingly important element in the technical role of overseas establishments is the need to establish and monitor interorganisational linkages and partnerships (Håkansson, 1987). This is now a key element in a firm's ability to maintain its competitive and technological advantage and forms an essential component in its technology strategy.

GLOBAL STRATEGIES AND PRACTICES FOR TECHNOLOGY FLOWS AND STRUCTURE

In this increasingly complex world, companies seek to develop strategies which allow an effective management and co-ordination of their core technological competences. There have been a number of alternative scenarios and strategies presented within this context. On a macro-, industry perspective there are the alternative scenarios presented by Porter and Reich in terms of how firms and industries respond to increasing globalization and the changing nature of technology (Lazonick, 1993). Thus Porter (1990) envisages that 'industry clusters' will emerge associated with relatively fixed concentrations of interfirm and interfunctional specialization in selected parts of the globe. By contrast Reich (1991) sees 'global webs' developing associated with the rise of locationally flexible stateless corporations who will seek to integrate various technologies and competencies from different parts of the world. On a micro level, Allen and Hauptman (1987) (see also Allen, 1977) discussing R&D organizations, contrast the benefits of 'functional organization' and 'project organization' in relation to communication, knowledge transfer, and R&D performance. 'Functional organization' involves clustering individuals from similar disciplines together working on different problems, whilst 'project organization' seeks to gather people from different specialities to work on the same problem. The rate and generation of new technology, the duration of the task involved and the degree of organizational co-ordination and interdependence (the three combining to produce an 'organizational structure space') will determine which of the two organizational forms is the best solution. Between these two levels, at a firm level, the author (see, for example, Howells, 1993; Howells and Wood, 1993) has sought to develop a basic bipolar strategy ensemble for multinationals seeking to overcome the problems of co-ordinating technological and knowledge competencies on a global scale. The distinction is between those multinationals which have sought optimal facilities/functions locations but with greater and more complex numbers of (difficult) cross-border technology transfers and flows—'global switching'—and those firms which have established a more concentrated pattern of facility/functional co-location producing fewer cross-border flows at the expense of less optimal and flexible location patterns for research and production—'global focusing'.

In relation to global switching, those companies which are truly developing global capabilities have to consider the issue of where research and technical capability reside. This is becoming less of an issue, both for the company itself and for the locality where such scientific and technical capability is based. For companies which are gradually evolving towards an integrated functional operation on a worldwide basis, whole sets of sites and countries are involved in the innovation and production chain. The essence of global switching is in the ability of companies to co-ordinate and 'boundary span' their different functional operations (i.e. research, development, manufacture, marketing, sales, administration) in an integrated fashion, on a global scale. The ability to 'switch' geographically between sites in terms of functional sequencing and link-ups is best exemplified and most impressive with the development cycle of a new product from initial discovery and invention through to first market launch. However, it can also occur on an intrafunctional level, where the manufacture of certain specific products can be switched from one plant to another plant located at opposite sides of the world. There are therefore basically two types of global switching: 'horizontal' and 'vertical'. Horizontal global switching is more limited in scope than vertical switching, involving international linkages on an intrafunctional basis only (for example, between production sites). By contrast vertical global switching involves vertical, functional integration on a worldwide basis, and a new product development cycle (from discovery through to final market launch) is perhaps the most challenging example of this.

The practice of horizontal global switching is much more established than vertical switching, particularly as it relates to embodied technologies and more codified knowledge. Horizontal switching essentially refers to intra-functional technology and material linkages between overseas establishments. In the case of manufacturing the level of international material and technical linkages and sourcing depends in part on the nature of the product and production process. Materials/components with low value-to-weight ratios are less likely to be involved in overseas intrafirm trading because of high shipping costs. Equally, some products tend to be produced in completely integrated manufacturing processes which cuts down international linkages between overseas subsidiaries. Many products do involve substantial material/component levels in their manufacture and where high transport costs have little impact on their overall cost. Here the phenomenon of horizontal global switching has been well established, certainly since the mid-1950s. Such a process has been further encouraged by factors, such as government policies (Blackbourn, 1974) and transfer pricing, which have also encouraged switching between manufacturing operations. Further growth in horizontal switching internationally has been seen in the increase in international sourcing and the growing standardization of components/materials between overseas sites producing similar products and product ranges (Levy and Dunning, 1993). This may lead to the creation of a single source (or dual source) for a particular component on a worldwide basis for a multinational company rather than a myriad of suppliers formed along national, market-specific lines. This is where horizontal global switching within a particular function (i.e. manufacturing) can lead to (vertically) integrated manufacturing production and assembly systems, where plants supply and receive ('switch') products, parts, and knowledge in an integrated worldwide supply chain. A much less common occurrence until recently, has been horizontal global switching in other corporate functions, such as R&D or sales/marketing. In R&D, global integration only effectively began in the 1980s with multinationals slowly starting to switch particular R&D activities on an international basis. Basic research would be undertaken in one site (or sets of sites), the development stage would then be switched to another site and testing and toxicology to a third or further site.

   At its most simple, vertical global switching involves a R&D–production–marketing–sales sequence of interfunctional linkages. Traditionally this vertical sequencing was undertaken mainly on one site or sets of closely inter-linked sites within a national territory. However increasingly large multinationals with functions spread across the world have had the ability to switch such sequencing across national boundaries. R&D, or indeed one part of the research process, may be undertaken in one country, initial production scale-up in another, full production and related component production in other sets of countries and first market launch in a completely different country. The co-ordination and integration of these different (within and between) function interfacing is at the best of times extremely difficult and such problems are heightened if this occurs on a global basis. However it provides considerable economic and technical benefits for corporations who have been able to exploit the different technical, manufacturing, and marketing skills of the various sites, as well as to ease international compatibilities.

The ability to 'switch' geographically between sites in terms of functional sequencing and link-ups is best exemplified and most impressive with the development cycle of a new product from initial discovery and invention through to first market launch. Information relating to the exact sequencing of the locational switching is difficult to come by, but one new product innovation introduced by Glaxo, Salmeterol, involved R&D at its site at Ware in the UK, followed by extensive clinical trial studies at sites across the world. The responsibilities for the scale-up of production for the active ingredients in the drug were transferred to Montrose in Scotland and then moved into full-scale primary production. Another primary production site in Singapore is also to come on-stream and both the Montrose and Singapore factories will supply secondary production and packaging operators in Evreux in France and Ware in the UK. The first market launch for the product was actually the UK, although it was closely followed by launches in other European countries.

In a similar context Hewlett Packard also displays the phenomenon of global switching in global product development and production. One example is of a new product introduction, relating to office systems, covering a span of countries. In the case of this new product, the initial basic development work was undertaken at the company's laboratory in Palo Alto, the development and application work was then taken up by its Bristol laboratory. The actual product was then manufactured in two plants in separate countries for worldwide distribution, and the product was finally launched in a fifth country. Examples of research and design work undertaken in its main laboratories in Japan or the UK, and flowing the other way in terms of development and manufacture, have also occurred. These switches have been facilitated by a more formalized life-cycle for new product development and more attention paid to critical 'hand-over' periods, such as 'manufacturing release' where responsibility for a new product is moved from R&D to that of manufacturing. A third example was that of Texas Instruments which has sixty major manufacturing facilities worldwide in eighteen countries. To support the effective co-ordination and integration of its resources worldwide the company has steadily built up its satellite-based communications network. For example, its integrated circuit (IC) design centres in Europe at Bedford, Freising, Nice, and Rieti are linked by real time data and communication systems to centres in the USA, India, and the Far East to enable the integrated use of new-product design technology. An example quoted by the company is that a chip may be designed in Europe or Japan (Tsukuba), then the chip specifications can be transferred by satellite to one of its major plants in

Texas, where the components are produced and sent to Kuala Lumpur or one of its other plants in East Asia for final integration.

The concept of vertical global switching involves the functional integration on a worldwide scale which is far removed from the hierarchical and lagged notions of the product life-cycle model. Under the product life-cycle model, manufacturing and research capacity are seen as gradually shifting from innovative domestic markets to foreign markets as products move from an 'early' or 'development' phase through to a 'growth' stage and onto a 'mature' phase of their life-cycles (Vernon, 1966). The basis of the model, as Vernon notes (1979: 41–5), is the need in the early stages of the major technological work to co-ordinate scientific, engineering, planning, financial, and marketing activities and to keep a close watch on the expensive and high-risk investments, all of which will induce both R&D and the initial stages of production to be kept at home. By contrast the notion of vertical global switching sees a set of global linkages and interactions between functions which have increasingly less to do with a domestic-oriented, hierarchical structure associated in turn with a filtering down of technical expertise from home base to overseas units. Instead it involves a more federated structure with increasing expertise and 'lead role' function situated in overseas affiliates. It also has important implications for notions relating to the benefits and spillovers of the innovation process on a local or national scale. Although many research and technical benefits do get manufactured locally, an increasing number do not; the notion of closed technical and production systems are breaking down. Thus, for example, in the UK both Motorola and Lucent Technologies have major R&D and design laboratories located in Swindon undertaking mobile and wireless telecommunications research, but the products derived from their research and technical work are incorporated into products manufactured outside the UK (although both companies do have manufacturing facilities in Britain: Motorola has a plant in Easterhouse, Scotland and Lucent Technologies has a factory in Malmesbury, Wiltshire).

Global focusing relates to the spatial concentration of research, production, and other key facilities specializing in a particular product, product group, or related technologies on a single or closely related set of sites in selected locations across the world. The origins of this phenomenon can often be traced to the establishment of particular product mandates for manufacturing plants (Roth and Morrison, 1996), but also links in with more recent issues associated with developing closer links with key suppliers (Wong, 1992) and customers. The main advantages of global focusing stem from its basic simplicity (Table 3.2). By allowing cross-functional specialisms to develop around a particular product group or technology, all the necessary expertise and intra- and interfirm linkages can be centred on a particular site, or set of neighbouring sites. Problems relating to interfunctional linkages within the firm, which are particularly important when developing new products, are

Table 3.2. Global focusing: Competitive advantages and disadvantages

---

ADVANTAGES
  1. Intrafirm: good interfunctional linkages within the firm.
  2. Intrafirm: good co-ordination of new product developments.
  3. Interfirm: ability to develop localized links with suppliers (backward linkages).
  4. Interfirm: potential for good contacts with lead, innovative customers (forward linkages).
  5. Potential to tap into international centres of excellence for particular products/ technologies.

DISADVANTAGES
  1. Problems of centric views and links.
  2. Associated with this, danger of missing new developments occurring elsewhere in the world.
  3. Susceptible to decline in specialist advantage due to decline in:
     • internal competences.
     • external competences   loss of interfirm, agglomerative advantages.
     • general long-term decline in product/technology specialism.
  4. 'Lumpy' nature of innovation and development.
  5. Danger of competition for key resources from other companies seeking to locate in same locality.

Source: Howells and Wood (1993: 150).

reduced. In addition the facility may be sited near to, or can seek to establish, a set of key local suppliers. Similarly it can gain benefits from good forward linkages with location at, or near to, 'lead', innovative customers. These inter-firm benefits of global focusing can be gained by locating production in an existing international centre of excellence for that particular sector or technology group. One example of this has been recent moves by European and North American companies to set up centres of excellence in research and production technologies in Japan, in such fields as advanced materials.

This localization strategy for products and technologies therefore over-comes many of the problems of distance associated with poor communication, interfacing, and co-ordination. Overall interaction on a formal and informal basis can be much greater, both on an intra- and interorganizational basis. Friedrikson and Lindmark (1979: 172) note that

. . . the supplies that are customer specific in one or more respects are often charac-terised by extensive technical co-operation between the buying and selling firms. This co-operation requires reliable and rapid communication of information, which is at present usually conveyed through personal contacts. These distance-sensitive contacts limit the geographical areas in which possible contractors should be located, if placing production with them is to be considered profitable. It may therefore be assumed that the production of non-standardized articles is largely placed with subcontractors located in the same geographical area as the buying firm. In the case of even more specific purchases there may be only a few suppliers available so the buyer is forced to look further afield despite this need for close co-operation.

However, although this obviously makes a highly desirable pattern of localized and specialized supplier/subcontractor network it often cannot be achieved or desired (Linge 1992: 326). A surprisingly large number of key suppliers are only effectively available from a highly restricted set of locations worldwide and on this basis would reduce the benefits, and ability to establish, local specialist subcontractor clusters.

The build up of global focusing by firms, allowing an international network of units to take on responsibility for the development of particular products/technologies, represents a move towards a more decentralized, 'networking' and away from a centralized, 'home-based' orientation. However, in a sense although it overcomes some of the problems of a centralized co-ordination system focused on the parent company's home-base, there are still dangers. The most obvious is that this strategy still retains a centralized vision, even if it is transposed out of the company's home market. The danger of missing key signals from other markets elsewhere in the world and the centre or unit becoming too inward-looking and complacent are still there. In addition the concentration of all the expertise in one main locale exposes the company to risks of the creative expertise or specialist advantage once built up in a single location starting to decline or drift away.

More generally by focusing a particular unit on one product group or technology exposes that establishment to downturns or fluctuations in demand which over the longer term could lead to closure as the markets or technologies move on. For the firm it also reduces its flexibility in allocating spare productive capacity. This would lead to a suboptimal allocation of the company's total resources and reduction in flexibility in terms of being able to move products and production runs between plants (Cordell 1971: 58; see also Haug, 1992). A further potential problem in global focusing could lie in its very success. When certain clusters become targeted by firms because of their perceived excellence in certain sectors/technologies, it can lead to increased competition for resources, particularly in relation to skilled scientific and technical manpower. Problems of staff poaching and high labour turnover may result, creating the additional problem of research confidentiality and appropriability.

It should be noted here though that the reason for opting for a global focusing strategy may only be due to one or two factors noted above. This applies equally to their chance of success and it is unlikely that companies will be able to gain or develop all the advantages listed in Table 3.2. In addition companies may only be opting for global focusing in a limited fashion. This strategy may be only partially implemented with the company, at least initially, focusing on specialist products/technologies where the expertise clearly lies outside the parent company's home base. Associated with this, the move to global focusing may have much to do with informal and evolutionary developments based on earlier designations of manufacturing plants to particular product mandates. The initial mandating of a factory to manufacture a particular product or family of products on a worldwide (or continental region) basis, often leads on to that unit building up expertise in other key functions, most notably R&D, general design/engineering, and marketing. Over time, therefore, plants associated with world product mandates have taken international responsibility for these functions (Håkanson, 1990: 257) to form the basis for global focusing by firms.

Lastly, global focusing may arise via merger and acquisition activity. A company may acquire a firm overseas which has a particular strength in a product range/technology over its existing operations. This strength may reside in basic R&D or close contact with the customers, and for this reason the acquiring company decides to focus long-term investment in this sector at that overseas site rather than transfer it to its existing operations. The parent company, therefore, in rationalizing its activity in this particular sector or division will often 'reverse' its existing operations into the newly acquired firm's operations, often leading to the closure or downgrading of its domestic and/or existing facilities elsewhere. As such this move towards global focusing is in direct contrast to a more evolutionary, product mandate process, which generally builds upon initial manufacturing capabilities of the subsidiary.

Gupta and Govindarajan (1995) have also tried to deal with the issue of technology and knowledge flows and link it into corporate strategy, this time more specifically focusing on the roles of the subsidiary in this structure. They identify four generic subsidiary roles:

- *Global Innovator*: where the subsidiary serves as the 'fountainhead' or lead role in knowledge for other units in a particular technology of product group.
- *Integrated Player*: where the subsidiary is both a key source for, but also a key user of, other subsidiaries in the firm.
- *Implementor*: where the subsidiary engages in little knowledge creation of its own and relies heavily on knowledge flows from sister subsidiaries.
- *Local Innovator*: where the subsidiary has almost complete local responsibility for the creation of relevant know-how in all key functional areas, however this knowledge is too idiosyncratic to be of use in other countries.

In addition Gupta and Govindarajan (1995) have been able to test these four types in a cross-section of seventy-nine US, Japanese, and European companies and have found support for their model. In particular they found significant intrafirm differences in the knowledge role and flow pattern of subsidiaries (see also Fleetwood and Mölleryd, 1992). This finding does not conflict with studies examining the research and technical role of overseas subsidiaries which suggests that these are located and function for different reasons, such as adaptive work, access to key consumers and suppliers, 'listening posts' and the tapping of scarce scientific and technical talent (see, for example, Behrman and Fischer, 1980; Haug *et al.*, 1983; Pearce and Papnastassiou, 1996). However, what it does suggest is that differences over the subsidiary location factors and technical roles not only occur by nationality, industrial sector, and firm type, but also vary widely *within* firms. This in turn indicates that the situation is even more complex than first described and that trying to uncover a more systematic and predictable pattern of strategy and practice in technology transfer and location is going to be difficult.

CONCLUSIONS

The focus of this discussion has been on intrafirm international technology and knowledge flows and has sought to show how this has influenced organizational and locational shaping. Internal technology and knowledge flows do have a significant and indeed increasing impact on the organization and location of firms with the shift towards the knowledge-based economy. Although this impact may be changing with the decline of the importance of the 'tyranny of distance', intrafirm knowledge and technology flows still have a profound impact on firm structure and geography albeit in more subtle and indirect ways. There is a clear materials and communications hierarchy here, with materials transport and logistics having overcome the distance tyranny better, and this is also true to a lesser extent with more codified information (what Thorngren (1970) has termed as 'programmed' information). However in more strategic and tacit areas of communication ('planned' and more particularly 'orientation' knowledge and information flows) where trust and shared learning are involved, face-to-face contact (involving high 'social presence') is still important and thus proximity continues to have a strong influence on organizational shape. New ICTs may now impart more social and tacit elements in the communication process, but it is a slow process and the issue of 'tacitness' continues to have a crucial role in binding certain functions and activities together in the firm.

Although the focus of the analysis has been on internal relations and flows within the firm, external linkages and impacts also have an influence on the development of a firm's technological competence (Sen and Rubenstein, 1990) and its organization and location, as has been highlighted in the discussion on strategy and practice. The knowledge and information 'richness' of certain local regions and economies has an influence both in terms of the initial location of activities, but also in terms of the evolutionary shaping and extending of inter-organisational networking. There is an important dynamic element in firm-local environment relations in terms of innovation which should not be neglected (Tödtling, 1995: 185). However, although the local innovation 'task environment' may be important in terms of research and technical linkages for some regions, firms and (given Gupta and Govindarajan's 1995 work) subsidiaries, it may not be in others. Some operations may have high levels of internal knowledge and technology flow with other parts of the firm (both domestically and overseas) but low external contact levels locally. Others, however, may just simply remain 'closed' operations with low levels of knowledge and technology flows internally or externally whether local, national, or international.

Lastly from this discussion it should be highlighted that the main local economic benefits and multiplier effects of innovations generated in one locality may not be gained there. The notion of geographically 'closed systems' of innovation combining both technological generation *and* gain, whether at national or more particularly at local level, is open to doubt and further research.

REFERENCES

Abler, R. (1971), 'Distance, Intercommunications, and Geography', *Proceedings of the Association of American Geographers*, 3: 1–4.

Allen, T. J. (1977), *Managing the Flow of Technology*, Cambridge, Mass.: MIT Press.

—— and Cohen, S. (1969), 'Information in R&D Laboratories', *Administrative Science Quarterly*, 14: 12–19.

—— and Hauptman, O. (1987), 'The Influence of Communication Technologies on Organizational Structure: A Conceptual Model for Future Research', *Communication Research*, 14: 575–87.

Antonelli, C. (1995), *The Economics of Localized Technological Change and Industrial Dynamics*, Norwell, Mass.: Kluwer.

Aoki, M. (1986), 'Horizontal Versus Vertical Information Structure of the Firm', *American Economic Review*, 76: 971–83.

Arcangeli, F. (1993), 'Local and Global Features of the Learning Process' in M. Humbert (ed.), *The Impact of Globalisation on Europe's Firms and Industries*, London: Pinter, 34–7.

Arora, A. and Gambardella, A. (1994), 'The Changing Technology of Technological Change: General and Abstract Knowledge and the Division of Innovative Labour', *Research Policy*, 23: 523–32.

Bartlett, C. A. (1986), 'Building and Managing the Transnational: The New Organizational Challenge', in M. E. Porter (ed.), *Competition in Global Industries*, Boston: Harvard Business School Press, 367–401.

—— and Ghoshal, S. (1989), *Managing Across Borders: The Transnational Solution*, Boston: Harvard Business School Press.

Behrman, J. N. and Fischer, W. A. (1980), *Overseas R&D Activities of Transnational Companies*, Cambridge, Mass.: Oelgeschlager, Gunn & Hain.

Blackbourn, A. (1974), 'The Spatial Behaviour of American Firms in Western Europe', in F. E. I. Hamilton (ed.), *Spatial Perspectives on Industrial Organisation and Decision-Making*, London: Wiley, 245–64.

Boisot, M. (1994), 'Is Your Firm a Creative Destroyer? Competitive Learning and Knowledge Flows in the Technological Strategies of Firms', *Research Policy*, 24: 489–506.

Brockhoff, K. K. and Schmaul, B. (1996), 'Organization, Autonomy and Success of Internationally Dispersed R&D Facilities', *IEEE Transactions on Engineering Management*, 43/1: 33–40.

Caves, R. E. (1982), *Multinational Enterprise and Economic Analysis*, Cambridge: Cambridge University Press.

Chesnais, F. (1992), 'National Systems of Innovation, Foreign Direct Investment and the Operations of Foreign Multinational Enterprises', in B.-Å. Lundvall (ed.), *National Systems of Innovation: Towards a Theory of Innovation and Interactive Learning*, London: Pinter, 265–95.

Chudnovsky, D. (1981), 'Pricing of Intra-firm Technological Transactions', in R. Murray (ed.), *Multinationals Beyond the Market: Intra-Firm Trade and the Control of Transfer Pricing*, Brighton: Harvester Press, 119–32.

Cordell, A. J. (1971), *The Multinational Firm: Foreign Direct Investment and Canadian Science Policy*, Ottawa: *Science Council of Canada*.

Creamer, D. (1976), *Overseas Research and Development by United States Multinationals, 1966–1995: Estimates of Expenditures and A Statistical Profile*, New York: The Conference Board.

Cusumano, M. A. and Elenkov, D. (1994), 'Linking International Technology Transfer with Strategy and Management: A Literature Survey', *Research Policy*, 23: 195–215.

De Meyer, A. (1993), 'Management of an International Network of Industrial R&D Laboratories', *R&D Management*, 23: 109–20.

Flaherty, M. T. (1986), 'Coordinating International Manufacturing and Technology', in M. E. Porter (ed.), *Competition in Global Industries*, Boston: Harvard Business School Press, 83–109.

Fleck, J. (1994), 'Learning by Trying: the Implementation of Configurational Technology', *Research Policy*, 23: 637–52.

Fleetwood, E. and Mölleryd, B. (1992), 'Parent Subsidiary Relationships in Transnational Companies: Aspects of Technical Development and Organisation', *International Journal of Technology Management*, 7: 97–110.

Friedrikson, C. G. and Lindmark, L. G. (1979), 'From Firms to Systems of Firms' in F. E. I. Hamilton and G. J. R. Linge (eds.), *Spatial Analysis, Industry and the Industrial Environment: Progress in Research and Application*, i. *Industrial Systems* London: Wiley, 155–86.

Gibson, D. V., Kehoe, C. A., and Lee, S.-Y. K. (1994), 'Collaborative Research as a Function of Proximity, Industry, and Company: A Case-Study of an R&D Consortium', *IEEE Transactions on Engineering Management*, 41: 255–63.

Granstrand, O., Håkanson, L., and Sjölander, S. (1993), 'Internationalisation of R&D: A Survey of Some Recent Research', *Research Policy*, 22: 413–30.

Grant, E. B. and Gregory, M. J. (1997), 'Tacit Knowledge, the Life-Cycle and International Manufacturing Transfer', *Technology Analysis & Strategic Management*, 9: 149–61.

Gupta, A. K. and Govindarajan, V. (1991), 'Knowledge Flows and the Structure of Control in Multinational Corporations', *Academy of Management Review*, 16: 768–92.

—— —— (1995), 'Organizing Knowledge Flows Within MNCs', *International Business Review*, 3: 443–57.

Håkanson, L. (1981), 'Organisation and Evolution of Foreign Multinationals', *Geografiska Annaler*, 63B: 47–56.

—— (1990), 'International Decentralisation of R&D: The Organizational Challenges', in C. A. Bartlett, Y. Doz, and G. Hedlund (eds.), *Managing the Global Firm*, London: Routledge, 256–78.

—— (1987), *Industrial Technological Development: A Network Approach*, London: Croom Helm.

Haug, P. (1992), 'An International Location and Production Transfer Model for High Technology Multinational Enterprises', *International Journal of Production Research*, 30: 559–72.

—— Hood, N., and Young, S. (1983), 'R&D Intensity in the Affiliates of US-Owned Electronics Companies Manufacturing in Scotland', *Regional Studies*, 17: 383–92.

Hedlund, G. (1986), 'The Hypermodern MNC: A Heterarchy', *Human Resource Management*, 25: 9–35.

Hirschey, R. C. and Caves, R. E. (1981), 'Research and Transfer of Technology by Multinational Enterprises', *Oxford Bulletin of Economics and Statistics*, 43: 115–30.

Hood, N. and Young, S. (1982), 'US Multinational R&D: Corporate Strategies and Policy Implications for the UK', *Multinational Business*, 2: 10–23.

Holstius, K. (1995), 'Cultural Adjustment in International Technology Transfer', *International Journal of Technology Management*, 10: 676–86.

Howells, J. (1993), 'Emerging Global Strategies in Innovation Management', in M. Humbert (ed.), *The Impact of Globalisation on Europe's Firms and Industries*, London: Pinter, 219–28.

—— (1995), 'Going Global: The Use of ICT Networks in Research and Development', *Research Policy*, 24: 169–84.

—— (1996), 'Tacit Knowledge, Innovation and Technology Transfer', *Technology Analysis & Strategic Management*, 8: 91–106.

—— and Wood, M. (1993) *The Globalisation of Production and Technology*, London: Belhaven/Wiley.

Hymer, S. (1972), 'The Multinational Corporation and the Law of Uneven Development', in J. N. Bhagwati (ed.), *Economics and World Order*, London: Macmillan, 80–106.

Hu, Y.-S. (1995), 'The International Transferability of the Firm's Advantages', *California Management Review*, 37/4: 73–88.

Kim, D. H. (1993), 'The Link Between Individual and Organisational Learning', *Sloan Management Review* (Fall), 37–50.

Kogut, B. (1990), 'International Sequencing Advantages and Network Flexibility', in C. A. Bartlett, Y. Doz, and G. Hedlund (eds.), *Managing the Global Firm*, London: Routledge, 47–68.

Lave, J. and Wenger, E. (1991), *Situated Learning: Legitimate Peripheral Participation*, Cambridge: Cambridge University Press.

Lazonick, W. (1993), 'Industry Clusters Versus Global Webs: Organizational Capabilities in the American Economy', *Industrial and Corporate Change*, 2: 1–24.

Le Heron, R. B. (1978), 'R and D in New Zealand Manufacturing Firms', *Pacific Viewpoint*, 19: 149–71.

Levy, D. and Dunning, J. H. (1993), 'International Production and Sourcing: Trends and Issues', *STI Review*, 13: 13–59.

Linge, G. J. R. (1992), 'Just-In-Time: More or Less Flexible?', *Economic Geography*, 68: 316–32.

Link, A. N. and Tassey, G. (1993), 'The Technology Infrastructure of Firms: Investments in Infratechnology', *IEEE Transactions on Engineering Management*, 40: 312–15.

Madeuf, B. (1984), 'International Technology Transfers and International Technology Payments: Definitions, Measurement and Firms' Behaviour', *Research Policy*, 13: 125–40.

Malecki, E. J. (1979), 'Locational Trends in R&D by Large US Corporations, 1965–1977', *Economic Geography*, 55: 309–23.

—— (1980), 'Corporate Organization of R&D and the Location of Technological Activities', *Regional Studies*, 14: 219–34.

Mansfield, E. and Romeo, A. (1984), ' "Reverse" Transfers of Technology from Overseas Subsidiaries to American Firms', *IEEE Transactions of Engineering Management*, EM 31: 122–7.

—— Teece, D., and Romeo, A. (1979), 'Overseas Research and Development by U.S.-Based Firms', *Economica*, 46: 187–96.

Menzler-Hokkanen, I. (1995), 'Multinational Enterprises and Technology Transfer', *International Journal of Technology Management*, 10: 293–310.

More, R. A. (1985), 'Barriers to Innovation: Intraorganizational Dislocations', *Journal of Product Innovation Management*, 3: 205–8.

Nonaka, I. (1994), 'A Dynamic Theory of Organizational Knowledge Creation', *Organization Science*, 5: 14–37.

—— Byosiere, P., Borucki, C. C., and Konno, N. (1994), 'Organizational Knowledge Creation Theory: A First Comprehensive Test', *International Business Review*, 3: 337–51.

Neff, P. J. (1995), 'Cross-Cultural Research Teams in a Global Enterprise', *Research Technology Management*, 38/3: 15–19.

Oujian, M. I. and Carne, B. (1987), 'A Study of the Factors Which Affect Technology Transfer in a Multilocational Multibusiness Unit Corporation', *IEEE Transactions on Engineering Management*, 34: 194–201.

Pearce, R. D. (1992), 'World Product Mandates and Multinational Enterprise Specialization', *Scandinavian International Business Review*, 1: 38–58.

—— and Papnastassiou, M. (1996), 'R&D Networks and Innovation: Decentralised Product Development in Multinational Enterprises', *R&D Management*, 24: 315–33.

Polanyi, M., 'Tacit Knowing: Its Bearing on Some Problems of Philosophy', *Review of Modern Physics*, 34: 601–16.

—— (1967), *The Tacit Dimension*, London: Routledge.

Porter, M. E. (1990), *The Competitive Advantage of Nations*, New York: Free Press.
Prahalad, C. K. and Doz, Y. L. (1987), *The Multinational Mission: Balancing Global Demands and Global Vision*, New York: Free Press.
Reich, R. B. (1991), *The Work of Nations: Preparing Ourselves for 21st-Century Capitalism*, New York: Knopf.
Roth, K. and Morrison, A. J. (1996), 'Implementing Global Strategy: Characteristics of Global Subsidiary Mandates', *Journal of International Business Studies*, 4: 715–35.
Ruggles, R. L. (1997), 'Tools for Knowledge Management: An Introduction', in R. L. Ruggles (ed.), *Knowledge Management Tools: Resources for the Knowledge-Based Economy*, Boston: Butterworth-Heinemann, 1–8.
Sen, F. and Rubenstein, A. H. (1990), 'An Exploration of Factors Affecting the Integration of In-house R&D With External Technology Acquisition Strategies of a Firm', *IEEE Transactions on Engineering Management*, 37: 246–58.
Senker, J. (1995), 'Networks and Tacit Knowledge in Innovation', *Economies et Sociétés*, 2/9: 99–11.
Shotwell, T. K. (1971), 'Information Flow in an Industrial Laboratory—A Case Study', *IEEE Transactions on Engineering Management*, EM 18: 26–33.
Slaughter, S. (1993), 'Innovation and Learning During Implementation: A Comparison of User and Manufacturer Innovations', *Research Policy*, 22: 81–95.
Sørensen, K. H. and Levold, N. (1992), 'Tacit Networks, Heterogeneous Engineers and Embodied Technology', *Science, Technology and Human Values*, 17: 13–35.
Taylor, G. D. (1994), 'Negotiating Technology Transfers Within Multinational Enterprises: Perspectives from Canadian History', in G. Jones (ed.), *The Making of Global Enterprise*, London: Frank Cass, 127–58.
Teece, D. J. (1976), *The Multinational Corporation and the Resource Cost of Technology Transfer*, Cambridge, Mass.: Ballinger.
—— (1977), 'Technology Transfer by Multinational Firms: The Resource Cost of Transferring Technological Know-How', *Economic Journal*, 87: 242–61.
Terpstra, V. (1977), 'International Product Policy: The Role of Foreign R&D', *Columbia Journal of World Business*, 12: 24–32.
Thorngren, B. (1970), 'How Do Contact Systems Affect Regional Development?', *Environment and Planning*, A2: 409–27.
Tödtling, F. (1995), 'The Innovation Process and Local Environment', in S. Conti, E. J. Malecki, and P. Oinas (eds.), *The Industrial Enterprise and its Environment: Spatial Perspectives*, Aldershot: Avebury, 171–94.
Urlich, D., Jick, T., and von Glinow, M. A. (1993), 'High-Impact Learning: Building and Diffusing Learning Capability', *Organizational Dynamics*, 22/2: 52–66.
Veugelers, R. and van den Houte, P. (1990), 'Domestic R&D in the Presence of Multinational Enterprises', *International Journal of Industrial Organization*, 8: 1–15.
Vernon, R. (1966), 'International Investment and International Trade in the Product Cycle', *Quarterly Journal of Economics*, 80: 190–207.
—— (1977), *Storm over the Multinationals: The Real Issues*, London: Macmillan.
—— (1979), 'The Product Cycle Hypothesis in a New Institutional Environment', *Oxford Bulletin of Economics and Statistics*, 4: 255–67.
—— and Davidson, W. H. (1979), 'Foreign Production of Technology-Intensive Products by US-Based Multinational Enterprises', Working Paper No. 79–5,

Division of Research, Graduate School of Business Administration, Harvard University.

von Hippel, E. and Tyre, M. (1993), 'How the "Learning-by-doing" is Done: Problem Identification in the Novel Process Equipment', Sloan School Management Working Paper No. BPS 3521–93.

Wei, L. (1995), 'International Technology Transfer and Development of Technological Capabilities: A Theoretical Framework', *Technology in Society*, 17: 103–20.

Wong, P. K. (1992), 'Technological Development Through Subcontracting Linkages', *Scandinavian International Business Review*, 1: 28–40.

Young, S., Hood, N., and Dunlop, S. (1988), 'Global Strategies, Multinational Subsidiary Rules and Economic Impact in Scotland', *Regional Studies*, 22: 487–97.

—— —— and Peters, E. (1994), 'Multinational Enterprises and Regional Economic Development', *Regional Studies*, 28: 657–77.

4. New Technology and Jobs*

Mario Pianta

1. INTRODUCTION

The growing literature on innovation has only recently addressed the issue of the employment impact of technological change. With unemployment reaching 18 million in the European Union and 35 million in OECD countries, this is a much needed development. Important changes in both innovation and employment patterns have emerged in the 1990s and new research and policy questions have to be addressed.

Innovation patterns

In the 1980s, the industrialized countries increased their technological activities substantially, as measured by several indicators such as R&D expenditure, number of researchers, number of patents, and direct surveys on innovation. Growing investment and use of new intermediate goods led to a large-scale adoption of a range of new technologies—information and communication technologies (ICTs), new materials, new manufacturing systems—across the whole economy.

With the recession of the early 1990s this growth was reversed. Public and private spending in research and development declined in real terms for the first time in most OECD countries. Government budget restraints on the one hand and the need for companies to restructure themselves on the other did not offer much scope for expanding R&D budgets even in the subsequent recovery. At the same time, the international diffusion of new technologies, especially those linked to ICTs, increased rapidly, pervading most economic activities, from manufacturing to services, as well as new emerging consumption patterns. While many studies have investigated the contribution that such innovative efforts have made to the competitiveness and growth of countries, industries, and firms,[1] much less attention has been paid to the employment consequences.

* I am grateful to Rinaldo Evangelista for his comments and to Leopoldo Nascia for his assistance in the statistical work and the preparation of figures.

[1] Amongst a large literature, the effects at the country level are reviewed in Fagerberg (1994) and Pianta (1995); at the sectoral level see Dosi, Pavitt, and Soete (1990), Scherer (1992), and Amendola, Guerrieri, and Padoan (1992).

Employment patterns

Most recent studies of unemployment have largely confined themselves to developments within the functioning of the labour market, focusing on the short-term impact of demand factors, wage levels, or the 'mismatch' between demand and supply of labour due to the skill composition of the workforce or the lack of flexibility of labour-market regulations. Such approaches ignore a key cause of present unemployment, that is the role of technological change, with its long-term impact on growth, the economic structure, and its direct and indirect effects on the use of labour.[2]

The question of technological unemployment returned to the research and policy agenda in Europe with the recession of the early 1990s, and the emergence of an unprecedented pattern of 'jobless growth'. For the first time in post-war history the recovery of production and profits was not matched by a recovery in jobs, pointing out a fundamental change in the mechanisms of growth. In the United States and Japan the unemployment problems have been partly hidden by different statistical definitions and social arrangements; in the former the growth of part-time and low-wage jobs has led to a serious polarization of incomes, while in the latter the economic dynamism has faded and the need to adjust the social model is emerging.

At the root of such changes are two main factors: the role of new technologies and the globalization of economic activities. This chapter investigates how and why technological change has led to such worrying consequences for employment.

The structure of the chapter is as follows: after outlining a conceptual framework in the next section, the empirical evidence in Section 3 consists of an analysis of the employment changes in manufacturing sectors in the last decade in the six largest OECD economies—the United States, Japan, Germany, France, the United Kingdom, and Italy. They are related to the patterns of structural change in the sectoral composition of industry and to the different forms of technological change, namely that embodied in investment and the innovative outputs of a disembodied nature (proxied by patents). In order to overcome the limitations of such technology data, Section 4 uses the results of the recent innovation surveys carried out in several European countries, linking them to the more recent employment performance of manufacturing sectors. Section 5 offers some preliminary evidence on the employment consequences of technological change in the service sectors in the case of Italy, where a pioneering survey on innovation in

---

[2] Recent studies of technology and employment, using a variety of approaches, include Freeman, Clark, and Soete (1982); Freeman and Soete (1987, 1994); Leontief and Duchin (1986); Boyer (1988); Pasinetti (1981, 1990); Sylos Labini (1990); Meyer-Krahmer (1992); OECD (1994, 1996b, 1996c); Caracostas and Muldur (1995); Petit (1995a,b); Pini (1995); Rifkin (1995); Vivarelli (1995); *Science, Technology, Industry Review* (1996); and Pianta (1997).

services has just been completed. The conclusions, in Section 6, summarize the available evidence and outline directions for research and policy.

2. A CONCEPTUAL FRAMEWORK

While the issue of technological unemployment has been investigated at length by classical economists, in the high growth post-war decades it was widely assumed that the variety of 'compensation mechanisms' could more than offset the direct job losses due to technological change. In the last decade, however, slower growth, sluggish demand, strong innovation and increasing diffusion of new technologies have changed the economic landscape of the more advanced countries. The employment impact of innovation is now further complicated by the pressure of international competition on increasingly open economies and by the globalization of production and technology, all factors resulting in an acceleration of innovation and structural change, generally with a labour-saving bias.

How can the employment impact of new technologies be investigated empirically? Studies can follow three main paths of research.

1. First, they may focus on the direct effects of innovations in the firms (or industry) where they are introduced (see Evangelista, 1995; Vivarelli, Evangelista, and Pianta, 1996; Cesaratto and Stirati, 1996).

2. Second, they may explore the complex set of indirect effects on other competing firms, on upstream and downstream sectors, or on the macroeconomic level, developing a dynamic model for the whole economy. This is the most comprehensive approach, which is able to take into account the variety of 'compensation mechanisms' of technological unemployment. They include the positive impact on production and jobs which may be due to new machinery, new products, reduced prices, increased profits and investment, higher productivity, income effects, and overall expansion of demand. However, such studies tend to use very simple and aggregate technology indicators, neglecting the complexity of innovative activities and their differences across sectors and firms. They also tend to model a closed economy, not taking into account the increasing international integration and the globalization of technology and production (see Meyer Krahmer, 1992; Vivarelli, 1995; Pini, 1995).

3. Third, studies on the employment impact of innovation may focus on sectoral analyses, linking technological and structural change and investigating its specific nature and impact across industries. This approach (OECD 1996b,c; Pianta, Evangelista, and Perani, 1996) makes it possible to use more refined indicators of innovative activities and to account for the differences across sectors and countries of the relationship between technology and jobs. This approach will be the one followed in this chapter.

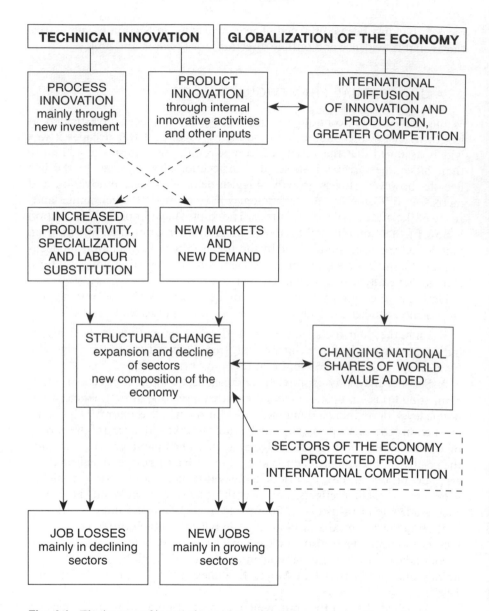

Fig. 4.1. The impact of innovation and structural change on employment
Source: Pianta, Evangelista, and Perani, 1996.

Figure 4.1 offers a framework for exploring the relationships between technological innovation, globalization, and employment. Process innovations (introduced mainly through new investment) and product innovation (based on internal innovative activities as well as on new intermediate or capital goods) lead to the well-known contrasting effects of increasing productivity and replacing labour on the one hand, and of creating new markets, demand, and production on the other hand, through different compensation mechanisms.

In a context of globalization of production and markets, however, innovations have a rapid international diffusion. The result is greater competition and a new international division of labour, both in terms of the sectors of a country's activity and of the different phases of production localized in each nation. This process changes countries' shares in the value added of global production. Greater competition reinforces the pressure to increase productivity, giving greater role to specialization advantages. This, together with the emergence of new innovation-led fields of activity, leads to the increased pace of structural change, resulting in a different sectoral composition of national economies.

The impact on employment is therefore the net result of, on the one hand, job losses due to the direct labour-displacing effect of innovation and to the decline of particular sectors, and on the other to job gains due to the employment-creation effect of technological change and of the growth of expanding sectors.

The part of the economy which is sheltered from global competition—many private services, the public sector, non-profit activities—should not be forgotten in this context, because here many compensation mechanisms operate and these sectors are at the centre of structural change in advanced economies, creating a large proportion of new employment opportunities.[3] This approach makes it possible to address the question of employment, looking at the combined impact of technological and structural change. The processes outlined above can be best investigated empirically through a sectoral analysis. First, a sectoral study can account for the structural change in the economy. Second, the sources and patterns of innovation and the forms of their introduction tend to be sector-specific. Third, for the purposes of international comparison the sectoral level offers adequate data and makes it possible to identify structural patterns in a more satisfactory way than can be learned from firm-level studies.[4] While the sectoral analysis should include

[3] Part of the growth of private services is associated with the transfer of activities previously carried out within large manufacturing firms; this may affect the patterns of structural change in a different way across sectors and countries.

[4] Firm-level analyses were presented at the US Commerce Department–OECD conference on 'The Effects of Technology and Innovation of Firm Performance and Employment', Washington, 30 Apr.–2 May 1995; while these show that the most innovative firms perform better in employment terms, they cannot identify the net effect that technological change has on employment at the sectoral (or aggregate) level.

the whole economy, in the next two sections the focus is on manufacturing industry, due to the availability of data, but also to the nature of innovative activities. In most manufacturing sectors the internal generation of know-how and the adoption of innovations first introduced elsewhere are combined in the process of technological change, while in most other sectors—agriculture, private services, and government—the latter is by far the dominant form of innovation.

Finally, the examination of the six largest OECD economies makes it possible to identify the different outcomes that the processes outlined above may have. Far from being a deterministic process, the economic and employment outcomes of technological change are the result of social processes, where institutions, government policies and social relations play a major role, alongside the developments in technology and the strategies of firms. Therefore we expect to find different patterns and performances across countries, rooted also in their structural differences.

3. THE EMPLOYMENT IMPACT OF TECHNOLOGICAL AND STRUCTURAL CHANGE

The results of a recent study (Pianta, Evangelista, and Perani, 1996) shed light on the relationships between innovation, structural change and employment in the long cycle of growth from the early 1980s to the early 1990s. Employment, value added and productivity data for thirty-six manufacturing sectors[5] for the six largest OECD countries (USA, Japan, Germany, France, United Kingdom, and Italy) were considered. The evidence is summarized in three figures. Figure 4.2 shows for the aggregate of the six countries (G6) the rates of change of value added and employment, illustrating the overall pattern of structural change which has taken place in the last decade. Manufacturing classes scatter along a positive relation, with a few sectors showing growth in both value added and employment, a few showing a decline in both, and the majority combining job losses and increased value added.[6] The growth sectors appear to be associated with greater technologi-

---

[5] The source is the OECD STAN database, with data for ISIC classes. The variables considered include value added (in constant prices), employment (number engaged) and productivity (value added per employee), measured as average annual rates of change from 1980–2 to 1990–2. The three-year averages are introduced in order to avoid the cyclical effects and to provide a solid picture of the changes in the industrial structure of the last decade.

[6] The three clusters are the following: (a) Growth sectors, where value added and employment have both increased, including plastic, printing, office computing, aircraft, drugs, electrical apparatus, food, motor vehicles, and other chemicals; (b) declining sectors, with an opposite pattern, of a fall in both value added and employment, including leather, footwear, iron and steel, petroleum refining, and tobacco; (c) sectors in restructuring, with growth in production and fall in employment, include all remaining sectors.

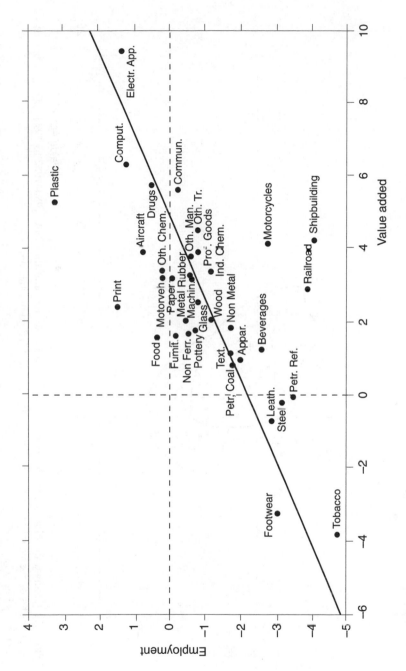

Fig. 4.2. Changes in value added and employment in G6 countries, 1980–1982 to 1990–1992 (percentage annual rates of change). G6 = United States, Japan, Germany, France, United Kingdom, and Italy.
Source: As Fig. 4.1.

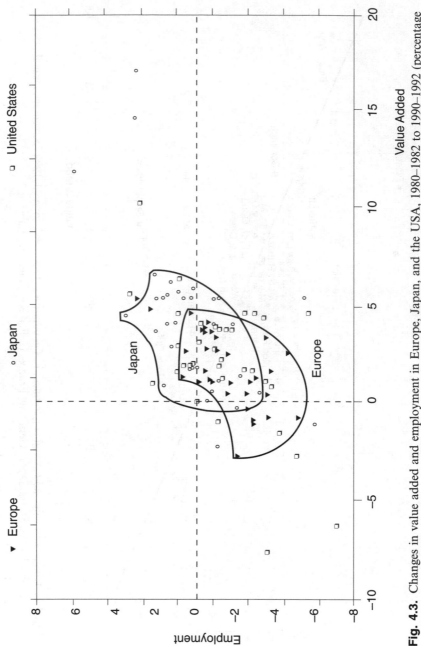

Fig. 4.3. Changes in value added and employment in Europe, Japan, and the USA, 1980–1982 to 1990–1992 (percentage annual rates of change). Europe = Germany, France, United Kingdom, and Italy
Source: As Fig. 4.1.

cal intensity, an issue already pointed out in the OECD studies (OECD, 1994, ch. 4; 1996b).

If we look behind the G6 aggregate, the patterns of the USA, Japan, and the four European countries show a rather different distribution, presented in Figure 4.3.[7] It is striking that Japan has a large number of its manufacturing sectors in the growth quadrant, while Europe has most of its industries in the restructuring quadrant, with the USA showing an intermediate position.

The contrasting performances of Europe and Japan are even more evident when the growth of productivity is plotted against changes in employment, as shown in Figure 4.4.[8] While for Japan no association is evident and several sectors show positive employment and productivity changes, for Europe a clear negative relationship emerges; the manufacturing sectors where productivity has increased tend to be those where employment has fallen. Again the distribution of the USA is intermediate between these two cases.

This evidence is coherent with the studies by Appelbaum and Schettkat (1995, 1996) which pointed out that the relationship between productivity and employment has turned from a positive one in the 1970s to a negative one in the 1980s, due to the changed pattern of growth and demand, and to the new wage and labour-market conditions. With slower growth and sluggish demand in Europe, the innovation-led process of productivity growth has mainly taken the form of labour-saving innovative strategies by firms, resulting in large job losses in most manufacturing sectors.

In the comparison of the six major OECD countries two technology variables have been included: gross fixed capital formation[9] and the number of patents granted in the USA to inventors of the six countries.[10] In order to use

[7] For total manufacturing, the rates of change of value added and employment differ significantly across the three areas. Employment has increased by an annual rate of 1.09% in Japan and fallen by -0.58% in the USA and by –1.08% in Europe. Value added has increased by 5.68% in Japan, 2.38% in the USA, and 1.94% in Europe.

[8] For manufacturing industry as a whole, Japan shows a higher elasticity of employment relative to value added than the USA and Europe. Conversely, the same increase in productivity leads to higher job losses in Europe than in the USA, and to small job gains in Japan.

[9] Data—expressed as average annual rates of change between the 1980–2 and 1990–2 averages—are drawn from the same STAN database, and converted to 1985 prices using GDP deflators. Data on investment in machinery and equipment alone would have been preferable, but were not available. Investment plays a double role; first, it is an indicator of process innovations and of the technological changes embodied in new capital goods, generally acquired from other sectors; second, it is an indicator of the expansion of production capacity due to the patterns of structural change and to product innovations. These two roles have contrasting effects on employment, a negative one for the former and a positive one for the latter. From the pattern of association with other variables the dominant role will be identified.

[10] Data are drawn from the US Patent and Trademark Office database. Patents are an indicator of the internal innovative activities of individual sectors, which are directly associated with product innovations; data at the sectoral level are closely correlated with R&D expenditure. The number of patents granted in the USA is one of the most widely used technology indicators. The USA is the largest and most advanced market for technology and for foreign countries the patents obtained in the USA are a good indicator of their technological activities at the international level. The data however are less reliable as an indicator for the USA itself, as they record

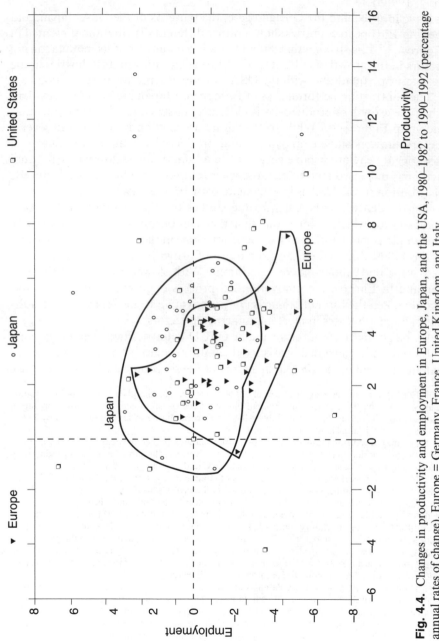

Fig. 4.4. Changes in productivity and employment in Europe, Japan, and the USA, 1980–1982 to 1990–1992 (percentage annual rates of change). Europe = Germany, France, United Kingdom, and Italy *Source: As* Fig. 4.1.

Table 4.1. Correlations between growth rates of economic, technological, and employment variables (real annual rates of change from 1980–2 to 1990–2 averages; 19 manufacturing sectors)

Correlations between:	G6	Europe 4	USA	Japan	Germany	France	UK	Italy
Employment								
Value added	0.57^c	0.62^c	0.53^c	0.52^b	0.63^c	0.48^b	0.59^c	0.18
Productivity	−0.28	−0.51^b	−0.28	−0.06	−0.55^c	−0.61^c	−0.32^a	−0.65^c
Investment	0.87^c	0.75^c	0.66^c	0.67^c	0.64^c	0.42^b	0.72^c	0.07
Patents	0.50^b	0.69^b	0.14	0.32^a	0.86^c	0.77^c	0.54^c	−0.04
Value added								
Productivity	0.55^c	0.35^a	0.67^c	0.82^c	0.24	0.39^b	0.56^c	0.60^c
Investment	0.58^c	0.61^c	0.23	0.22	0.32^a	0.42^b	0.60^c	0.02
Patents	0.56^c	0.40^b	0.23	0.66^c	0.50^b	0.25	0.47^b	0.37^b
Productivity								
Investment	−0.09	−0.24	−0.32^a	0.13	−0.29	−0.09	−0.01	0.002
Patents	0.28	−0.39^b	0.12	0.57^c	−0.62^c	−0.55^c	0.07	0.28
Investment								
Patents	0.45^b	0.63	0.21^c	0.31	0.40^b	0.24	0.57^c	−0.38^a

Notes: Significance levels = ^{a} 90%, ^{b} 95%, ^{c} 99%. G6 includes all six countries; Europe 4 includes Germany, France, the United Kingdom, and Italy.

Source: Pianta, Evangelista and Perani, 1996.

these variables a higher level of aggregation was required and all variables were considered for nineteen manufacturing sectors.[11] Table 4.1 provides an overview of the relationships between the five variables; simple correlation coefficients were calculated across the nineteen sectors for the six countries considered. For the G6 aggregate the growth rates of employment, value added, investment, and patents always have strong (and significant) correlations. Productivity grows in parallel with value added (partly due to the way the variable is defined) and has a small (non-significant) negative link to employment.

The same pattern of relationships is broadly common to the USA, Japan, and to the group of four European countries. In the USA however value added and investment are unrelated and patents show no association to other

the patents obtained in the domestic market, which tend to be in higher numbers, of lower quality, and of more uniform distribution across sectors than patents obtained abroad (see Archibugi and Pianta, 1992, 1996).

[11] All STAN-based variables (employment, value added, productivity, and investment) were considered in the 22 ISIC classes disaggregation. US patent data are available by 41 SIC classes and a preliminary concordance has been established, covering 19 of the 22 ISIC classes (leaving out the ISIC classes of Wood products and furniture; Paper and printing; and Other manufacturing). For patents, the SIC classes of Ordnance and Other industries were excluded, while the rest were attributed to the 19 ISIC classes considered.

variables (probably due to the use of domestic US patents). In Japan patents are linked to productivity rather than investment.

In Europe the only difference from the G6 is that the negative relationship between employment and productivity is stronger and significant. Looking at individual European countries, the same structure of relationships emerges in Germany, France, and the UK, with differing patterns found only for patents. In Italy, however, the pattern of associations is markedly different. The only strong and highly significant correlations are the negative one between productivity and employment growth and the positive one between productivity and value added.

A regression analysis has been carried out, interpreting the changes in employment as the result of technological innovation and structural changes in the sectoral composition of economies. The latter is accounted for by the changes in sectoral value added; the impact of product innovations and, more generally, of innovative activity internal to sectors can be proxied by the growth of patenting; finally investment represents more the expansion of production capacity than the relevance of process innovations.[12] In the regression analysis therefore we expect positive signs from all three variables.

First the analysis is carried out pooling the six countries and the nineteen sectors. Then the regressions are repeated separately for each country on the nineteen sectors available; Table 4.2 shows the results.

In the pooled analysis, all three variables have a positive sign and highly significant coefficients (the adjusted R-squared is 0.45). Even when the value added variable is removed (col. b) the regression maintains its strength; the two coefficients remain positive and increase their significance (the adjusted R-squared is 0.41), suggesting that the effect of structural change is largely captured by the changes in sectoral investment patterns. These results suggest that the effects of technological and structural change are closely associated (and difficult to disentangle with the available indicators). They explain to a large extent the employment changes in manufacturing sectors of the six largest advanced economies.

The relevance of technological and structural change points to a fundamental, long-term dynamics shaping employment patterns and leaves little room for explanations based only on short-term labour-market patterns.

This role of technological and structural change also emerges from the different results obtained from the regressions for the six countries. The growth of value added appears moderately significant only in the USA and Germany (as well as in the Europe aggregate). Investment has the greatest and most generalized positive impact on employment growth, accounting for much of the process of structural change, with the only exceptions being France and Italy. Patents show a positive and significant link to employment only in

---

[12] The strong association shown above between investment, value added, and employment suggests that the dominant factor in investment patterns is the 'expansionary effect'.

Table 4.2. Regression estimates (dependent variable: rate of change of employment)

	Pool of 6 countries and 19 sectors		USA	Japan	Europe	Germany	France	UK	Italy
	(a)	(b)							
Constant	-2.603	-2.268	-1.684	-2.017	-3.133	-2.896	-4.47	-3.68	-1.669
Value added	0.204		0.314	0.151	0.231	0.28	0.269	0.191	0.296
	(2.951)c		(2.384)c	(1.038)	(2.416)b	(2.022)a	(1.522)	(0.989)	(1.045)
Investment	0.227	0.258	0.369	0.342	0.228	0.211	0.103	0.35	0.027
	(4.618)c	(5.181)c	(3.344)c	(2.505)b	(3.670)c	(3.277)c	(0.944)	(2.147)b	(0.118)
Patents	0.152	0.226	-0.072	-0.029	0.392	0.681	0.75	0.141	-.076
	(2.460)b	(3.872)c	(0.402)	(0.151)	(4.234)c	(5.865)c	(4.271)c	(0.717)	(0.296)
Adjusted R-squared	0.449	0.409	0.505	0.393	0.448	0.858	0.624	0.479	-0.129
F-statistics	(30.582)c	(38.728)c	(7.111)c	(4.668)b	(20.447)c	(37.362)c	(10.422)c	(6.523)c	(0.389)
Number of cases	109	109	19	18	19	19	19	19	18

Notes: T-statistics in brackets. Significance levels = [a] 90%, [b] 95%, [c] 99%.

Germany and France. The lack of association for Japan may be due to the high growth rates of patenting in the USA experienced by most sectors, even of lower technological intensity.

Overall, the regressions largely account for the employment changes of all countries, with the exception of Italy where no variables were significant. Only in Italy were the increases in production and the technological activities of manufacturing sectors unrelated to the employment changes of the last decade. While for the advanced countries as a whole the expansion of innovation-led activities in growing sectors has partially offset the job losses due to technological change and greater competition, in Italy there is no evidence of such a compensation mechanism.

For the advanced economies in aggregate in the 1990s, the sectors showing the highest rates of investment and innovation experienced greater growth of output and employment. Technology, in other words, has accompanied the process of structural change, favouring the emergence of new fields of activity which have provided new job opportunities.

However, such a process becomes more uneven when the individual countries—especially the European ones—are considered, because the benefits of the compensation effects are distributed as a result of a competitive process, which is affected also by the sectoral specialization of individual countries; this helps explain the weaker associations found at the country level. In Europe, and particularly in Italy the 'virtuous circle' between technology, growth, and employment is much weaker and the gains offered by productivity growth have resulted in job losses. In these countries, rather than leading to the expansion of new activities, investment and innovation have focused on the restructuring of traditional sectors of the economy, and are associated with large labour-saving effects.

The lack of detailed sectoral data for recent years makes it difficult to replicate this investigation for the economic cycle of the 1990s, but there is some evidence of a change in the sectoral patterns shown above. Both in Europe and elsewhere, it is no longer clear whether 'high-tech' sectors have had better than average employment performances. And the very definition of 'high-tech' needs to be improved, with a more comprehensive view of innovative activities. These issues are addressed in the following section.

4. INNOVATION SURVEY DATA AND EMPLOYMENT IN EUROPE IN THE 1990s

A major limitation of the studies on the employment impact of innovation, including the analysis of the previous section, is that the technological indicators—patents, R&D, and gross investment—used as proxies for disembodied and embodied technological activities, account for only some aspects of the complex innovation process. In particular, activities such as non-formalized research, design, and engineering are not covered by such variables, nor is it possible to identify the part of investment related to innovation. A solution to such a problem is offered by the use of innovation survey data, which provide an enlarged set of quantitative and qualitative indications on firms' innovative activities (for early uses see Evangelista, 1995; Vivarelli, Evangelista, and Pianta, 1996).

Innovation surveys have been carried out in several European countries in the framework of the EU-sponsored Community Innovation Survey (CIS). They identify the firms which have introduced innovations (at least one product or process innovation) in the period 1990–2.[13] In this section the relationship between technological change and employment is examined for five European countries (Italy, Germany, the Netherlands, Denmark, and Norway)[14] in the early 1990s at the level of twenty manufacturing sectors, using data on the total expenditure for innovation in 1992 and its main components (R&D, innovative investment, etc.). The innovative intensities of individual sectors have been calculated and related to the changes in economic and employment variables from 1989 to the latest available year.[15] In order to point out the variety of patterns shown by European countries, changes in employment are plotted against the innovative intensities of sectors for the extreme cases of Italy and Germany in Figures 4.5 and 4.6. In the latter we find a rather dispersed distribution, while for Italy a negative

[13] First results of the Community Innovation Survey (CIS) were presented at the Conference on 'Innovation Measurement and Policies', organized by Eurostat and the European Commission DG XIII, held in Luxembourg on 20–1 May 1996. For an evaluation of the survey see Archibugi et al. (1995). A major progress in technology indicators made possible by CIS is the definition of the total expenditure devoted to innovation by firms, including expenditure for R&D, design, trial production, innovative investment, acquisition of patents and licences, and exploratory marketing. The nature and structure of this expenditure is described in the research report by ISRDS-CNR and STEP (Evangelista, Sandven, Sirilli, and Smith, 1996) from which the data used here are taken. An overview of studies based on innovation surveys is in Archibugi and Pianta (1996). The analysis of the results of the Italian survey is in Archibugi et al. (1996).

[14] These are the countries with the more solid statistical results from the innovation surveys. In Italy 22,787 firms responded to the innovation survey, 7,553 of which were innovative. In Germany 3,879 firms responded and two-thirds had introduced an innovation in the 1990–2 period. The number of responses were 4,094 in the Netherlands, 674 in Denmark, and 982 in Norway. Other countries had lower numbers of replies and worse response rates, or did not include the question on innovation expenditure (France).

[15] Innovation expenditure data refer to the firms which had introduced an innovation in 1990–2. The innovative intensities were calculated by dividing the expenditure of the firms of a sector by the number of employees of the innovating firms of that sector (an alternative method, producing very similar results, is the use of the sales of innovating firms). These sectoral innovative intensities can be considered as an indicator of the innovative effort of individual industries, and are related to the performances of the whole of the sectors. It is difficult to estimate the lag between the innovative effort and the emergence of the economic impact; employment and output performances have been calculated using the average annual rates of change from 1989 (the start of the downturn) to the last available year (generally 1993). We can expect that the interindustry differences investigated here are likely to emerge even with an imperfect structure of lags.

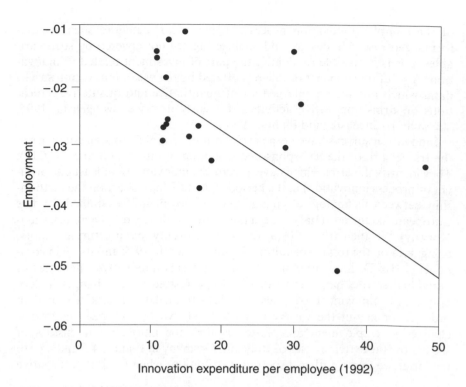

Fig. 4.5. Italy: Innovation expenditure and employment change (20 manufacturing sectors)

association emerges. This finding for Italy is affected by the specific industrial structure of the country, by the prevalence of labour-saving process innovations within firms' innovative efforts, and by the strong productivity growth obtained at the expense of employment also in high-tech industries (as seen above in Tables 4.1 and 4.2).[16] The innovation–employment relationship across industries in the five European countries has been investigated with a regression analysis where changes in employment are explained by changes in value added (accounting for structural change), gross investment per

[16] The negative employment impact of innovative activities in Italy is pointed out by Vivarelli, Evangelista and Pianta (1996) and Pianta (1996), with sectoral analyses. The study at the firm level by Cesaratto and Stirati (1996) compares 6,000 innovating and 9,000 non-innovating firms with the employment and economic performance of the 26,000 firms included in the survey on economic activity. The number of employees appears as an unreliable measure as it is gross of temporary lay-offs, and the number of hours worked by blue-collar workers is also investigated. Overall, innovation shows a negative relation to employment, although small innovating firms perform better than any other group in all indicators. The expected contrasting consequences of product and process innovations are also found.

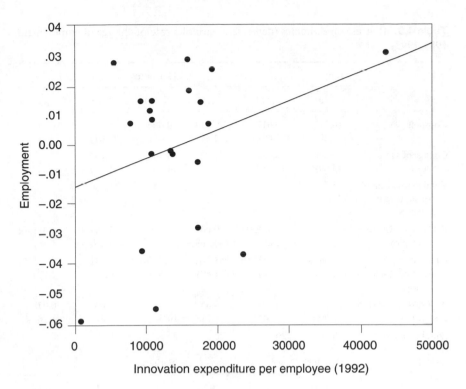

Fig. 4.6. Germany: Innovation expenditure and employment change (20 manufacturing sectors)

employee, and two indicators of technological intensities, total innovation expenditure per employee and R&D expenditure per employee, both drawn from the innovation surveys. The results are shown in Table 4.3.[17]

In all five countries employment changes follow the pattern of structural change shown by the evolution of value added, which always has a positive and significant impact. Total innovation expenditure per employee—the most comprehensive new indicator offered by the innovation surveys—has a negative sign in all countries but Germany, and is significant only in Italy. R&D intensities show a negative impact on employment in all countries but Norway, and the coefficients are significant in Italy and the Netherlands. Gross investment intensities have a positive and significant impact in Denmark; in the other countries it generally shows negative, non significant

[17] The list of variables is the following: average annual rate of change of employment, 1989–93 (dependent variable), Average annual rate of change of real value added, 1989–93; total innovation expenditure per employee in 1992; Expenditure for R&D per employee in 1992; gross fixed investment per employee, 1992.

Table 4.3. Regression estimates (dependent variable: rate of change of employment, 1989–1993)

	Italy			Germany		
	(a)	(b)	(c)	(a)	(b)	(c)
Constant	−0.013 (−2.40)[b]	−0.017 (−3.09)[c]	−0.014 (−2.41)[b]	0.006 (0.48)	0.01 (1.01)	−0.013 (−0.94)
Change of value added	0.256 (3.00)[c]	0.224 (2.33)[b]		0.702 (4.93)[c]	0.697 (5.17)[c]	
Total innovation expenditure per employee	−5.70E-04 (−241)[b]			2.94E-07 (0.63)		
R&D expenditure per employee		−7.49E-04 (−2.06)[a]	−0.001 (−3.168)[c]		−2.59E-06 (−1.26)	−4.38E-06 (−1.36)
Gross fixed investment per employee	−1.64E-10 (−0.37)	−6.16E-10 (−1.44)	−758E-10 (−1.60)	−5.55E-07 (−0.64)	6.24E-07 (0.07)	2.36E-06 (1.77)[a]
Adjusted R-squared	0.52	0.49	0.35	0.67	0.63	0.07
F-statistics	7.99[c]	7.04[c]	6.21[c]	10.68[c]	11.84[c]	1.75
Number of cases	20	20	20	20	20	20

	Denmark			Netherlands		
	(a)	(b)	(c)	(a)	(b)	(c)
Constant	−0.032 (−2.89)[b]	−0.032 (−3.13)[c]	−0.031 (−2.71)[b]	−0.002 (−0.13)	0.004 (0.44)	0.007 (0.60)
Change of value added	0.353 (2.06)[a]	0.359 (2.20)[b]		1.04 (2.49)[b]	1.127 (3.29)[c]	
Total innovation expenditure per employee	−5.01E-08 (−0.42)			−3.99E-04 (−0.39)		
R&D expenditure per employee		−4.03E-07 (0.33)	−2.83E-07 (−0.64)		−5.00E-03 (−2.80)[b]	−5.00E-03 (−1.93)[a]
Gross fixed investment per employee	4.19E-07 (1.92)[a]	4.67E-07 (2.18)[b]	4.64E-07 (1.93)[a]	−2.08E-07 (−0.27)	−2.76E-07 (−0.43)	1.94E-07 (0.25)
Adjusted R-squared	0.23	0.28	0.09	0.15	0.42	0.09
F-statistics	2.73[a]	3.18[a]	1.87	2.08	5.61[c]	1.9
Number of cases	18	18	18	20	20	20

	Norway		
	(a)	(b)	(c)
Constant	−0.05	−0.05	−0.044
	(−6.06)[c]	(−6.06)[c]	(−5.14)[c]
Change of value added	0.576	0.554	
	(2.27)[b]	(2.16)[b]	
Total innovation expenditure per employee	−0.002		
	(−0.07)		
R&D expenditure per employee		0.012	0.106
		(0.13)	(1.11)
Gross fixed investment per employee	−2.30E-08	−2.06E-08	1.16E-08
	(−0.23)	(−0.20)	(0.11)
Adjusted R-squared	0.14	0.14	−0.42
F-statistics	2.05	2.05	0.62
Number of cases	20	20	20

Notes: T-statistics in brackets. Significance levels = [a] 90%, [b] 95%, [c] 99%.

coefficients; in Germany, the Netherlands, and Norway the sign turns positive when changes in value added are removed from the equations.

While differences across countries are substantial, a common result is the (counter-intuitive) generally negative impact of innovation intensities on employment. When we control for the dynamics of structural change, the sectors characterized by greater innovation intensity, in all its components, tend to show worse employment performances in the early 1990s. This is mainly the result of the negative patterns shown by several high-technology sectors in Europe.

In interpreting such results it should be borne in mind that total innovation expenditure includes a broader range of innovative activities than is the case with previously available indicators. Such activities result from a larger variety of technological strategies of firms, pursuing different aims. In the recession of the early 1990s innovation choices may have been affected by the overall process of restructuring and job reduction in manufacturing all over Europe. Technological change may have been part of the reorganization of industry, with serious labour-saving effects.

The question remains whether this outcome was the result of a cyclical recession or of a new, long-term pattern of 'jobless growth' with technological unemployment in Europe.

Recent evidence on Italy

A partial answer comes from the availability of more recent employment data for Italy. Several years after the end of the recession, the negative relationship between sectoral innovation intensities and job performances is confirmed. When employment changes from 1992 to 1996 (an appropriate period to search for the impact of the innovative efforts of 1992) are investigated, their relationship to the innovation intensity of manufacturing sectors remains the same shown (for an earlier year) in Figure 4.5 and in the regressions of Table 4.3.[18] The evidence on the persisting labour-saving nature of technological change is therefore extensive in the case of Italy, and parallel updated analyses on other European countries are needed.

While all the evidence so far provided concerns manufacturing industry, a look at employment changes in the whole economy may set the question of technological unemployment in a broader context. Again this is done here using recent data for Italy.

Figure 4.7 shows the rate of change of total employment in the main sectors of the economy from 1989 to 1995. Positive job growth can be found only in six fields of the service sector, while other private services, public administration, and construction show moderate job losses. All sixteen manufacturing industries, as well as the energy, communication and agricultural sectors, show substantial job losses, at a rate ranging from 1 to 4 per cent a year. It is remarkable that the manufacturing fields with the highest innovative intensity generally appear at the bottom of the figure.

The aggregate result for Italy is a loss of 1.3 million jobs from late 1991 to early 1995. From then to January 1997 the fall in employment halted, but job growth has been minimal (at 140,000). The greater employment dynamism of services raises the question of whether this is mainly the outcome of a structural change which expands demand and supply of service activities, or whether technological change is also having a positive impact on employment, differently from the case of manufacturing. For the first time, this question can be addressed empirically using the results of the innovation survey on services recently completed in Italy.

5. INNOVATION AND EMPLOYMENT IN SERVICES

The first Istat innovation survey on services in Italy (see Evangelista and Sirilli, 1997) provides data on the consequences of the introduction of inno-

---

[18] The regression analysis shows that the changes in employment from 1992 to 1996 are positively affected by changes in value added in the same period (with a significant coefficient) and negatively affected by the total innovation expenditure per employee.

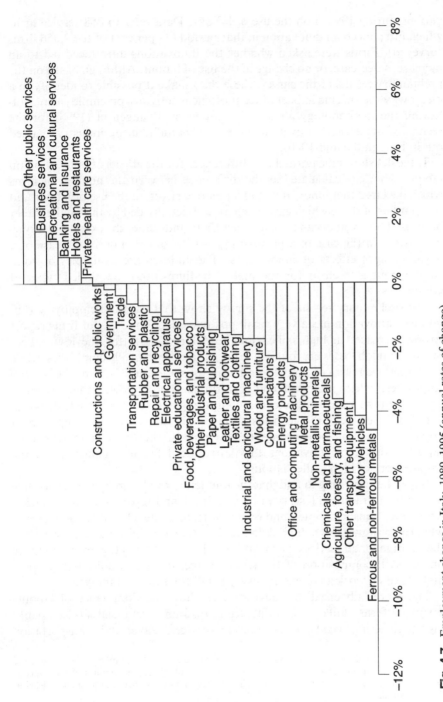

Fig. 4.7. Employment change in Italy, 1989–1995 (annual rates of change)

vations during 1993–5 on the use of labour. Data refer to 758 service firms which introduced an innovation in that period (37 per cent of the 2,056 firms surveyed). Firms were asked whether the innovations introduced led to an increase, a decrease, or no change in the use of labour. Although based on the preliminary results of the survey, these data make it possible to identify in a direct way the specific impact of technological activities on employment, following the methodology already developed by Evangelista (1995) for the results of the earlier innovation survey on manufacturing industry, carried out in Italy in the mid-1980s.

Table 4.4 shows the normalized differences for the effects of innovation on labour. They are calculated as the difference between the number of firms which declared that innovation had a positive effect on the use of labour and the number of those which gave a negative effect, divided by the total number of firms. These values can be read as synthetic indexes of the extent of labour-increasing (in the case of a positive sign) or labour-saving (in the case of a negative sign) effects of innovations. The indexes are available for total employment as well as for the high-, medium-, and low-skilled types of labour.[19]

The preliminary results of the survey show that for total employment in services innovation has a very small positive effect on jobs, but firms report strong increases in high-skilled jobs and large losses for the low-skilled. Substantial job losses are found in firms with more than 500 employees, while the largest increases of innovation-based jobs are found in firms below 100 employees, where the skill composition is slightly lower than average. Looking at the sectoral differences, computing and software, waste disposal, and R&D services are the fields showing the most positive employment impact of technological change (about half of the firms in these sectors reported that the innovations they introduced led to an increase in the employment of high-skilled labour).

It may be surprising to find that the impact on total employment is positive for firms in 'traditional' services such as trade and repair of motor vehicles, wholesale, transport, hotels and restaurants, retailing, cleaning, and security, which also show gains in high skills and losses in low skills that are lower than the average for all services. Such data should be examined together with those on the skill composition of the labour force; in such 'traditional' services highly skilled workers represent a very small fraction of employees.

The more 'advanced' business services show the dominance of labour-saving patterns similar to manufacturing. Insurance, financial services, banking, engineering, legal and accounting services, travel and transportation

[19] It should be pointed out that these indexes are calculated on the number of firms reporting different employment impacts, and no information is available on the amount of job gains or losses. For relatively large numbers of firms, however, it can be assumed that frequency distributions are similar.

Table 4.4. Effects of innovative activities on the use of labour in services by firm size and sector, 1993–1995

Size classes and sectors	Normalized differences[a]			
	Total employment	High-skilled	Medium-skilled	Low-skilled
Size classes:				
20–49	0.17	0.22	0.16	−0.02
50–99	0.14	0.24	0.16	−0.03
100–199	0.07	0.38	0.25	−0.14
200–499	−0.03	0.23	0.10	−0.22
500–999	−0.25	0.25	0.02	−0.40
1000 and over	−0.21	0.33	0.08	−0.53
Sectors:				
Computing and software	0.36	0.52	0.15	−0.09
Waste disposal	0.31	0.42	0.31	−0.08
R&D	0.23	0.46	0.23	−0.15
Trade and repair of motor vehicles	0.17	0.13	0.36	0.17
Wholesale trade (excl. motor vehicles)	0.16	0.21	0.23	−0.04
Transport (excl. air)	0.14	0.17	0.19	−0.05
Hotels and restaurants	0.14	0.23	0.14	0.03
Retail trade	0.10	0.22	0.06	−0.12
Cleaning and security	0.09	0.21	0.18	−0.03
Business services and advertising	0.06	0.38	0.19	−0.19
Travel and transport services	−0.06	0.33	0.20	−0.25
Legal, accounting	−0.06	0.36	0.13	−0.33
Engineering	−0.16	0.44	−0.11	−0.28
Banking	−0.19	0.12	−0.01	−0.35
Other financial	−0.25	0.42	0.08	−0.08
Insurance	−0.29	0.46	0.04	−0.62
TOTALS	0.04	0.25	0.13	−0.16

[a] Number of firms which have increased the use of labour minus the number of firms which have decreased the use of labour/total number of innovating firms.

Source: Evangelista and Sirilli, 1997.

Note: Some sectors are excluded due to the very low number of firms.

services introduced innovations which led mainly to job losses. These sectors are also the heaviest users of information and communication technology (ICT) and are among the largest buyers of ICT equipment, which is a crucial part of the innovations they introduced. Only other business services and advertising has a modest positive index. In these fields strong positive values for high-skilled labour are matched by equally large job losses for the low-skilled.

Important differences therefore emerge between services and manufacturing in the direct employment impact of innovation in the firms introducing them, with business services appearing to be closer to the pattern found in manufacturing, where innovation is largely associated with the process of restructuring, in spite of the growing size of such services in terms of both value added and employment.[20]

6. CONCLUSIONS

The evidence presented in this chapter shows that the employment impact of technological change varies widely across countries and sectors, and between manufacturing and services. In the 1990s there is evidence of widespread negative consequences of innovation in Europe, marked by unprecedented unemployment levels and a new pattern of 'jobless growth'. In the long cycle of growth from the early 1980s to the early 1990s, employment changes in manufacturing sectors of the six largest OECD economies are found to be closely associated to the effects of technological and structural change, measured by indicators such as value added, investment, and patents. Such factors are crucial in shaping the long-term development of employment, much more than the short-term operation of labour markets.

Across manufacturing sectors, technological change appears to have accompanied in the 1980s the process of structural change, favouring the emergence of new activities which have offered new employment. Such growth opportunities, however, are captured by countries after a strongly competitive process, where national specializations and technological advantages are crucial. European countries are less present in the most dynamic sectors at the world level. They therefore found it harder to benefit from the 'virtuous circle' between technology, growth, and employment which appears

---

[20] In a similar study in the case of manufacturing (Evangelista, 1995; Vivarelli, Evangelista, and Pianta, 1996), the direct employment impact of innovations was found to be moderately negative, with positive values in about one-third of industries, including aircraft, drugs, electronics, and machinery. Exploring the determinants of the employment impact of innovation in manufacturing across thirty industries, it was found that a positive effect on the use of labour is associated with higher innovation costs, and in particular with design and engineering expenditure, as well as with the share of product innovations, while a negative link emerges for process innovation.

to have operated at the global level. Conversely, some negative effects of technological change (process innovations in particular) have emerged more clearly.

More detailed indicators, drawn from the Community innovation surveys, show that in several European countries some evidence of a generally negative impact of technology on employment is found in the 1990s. Sectors with a higher intensity of total innovation expenditure have often experienced greater job losses, once changes in output are controlled for. This appears to be the result of the labour-saving bias of the innovation strategies carried out by European firms and of a macroeconomic context marked by slower growth and sluggish demand. Such evidence raises the worrying perspective of a long-term pattern of 'jobless growth' with technological unemployment in Europe.

An exploratory analysis of the results of the innovation survey on services in Italy shows that business-oriented services do not differ significantly from the labour-saving pattern typical of manufacturing, although for the whole of the service sector the innovations introduced by firms led to a moderate increase in the use of labour in the 1993–5 period. While more systematic evidence is still needed on the developments in Europe in the 1990s, a number of issues emerge as deserving attention in both research and policy work.

(i) *The importance of structural change.* A fundamental reason for the worse employment performance of Europe relative to the USA and Japan has been the European weakness in the manufacturing (and service) sectors marked by the highest growth rates of output and employment, which include the fields associated with ICTs. Favouring a process of structural change towards such activities may contribute to creating the conditions for long-term employment growth.

(ii) *The potential of ICTs.* In the emergence of a new technological paradigm based on ICTs, the job losses associated with the decline of old sectors and the restructuring of industrial processes appear to outweigh, especially in Europe, job gains in new activities and markets. The modest rate of product and service innovation, the slow pace of changes in demand and the slow learning by users and consumers, are all factors that are likely to contribute to the lack of development of the new ICT-based markets. Another, more fundamental reason, however, is the mismatch and lack of co-ordination between the technological, organizational, institutional, and social innovations which are required for the successful emergence of a new technological paradigm (see Freeman, Clark, and Soete, 1982).

(iii) *The nature of the innovative process.* With innovations in all industries dominated by the new information and communication technologies, the use and adaptation of innovations developed elsewhere, the process and organizational innovations may be more relevant than the traditional model of technological change dominated by R&D-led product innovations, leading to the

emergence of new markets and sectors of economic activity. A reconceptual-
ization of the range of innovative efforts, of their economic impact, and of the
policies supporting them, may therefore be required.

(iv) *Working time reduction and new employment sources*. Historically, technological change has always led to reductions in working time. More attention
should be devoted to the evolution of the number of hours worked, which are
a better indicator of the actual amount of labour used in the economic system.
From the available evidence, a reduction of the working time is essential to
prevent a further worsening of the employment situation in Europe (see
Vivarelli and Paladino, 1997). A crucial issue in this context is the way in
which the productivity gains offered by technological change are redistributed
to workers (in the form of higher wages and lower hours) and to society at
large (in the form of lower prices and greater resources available for socially
useful activities). The latter may contribute to opening up new employment
opportunities in labour-intensive activities somewhat sheltered from international competition, responding to unmet needs and demands, such as the
'third sector' and non-profit, socially useful activities (see Rifkin, 1995).

(v) *The coherence between macroeconomic and innovation policies*. While
technology and industrial policies have spurred innovation and competitiveness on the supply side, the importance of demand factors has been neglected.
Technological and structural change—and employment growth—cannot be
achieved without a combination of supply-push and demand-pull effects, and
without a coherence between technological change and macroeconomic conditions, including the pace of growth and distribution patterns. The current
constraints on the expansion of demand, set by the convergence criteria for
European Monetary Union, and the increasingly uneven distribution of
income, may turn out to be equally important factors preventing the evolution of economic structures consistent with the potential offered by technological change.

In terms of policy, these are directions that might be pursued in order to
secure the job-creating potential of innovation and to redistribute to the
whole of society the benefits promised by the new technologies.

REFERENCES

Amendola, G., Guerrieri, P., and Padoan, P. C. (1992), 'International Patterns of
    Technological Accumulation and Trade', *Journal of International and Comparative
    Economics*, 1/1.
Appelbaum, E. and Schettkat, R. (1995), 'Employment and Productivity in
    Industrialized Economies', *International Labour Review*, 134/4–5: 605–23.
—— —— (1996), 'Product Demand, Productivity and Labour Demand in a
    Structural Model', Paper for the TSER conference 'Technology, Economic
    Integration and Social Cohesion', Cepremap, Paris, 22–3 Nov. 1996.

Archibugi, D. and Pianta, M. (1992), *The Technological Specialization of Advanced Countries*, Dordrecht: Kluwer.

—— —— (1996), 'Innovation Surveys and Patents as Technology Indicators: The State of the Art', in OECD, *Innovation, Patents, and Technological Strategies*.

—— Cohendet, P., Kristensen, A., and Schaffer, K.-A. (1995), *Evaluation of the Community Innovation Survey*, Brussels: European Innovation Monitoring System (EIMS).

—— Evangelista, R., Perani, G., and Rapiti, F. (1996), 'Nature, Determinants and Obstacles of Innovation Activities: An Analysis of the Italian Innovation Survey', Paper for the Schumpeter Society Conference, Stockholm, June 1996.

Boyer, R. (1988), 'Formalizing growth regimes', in G. Dosi (eds.), *Technical Change and Economic Theory*, London: Pinter, 603–35.

Caracostas, P. and Muldur, U. (1995), 'Long Cycles, Technology and Employment: Current Obstacles and Outlook', *STI Review*, 15.

Cesaratto, S. and Stirati, A. (1996), The Impact of Innovation on Employment in the Manufacturing Sector in Italy: Results from CIS', Paper for the Eurostat-DG XIII Conference on 'Innovation Measurement and Policies', Luxembourg, 20–1 May 1996.

Dosi G., Pavitt, K., and Soete, L. (1990), *The Economics of Technical Change and International Trade*, Hemel Hempstead: Harvester Wheatsheaf.

Evangelista, R. (1995), Innovazione e occupazione nell'industria italiana: un'analisi per imprese e settori, *L'Industria*, 1: 107–26.

—— and Sirilli, G. (1997), 'Innovation in the Service Sector: Results from the Italian Statistical Survey', Paper for the Conference on Technology Policy and Innovation, Macau, 2–4 July 1997.

—— Sandven, T., Sirilli, G., and Smith, K. (1996), 'Measuring the Cost of Innovation in European Industry', Paper for the Eurostat-DG XIII Conference on 'Innovation Measurement and Policies', Luxembourg, 20–1 May 1996.

Fagerberg, J. (1994), 'Technology and International Differences in Growth Rates', *Journal of Economic Literature*, 32: 1147–75.

Freeman, C. and Soete, L. (1987) (eds.), *Technical Change and Full Employment*, Oxford: Blackwell.

—— —— (1994), *Work For All or Mass Unemployment?*, London: Pinter.

—— and Clark, J. (1982), *Unemployment and Technical Innovation*, London: Pinter.

Leontief, W. and Duchin, F. (1986), *The Future Impact of Automation on Workers*, Oxford: Oxford University Press.

Meyer-Krahmer, F. (1992), 'The Effects of New Technologies on Employment', *Economics of Innovation and New Technology*, 2: 131–49.

OECD (1994), *The OECD Jobs Study, pt. 1: Labour Market Trends and Underlying Forces of Change*, Paris: OECD.

—— (1996a), *Innovation, Patents and Technological Strategies*, Paris: OECD.

—— (1996b), *Technology, Productivity and Job Creation*, 2 vols., Paris: OECD.

—— (1996c), *Technology and Industrial Performance*, Paris: OECD.

Pasinetti, L. (1981), *Structural Change and Economic Growth*, Cambridge: Cambridge University Press.

—— (1990), 'Structural Change and Unemployment', *Structural Change and Economic Dynamics*, 1/1.

Petit, P. (1995a), 'Employment and Technical Change', in P. Stoneman (ed.), *The Economics of Innovation and Technical Change*, Oxford: Blackwell.

Petit, P. (1995b), 'Technology and Employment: Key Questions in a Context of High Unemployment', STI Review, 15.

Pianta, M. (1995), 'Technology and Growth in OECD Countries, 1970–1990', Cambridge Journal of Economics, 19/1: 175–87; repr. in D. Archibugi and J. Michie (1997) (eds.), Technology, Trade and Growth, Cambridge: Cambridge University Press.

—— (1996), 'L'innovazione nell'industria italiana e gli effetti economici e occupazionali', Economia e Politica Industriale, 89.

—— (1997) (ed.), Tecnologia e occupazione: Le analisi dell'Ocse e il dibattito italiano, Rome: ISRDS-CNR.

—— Evangelista, R. and Perani, G. (1996), 'The Dynamics of Innovation and Employment: An International Comparison', Science, Technology Industry Review, 18.

Pini, P. (1995), 'Economic Growth, Technological Change and Employment: Empirical Evidence for a Cumulative Growth Model With External Causation for Nine OECD Countries, 1960–1990', Structural Change and Economic Dynamics, 6: 185–213.

Rifkin, J. (1995), The End of Work: The Decline of the Global Labor Force and the Dawn of the Post-market Era, New York: Putnam.

Scherer, F. M. (1992), International High-Technology Competition, Cambridge, Mass.: Harvard University Press.

Science, Technology, Industry Review (1996), special issue on 'Technology, Productivity and Employment', 18, Paris: OECD.

Sylos Labini, P. (1990), 'Technical Progress, Unemployment and Economic Dynamics', Structural Change and Economic Dynamics, 1: 41–55.

Vivarelli, M. (1995), The Economics of Technology and Employment, Aldershot: Elgar.

—— Evangelista, R., and Pianta, M. (1996), 'Innovation and Employment in Italian Manufacturing Industry', Research Policy, 25: 1013–26.

—— and Paladino, S. (1997), 'Growth and Employment: Some Evidence on G-7 Economies', Paper for the TSER Conference on 'Technology, Economic Integration and Social Cohesion', MERIT, Maastricht, 18–19 Apr. 1997.

Part II

Innovation and Growth

Part II

Innovation and Growth

5. Markets, Competition, and Innovation*

Michael Kitson and Jonathan Michie

1. INTRODUCTION

Although the overall growth rate of the UK economy in the 1980s and 1990s was similar to that of the other advanced countries, this is hardly an indicator of success.[1] Output per person is lower for the UK than for any of the other G7 group of countries, and it is also below the OECD average. This output 'gap' indicates a potential for 'catching-up' growth. Lagging countries, such as the UK, could in principle borrow and adopt new technologies and management techniques from leading countries. This should enable lagging countries to achieve superior growth *rates* compared to the leading countries, at least until the output gap is closed. We have argued elsewhere (Kitson and Michie, 1996*a*,*b*, 1997) that this failure of the UK to catch up with the other industrialized countries is due in part at least to a failure of economic policy as well as to the debilitating grip of various institutional constraints.

Politicians of all hues pay lip-service to the need to create a competitive economy. This is often presented, in Britain at least, as requiring deregulation and the 'freeing-up' of markets. Behind such policy proposals often lies a picture of economic processes where firms compete in markets with large numbers of customers and competitors, and where keen prices and low costs are the key determinants of success. This misrepresents the character of the competitive process in most sectors. This chapter—using evidence from the recent innovation survey carried out by Cambridge University's ESRC Centre for Business Research (Cosh and Hughes, 1996)[2]—shows that factors such as trust and co-operation can play an important role in competitive success and may actually be undermined by a policy approach which prioritizes deregulation.

* We are grateful to Eric Wood for advice, particularly regarding the CBR data on which he has worked, to Renée Prendergast for some of the points made in Section 6 (which are developed in more detail in Michie and Prendergast, 1997), and to Keith Cowling, John Grieve Smith, Laurence Harris, Mario Pianta, and Brian Reddaway for helpful comments on an earlier version of this chapter.

[1] Particularly given the scale of North Sea oil production and employment, and the contribution made by North Sea oil to Britain's trade account and government revenues over these decades.

[2] See also Eric Wood, Chapter 6, this volume.

In the following three sections we report the reality of the competitive process as perceived, at any rate, by those firms responding to the CBR survey: Section 2 reports on the relatively small number of major competitors which most firms are dealing with—a far cry from a perfectly competitive world of price-takers. The role of price competition is considered explicitly in Section 3, as against other forms of (non-price) competition. Section 4 then investigates the role of co-operation and innovation. In considering the theory of market competition, Section 5 argues that the empirical findings of the CBR's work, as discussed in Sections 2–4, actually matches rather well with much political economy literature—albeit at odds with the 'Austrian' theory underpinning UK Government policy under the Thatcher/Major administrations. Finally, Section 6 discusses the policy implications, including the need in Britain for policies to tackle short-termism and boost investment. This would be in stark contrast to the market-oriented reforms introduced since 1979 which have discouraged links between investors and firms. More immediately it would contrast with investment in manufacturing—which still dominates world trade—having fallen by 8 per cent in 1996 while public investment fell by 20 per cent.

2. THE DATA

The analysis in this chapter (and the following chapter by Eric Wood) is based on surveys carried out by the ESRC Centre for Business Research (CBR) at the University of Cambridge (and its predecessor, the Small Business Research Centre).[3] These surveys were intended to provide a comprehensive picture of British business, considering such factors as competitive structures, employment and skills, innovation, finance, and growth.

The first survey was conducted in 1991 and was designed to provide a sample of 2,000 independent businesses employing less than 500 workers, equally split between business services and manufacturing. The sampling frame used was the Dun and Bradstreet database (see Bullock, Duncan, and Wood (1996) for a discussion of the advantages and disadvantages of this database). Originally, 8,050 firms were approached, 1,880 were discarded as they were too large, subsidiaries, had ceased trading, or were otherwise outside the survey's scope. Of the 6,170 firms that were surveyed, 2,028 returned useable questionnaires, a response rate of 32.9 per cent. The results of this survey (SBRC, 1992) provided the first comprehensive analysis of the UK small and medium-sized firm (SME) sector since Bolton (1971).

A second survey was conducted in 1993, using a short questionnaire focusing on a few key variables. A third survey was conducted in 1995. It is the

---

[3] See Bullock, Duncan, and Wood (1996), and Cosh, Duncan, and Hughes (1996) for more detail of the surveys.

results of this third survey, using a questionnaire similar in scale to the first survey, which forms the basis of most of the analysis in this chapter. Continued monitoring of the respondents to the original survey enabled identification of firms which had failed, or were failing. Of the original 2,018 respondents, 436 firms were excluded because of failure or because they were now outside the survey's scope. Of the 1,592 firms surveyed, 681 firms returned the full postal questionnaire, and 317 firms completed shorter questionnaires, a total response rate of 62.7 per cent.

In order to draw a comparative picture the respondents' characteristics are analysed according to a variety of categories: two sectors (manufacturing and business services); four size groups based on 1990 employment (micro, 0–9 employees; small, 10–99 employees; medium, 100–199 employees; and larger, 200 employees); three employment growth categories between 1990 and 1995 (stable/declining—zero or negative growth; medium growth—greater than zero but less than 35 per cent; fast growth—over 35 per cent); two innovation categories[4] (based on whether the firm innovated or not during the period 1992–5); and two collaboration categories[5] (based on whether the firm entered into a collaborative arrangement during the period 1992–5).

3. THE COMPETITIVE ENVIRONMENT

Firms operate in a range of competitive environments. At one extreme firms may compete in atomistic markets, with a large number of customers and competitors, and where competition is driven by price and cost factors. At the other extreme firms may operate in monopolistic or monopsonistic markets with no effective competitors, or with only one customer. The evidence from the CBR survey indicates that, although firms operate in diverse markets, the norm is for increasingly segmented markets—with firms relying on a few main customers and facing a limited number of competitors.

Table 5.1 shows that in 1995, 33 per cent of firms relied on just one customer for 25 per cent or more of their sales. The most apparent contrast is by firm size—micro and small firms are more likely to depend on just a few customers for the bulk of their business. Additionally, innovating firms are less likely to be dependent on a single customer than are non-innovating firms;

[4] Firms were classified as innovators or non-innovators on the basis of their answers to the following questions: (i) Has your firm introduced any innovations in products (goods or services) or processes during the last three years which were new to your firm? (ii) if you introduced a product (process) innovation was it, to the best of your knowledge, already in use in other firms either in (a) your industry or (b) other industries? If you made more than one product innovation please answer with respect to your most important product (process) innovation.

[5] Firms were classified as collaborators or non-collaborators on the basis of their answer to the following question: Has your firm in the last three years entered into formal or informal collaborative or partnership arrangements with any other organizations?

MICHAEL KITSON AND JONATHAN MICHIE

Table 5.1. Concentration of sales in 1995 (percentage distribution of firms)

Percentage of sales to largest customer	Less than 10	10–24	25–49	50–100	No. of firms
Micro	19.7	38.2	29.2	13.0	169
Small	25.8	43.0	20.1	11.2	375
Medium	40.3	32.8	14.9	11.6	65
Large	41.3	34.8	15.2	9.7	44
Manufacturing	26.8	41.2	19.6	12.4	347
Services	26.6	39.5	23.5	10.4	309
Innovators	28.8	40.7	21.8	8.8	441
Non-innovators	21.7	40.1	20.7	17.5	206
All	26.7	40.4	21.4	11.5	656

Source: University of Cambridge, ESRC Centre for Business Research, 1995 Survey into Growth, Innovation, and Competitive Advantage in Small and Medium-Sized Firms.

31 per cent of innovating firms—compared with 38 per cent of non-innovating firms—depend on just one customer to provide 25 per cent or more of their sales. In general, then, most firms have just a few key customers—indicating the importance to these firms of fostering their relations with customer-firms. Furthermore, as shown in Table 5.2 the majority of firms operate in rather segmented markets—with nearly two-thirds of firms having less than ten serious competitors.[6]

So, for the bulk of British business, the notion that firms are competing with a vast array of other enterprises—like the concept of perfect competition presented in economic textbooks—is a myth. Most firms are operating in segmented and niche markets.

4. HOW FIRMS COMPETE

How firms compete also reveals that any notion that prices and costs are the key to competitive success is at best simplistic. As shown in Table 5.3, when firms were asked to identify the sources of their competitive advantage the key factors were 'personal attention to client needs', 'reputation', and 'product quality'. 'Cost advantage' was the lowest-ranked factor, especially amongst those firms with the fastest rate of growth.

There are large and significant differences in competitive strategy between innovating and non-innovating firms. As shown in Table 5.3, in 1995 there

---

[6] There is some evidence of fewer competitors in manufacturing than in services, although there is no clear pattern in the differences between innovators and non-innovators, or between collaborators and non-collaborators.

Table 5.2. Competitive structures in 1995 (percentage distribution of firms)

Number of serious competitors	All	Manufac- turing	Services	Innovators	Non- innovators	Collabor- ators	Non- collaborators
0 (monopoly)	3.3	2.9	3.6	2.5	5.0	2.0	4.3
1–9 (highly segmented)	61.3	69.1	52.4	60.9	63.9	60.5	61.2
10–49 (partially segmented)	27.3	23.6	31.5	29.3	20.6	29.0	26.3
50–99 (partially atomistic)	2.6	1.2	4.3	2.5	3.0	3.6	2.1
100+ (highly atomistic)	5.5	3.3	8.2	4.8	7.5	4.8	6.2

Source: Authors' calculations from University of Cambridge, ESRC Centre for Business Research, 1995 Survey into Growth, Innovation, and Competitive Advantage in Small and Medium-Sized Firms database.

are statistically significant differences between the two sectors for seven out of the eleven competitiveness factors. The largest differences, in terms of rank as well as scores, were for product design, flair and creativity, product quality, specialized expertise or products, and range of expertise or products; all these factors were more important for innovating firms than they were for non-innovating firms. Further evidence of the differences in competitive factors is provided in Table 5.4, which shows the percentage of firms rating the factors as 'very significant' or 'crucial'. Innovating firms were far more likely to rank highly such factors as product design, flair and creativity, and specialized expertise or products, compared to non-innovating firms.

Overall, innovating firms stress the importance of higher-order qualitative factors which require investment in skills and technical capability. Conversely, in terms of rankings, they put less emphasis on cost and price factors compared with non-innovating firms. These major differences were also evident in an earlier Survey which assessed competitive advantage in 1990 (SBRC, 1992). This suggests that such differences do not merely reflect the contrast between firms that innovate and those that do not, but they also reflect differences between those firms that *intend* to innovate, or are receptive to such developments, and those that do not or are not.

One of the important ingredients for achieving competitive success appears to be to establish effective collaboration with others—customers, suppliers, higher education establishments, and so on. Such collaboration allows firms to expand their range of expertise, develop specialist products, and achieve various other corporate objectives.[7]

---

[7] This issue of collaboration between firms raises a separate issue not discussed in the current chapter, namely the question of when collaboration becomes collusion, and how this is (and should be) handled in the context of competition policy. Oughton and Whittam (1996) contains

Table 5.3. Assessment of key factors which contribute to competitive advantage, 1995 (average score and ranking)

	All		Manufacturing		Services		Innovators		Non-innovators		Stable/declining		Medium growth		Fast growth	
	Score	Rank	Score	Rank	Score	Rank	Score	Rank	Score	Rank	Score	Rank	Score	Rank	Score	Rank
Personal attention to client needs	4.4	1	4.3**	1	4.6**	1	4.4	1	4.5	1	4.5	1	4.4	1	4.4	1
Established reputation	4.2	2	4.1*	3	4.2*	2	4.2	=2	4.2	2	4.2	2	4.1	3	4.1	=3
Product quality	4.1	3	4.2**	2	4.0**	4	4.2**	=2	3.9**	4	4.1	3	4.3	2	4.2	2
Speed of service	4.0	4	4.0	4	3.9	5	3.9*	5	4.1*	3	4.0	4	4.0	4	3.9	5
Specialized expertise or products	3.9	5	3.8**	5	4.1**	3	4.0**	4	3.7**	5	3.9	5	3.9	5	4.1	=3
Range of expertise or products	3.6	6	3.5	=6	3.6	7	3.7**	6	3.4**	7	3.6	6	3.5	6	3.7	6
Price	3.4	=7	3.5**	=6	3.2**	=9	3.3**	9	3.5**	6	3.4*	7	3.4*	7	3.2*	=8
Flair and creativity	3.4	=7	3.0**	10	3.7**	6	3.5**	7	3.0**	9	3.2**	=8	3.3**	8	3.6**	7
Product design	3.2	9	3.2	8	3.2	=9	3.4**	8	2.7**	11	3.2	=8	3.2	=9	3.3	10
Marketing	3.1	10	2.9**	11	3.3**	8	3.2**	10	2.9**	10	3.0	=10	3.2	=9	3.2	=8
Cost advantage	3.0	11	3.1**	9	2.9**	11	3.0	11	3.1	8	3.0	=10	3.1	11	2.9	11
Range (highest score–lowest score)	1.4		1.4		1.7		1.4		1.8		1.5		1.3		1.5	
TOTAL RESPONSES	652		350		302		208		437		341		140		157	

Notes: A* significant at 10% level.   ** significant at 5% level.   F-test of difference between groups.

Source: As Table 5.1.

Table 5.4. Competitive advantage: factors rated very significant or crucial, 1995 (percentage of respondents)

	All	Innov-ators	Non-innovators	Collabor-ators	Non-collaborators
Personal attention to client needs	90.1	88.9	93.2	87.4	91.9
Product quality	85.2	87.6	78.9	87.0	83.7
Established reputation	83.4	82.7	84.9	82.2	83.9
Specialized expertise or products	75.2	79.1	67.5	80.5	71.7
Speed of service	75.2	73.5	79.9	66.0	81.8
Range of expertise or products	60.9	64.2	54.3	62.6	59.4
Price	46.8	43.6	53.3	37.8	53.0
Flare and creativity	50.1	55.1	39.5	55.4	45.8
Product design	51.8	57.5	35.7	58.0	47.0
Marketing	38.5	41.0	33.8	45.1	34.6
Cost advantage	34.3	33.8	34.9	26.9	38.9

Source: As Table 5.2.

5. COLLABORATION, INNOVATION, AND CORPORATE PERFORMANCE

Innovation is a key element in long-term economic growth. And, collaboration is one of the most important means of fostering innovation—as shown in Figure 5.1, half of the innovating firms in the CBR survey had entered into collaborative partnerships, whereas only one in six of the non-innovating

an interesting discussion of the relation between co-operation between firms on the one hand and competition policy on the other, combined with an analysis of the benefits to be had from reaping internal and external economies of scale. Co-operative external economies of scale enable small and medium-sized enterprises to pool fixed costs which can result not only in greater efficiency but also, by overcoming entry barriers, thereby increase competition. Thus public sponsorship of such co-operative industrial activities should not be seen as necessarily at odds with promoting competition. But a failure to appreciate this point could lead to a simple minded competition policy failing to promote such co-operation—or even outlawing it—thus actually undermining the conditions for healthy competition. On these issues of competition policy, see also Deakin, Goodwin, and Hughes, 1997; and Anderman, 1997. This discussion also cuts across the distinction that can be made between the different views of the innovation process—and the roles played within this by competition on the one hand, and large firms able to fund R&D on the other—within Schumpeter's *Capitalism, Socialism and Democracy* (1947) and *The Theory of Economic Development* (1961), on which see Michie and Prendergast (1997).

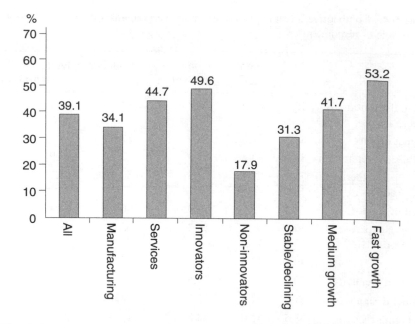

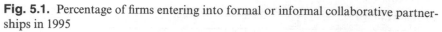

Fig. 5.1. Percentage of firms entering into formal or informal collaborative partnerships in 1995

Source: University of Cambridge, ESRC Centre for Business Research, 1995 Survey into Growth, Innovation, and Competitive Advantage in Small and Medium-Sized Firms.

firms had entered into such arrangements. Also, collaboration is particularly important for firms facing foreign competition; as the process of globalization continues apace such collaborative behaviour may become more important as domestic firms face stiffer competition in both home and overseas markets.

Figure 5.2 shows that firms undertake collaboration for a range of reasons. The four most important were to help expand the range of expertise and products, to assist in the development of specialist services and products required by customers, to provide access to UK markets, and to provide access to overseas markets. The process of collaboration allows firms to exploit economies of scale and scope. The reason given for collaboration that has shown the greatest increase since 1990 (from 29 to 38 per cent) is to help keep current customers. This suggests that collaboration may have increased for defensive reasons—perhaps in response to increased domestic and international competition.

Figure 5.3 shows the reasons for collaboration according to whether firms were innovators or non-innovators. In general, innovating firms are more likely to collaborate for all reasons compared to non-innovating firms. The one exception is to help keep current customers, suggesting that non-innovators are more defensive in regard to maintaining market share. Additionally, and not surprisingly, the reason for collaboration for non-innovators that has shown the greatest fall is the sharing of research and development.

The overall impact of increased innovation and collaboration is improvements in both output and employment growth rates—for individual businesses as well as for the economy as whole.[8] In terms of employment, fast-growth firms were almost twice as likely to have collaborated compared to firms with negative or no growth. Figures 5.4(a) and (b) give the distribution of employment growth in first, innovating and non-innovating firms and

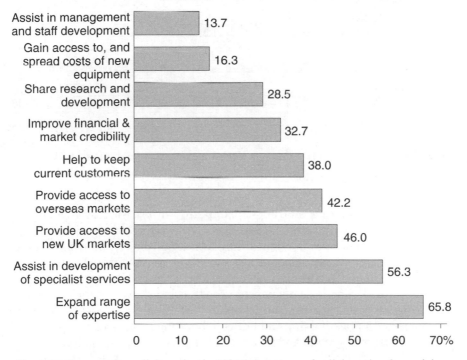

Fig. 5.2. Reasons for collaboration in 1995 (percentage of collaborating firms giving these reasons)

Source: As Fig. 5.1.

---

[8] Note that our data are all for small and medium-sized enterprises. There is a mass of evidence to suggest that collaboration between firms of roughly comparable size tends to be of a very different nature from that between large and small firms where the power relations are quite different. We are grateful to Keith Cowling for making this point. See also the discussion by Oliver and Blakeborough (this volume).

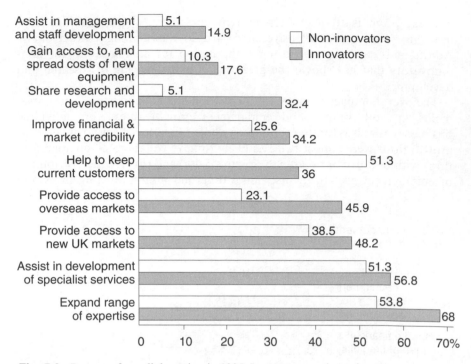

Fig. 5.3. Reasons for collaboration in 1995: Innovators and non-innovators
Source: As Fig. 5.1.

secondly, collaborating and non-collaborating firms; as shown in Figure 5.4(*a*), innovating firms were far less likely to have zero or negative employment growth than were non-innovating firms. Conversely, innovators were far more likely to have achieved fast growth in employment. Figure 5.4(*b*) indicates a similar picture in the contrast between collaborators and non-collaborators—superior employment growth being shown by the collaborators. Figures 5.5(*a*) and (*b*), and 5.6(*a*) and (*b*), show that this superior performance of innovating firms and of collaborating firms is also apparent in terms of turnover growth and in terms of the growth of profit margins.[9]

6. THE THEORY OF MARKET COMPETITION

What might explain these results, of market competition apparently benefiting from co-operation? The issue of whether the competitive environment

[9] For further discussion of these employment, turnover, and profit data see Cosh, Hughes, and Wood (1996).

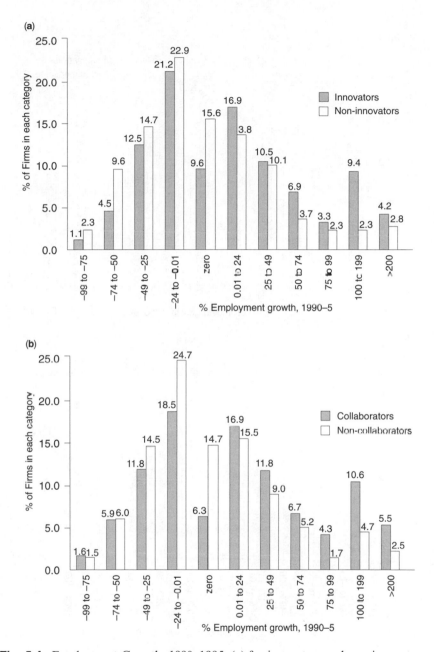

Fig. 5.4. Employment Growth, 1990–1995. (a) for innovators and non-innovators; (b) for collaborators and non-collaborators

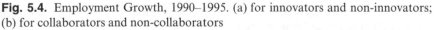

Source: Authors' calculations from University of Cambridge, ESRC Centre for Business Research, 1995 Survey into Growth, Innovation, and Competitive Advantage in Small and Medium-Sized Firms database.

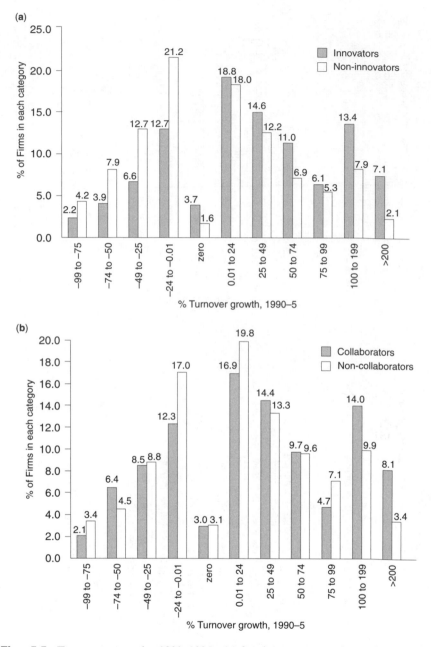

Fig. 5.5. Turnover growth, 1990–1995. (a) for innovators and non-innovators; (b) for collaborators and non-collaborators

Source: As Fig. 5.4.

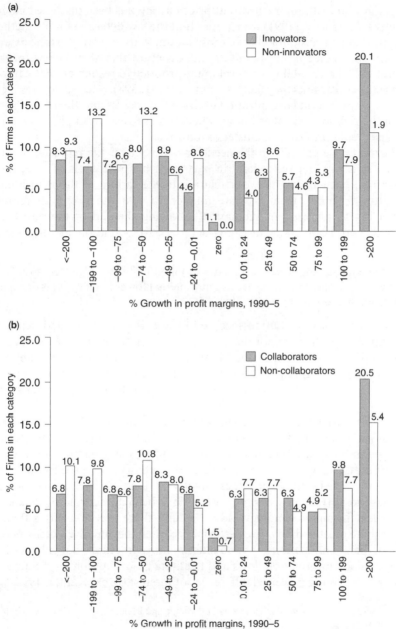

Fig. 5.6. Growth in profits margins, 1990–1995. (a) for innovators and non-innovators; (b) for collaborators and non-collaborators

Source: As Fig. 5.4.

promotes innovation or cut-throat price cutting has been discussed independently by Lazonick (1991) who argues that the key determinant of whether or not the firm's decision-makers choose an innovative strategy is the extent to which 'they control an organisational structure that they believe provides them with the capability of developing productive resources that can overcome the constraints they face' (Lazonick, 1991: 328). Such structures include not only the internal organization of firms themselves and their relationships with the public authorities but also networks of relationships between firms in a particular industry or cluster of industries.[10]

Lazonick's emphasis on the need for control over the requisite organizational structure derives at least in part from his own work as an economic historian, particularly his work relating to the failure of the British cotton industry to innovate in the late nineteenth and the twentieth centuries. Referring to a period of stagnation following the end of the post-Second World War boom, Lazonick characterizes the situation in the following terms:

The fundamental problem was an industry mired in its own highly competitive and vertically specialised structure, lacking any internal forces to set organisational transformation in motion. (Lazonick, 1986: 35).

The vast majority of businesspeople in the cotton industry had neither the incentive to participate nor the ability to lead in the internal restructuring of their industry (ibid. 45). Given this absence of leadership from within private industry, what was required was the visible hand of co-ordinated control not the invisible hand of the self-regulating market (Elbaum and Lazonick, 1986: 10–11).

The issue of the relationship between industry structure and the capacity for innovation is a complex one. On the one hand, there is evidence that forms of long-term relationship between independent firms may be superior to vertical integration as a means of co-ordinating the activities required for innovation especially where these activities involve a high degree of technological 'strangeness' (Gomes-Casseres, 1994: 63). These new forms of alliance are prevalent in high-technology industries and there are indications that they contribute most to innovative performance when they involve a dense network of interpersonal relationships and internal infrastructures that enhance learning, unblock information flows and facilitate co-ordination by creating trust and by mitigating perceived differences of interest (Moss Kanter, 1994: 97).[11]

---

[10] These points are argued in more detail by Michie and Prendergast (1997) on which this section draws.

[11] For further discussion of the role of trust see the March 1997 Special Issue of the *Cambridge Journal of Economics* on 'Contracts and Competition', and in particular the 'Introduction' by Deakin and Michie and the papers by Arrighetti, Bachmann, and Deakin; Lane; and Burchell and Wilkinson. See also Deakin and Michie (1997b), Deakin, Goodwin, and Hughes (1997), Michie (1997), and Deakin and Wilkinson (1997).

These points regarding information flows and so forth were also brought out by Dore (1983) in his discussion of the 'obligated relational contracting' found between Japanese firms. This involves long-term trading relations in which goodwill (with 'give and take') is expected to temper the pursuit of self-interest, although this and other labour-market practices have since come under strain, especially following the relatively slow economic growth of the 1980s.[12] In his 1983 article Dore argued that such relations were more common in Western economies than is generally recognized. While it may be objected that relational contracts lead to price distortions and hence to a loss of allocative efficiency, they do lead to high levels of other kinds of efficiency. Specifically, 'the relative security of such relations encourages investment in supplying firms', 'the relationships of trust and mutual dependency make for a more rapid flow of information', and 'a by-product of the system is a general emphasis on quality'. This discussion links to a number of classic papers (such as Richardson, 1972; and Mariti and Smiley, 1983), with Dore citing Macaulay's 1962 paper as demonstrating that relational contracting is indeed valued by firms in the USA as well as in Japan.[13]

With these apparent benefits of collaboration, why don't more firms enter into such arrangements? In part the answer may lie in the short-termism that prevails in many firms and industries, and a financial system more geared to quick pay-back periods and a high priority to maintaining dividend payout levels than to long-term investment commitments.[14] In particular, the attempt to squeeze productivity growth out of UK firms during the 1980s and 1990s via the intensification of competitive pressures allied with the opening up of cost-cutting competitive avenues may have had two contradictory effects—first, recording what have been interpreted by some as impressive and welcome productivity growth figures (Crafts, 1996; Eltis, 1996) while at the same time undermining the conditions for long-term, sustainable economic development.

7. POLICY IMPLICATIONS

The fostering of collaborative structures may be an important element in creating a competitive and successful economy—an economy capable of closing the output gap with its major competitors.[15] This opens up a very different

[12] A point taken up by Dore in Ch. 9, this volume.

[13] This literature is discussed in more detail in Buckley and Michie (1996).

[14] An additional problem of a principal-agent nature may occur where the financial sector is dealing with networks or other alliances of firms, the legal definition of which may not be entirely clear; we are grateful to Laurence Harris for drawing this point to our attention. The socio-legal context of contracting and some of the implications of this for competitive performance are discussed by Deakin and Michie (1997b).

[15] Indeed, when releasing a report in 1997 showing that British firms had reduced spending on innovation in 1996—at a time when the lifespan of their established products was falling—the

policy agenda than that which was pursued in the UK during the Thatcher and Major Governments of the 1980s and 1990s. Instead of the 'freeing up' of labour and product markets through policies of deregulation and casualization we need new industrial, innovation, and macroeconomic policies which will develop new forms of corporate finance and create effective mechanisms of corporate governance; provide a modern productive infrastructure which private firms can utilize, in many cases in a co-operative fashion; ensure a macroeconomic regime conducive to the creation of new industrial capacity, including low interest rates and a competitive exchange rate; ensure the expansion of employment opportunities so that investment in education and training will translate into the increased output levels which in the long run will repay such investments; and promote productive co-operation and industrial innovation. On this last point of promoting innovation, as suggested by Wood (Ch. 6, this volume), innovation policy could distinguish the different determinants of innovation between types of innovating firm so that the particular policy targets can be more effectively hit.

REFERENCES

Anderman, S. (1997), 'Commercial Cooperation, International Competitiveness, and EC Competition Policy', in S. Deakin and J. Michie (eds.), *Contracts, Co-operation, and Competition: Studies in Economics, Management, and Law*, Oxford: Oxford University Press.

Arrighetti, A., Bachmann, R., and Deakin, S. (1997), 'Contract Law, Social Norms and Inter-firm Cooperation', *Cambridge Journal of Economics*, 21/2 (Mar.), 171–95.

Bolton (1971), *Small Firms: Report of the Committee of Inquiry on Small Firms*, HMSO, London.

Buckley, P. and Michie, J. (1996), 'Introduction and Overview', in P. Buckley and J. Michie (eds.), *Firms, Organizations and Contracts: A Reader in Industrial Organization*, Oxford: Oxford University Press, 1–20.

Bullock, A., Duncan, J., and Wood, E. (1996) 'The Survey Method: Sample Attrition and the SME Panel Database', in Cosh and Hughes, *The Changing State of British Enterprise*.

Burchell, B. and Wilkinson, F. (1997), 'Trust, Business Relationships and the Contractual Environment', *Cambridge Journal of Economics*, 21/2 (Mar.), 217–37.

Cosh, A. and Hughes, A. (1996), *The Changing State of British Enterprise*, Cambridge: ESRC Centre for Business Research.

—— Duncan, J., and Hughes, A. (1996), 'Size, Age, Survival and Employment Growth', in Cosh and Hughes, *The Changing State of British Enterprise*.

UK's Confederation of British Industry warned manufacturers that they would go to the wall unless they invested in developing new products (as reported in the *Guardian* of 9 June 1997). Interestingly from the point of view of the analysis of the current chapter, this report also indicated that the growth in collaboration between manufacturing companies and academics, universities, and consultants had ended; (on the implications of this, see also Chapter 6 by Wood, this volume).

—— Hughes, A., and Wood, E. (1996), 'Innovation: Scale, Objectives, and Constraints', in Cosh and Hughes, *The Changing State of British Enterprise*.

Crafts, N. (1996), 'Deindustrialization and Economic Growth', *Economic Journal*, 106/434 (Jan.), 172–83.

Deakin, S. and Michie, J. (1997*a*), 'Contracts and Competition: An Introduction', *Cambridge Journal of Economics*, 21/2 (Mar.), 121–5.

—— —— (1997*b*), 'The Theory and Practice of Contracting', in S. Deakin and J. Michie (eds.), *Contracts, Co-operation, and Competition: Studies in Economics, Management, and Law*, Oxford: Oxford University Press.

—— and Wilkinson, F. (1997), 'Markets, Cooperation, and Economic Progress', *New Economy*, 4/3 (Autumn).

—— Goodwin, T., and Hughes, A. (1997), 'Co-operation and Trust in Inter-firm Relations: Beyond Competition Policy?', in Deakin and Michie (eds.), *Contracts, Co-operation, and Competition*.

Dore, R. (1983), 'Goodwill and the Spirit of Market Capitalism', *British Journal of Sociology*, 34/4, 459–82; repr. in Buckley and Michie (eds.), *Firms, Organizations and Contracts*, 359–82.

Elbaum, B. and Lazonick, W. (1986) (eds.), *The Decline of the British Economy*, Oxford: Clarendon Press.

Eltis, W. (1996), 'How Low Profitability and Weak Innovativeness Undermined UK Industrial Growth', *Economic Journal*, 106/434 (Jan.), 184–95.

Gomes-Casseres, B. (1994), 'Group Versus Group: How Alliance Networks Compete', *Harvard Business Review* (July–Aug.), 62–74.

Kitson, M. and Michie, J. (1996*a*), 'Britain's Industrial Performance Since 1960: Underinvestment and Relative Decline', *Economic Journal*, 106/434 (Jan.), 196–212.

—— —— (1996*b*), 'Manufacturing Capacity, Investment and Employment', in J. Michie and J. Grieve Smith (eds.), *Creating Industrial Capacity: Towards Full Employment*, Oxford: Oxford University Press

—— —— (1997), 'Does Manufacturing Matter?', *International Journal of the Economics of Business*, 4/1, 71–95.

Lane, C. (1997), 'The Social Regulation of Inter-firm Relations in Britain and Germany: Market Rules, Legal Norms and Technical Standards', *Cambridge Journal of Economics*, 21/2 (Mar.), 197–215.

Lazonick, W. (1986), 'The Cotton Industry', in Elbaum and Lazonick (eds.), *The Decline of the British Economy*.

—— (1991), *Business Organisation and the Myth of the Market Economy*, Cambridge: Cambridge University Press.

Macaulay, S. (1962), 'Non-Contractual Relations in Business: A Preliminary Study', Paper read at the Annual Meeting of the American Sociological Association, Aug. 1962; rev. and repr. in Buckley and Michie (eds.), *Firms, Organizations and Contracts*, 339–58.

Mariti, P. and Smiley, R. H. (1983), 'Co-operative Agreements and the Organization of Industry', *Journal of Industrial Economics*, 31: 437–51; repr. in Buckley and Michie (eds.), *Firms, Organizations and Contracts*, 276–92.

Michie, J. (1997), 'Cooperate or Compete?', *New Economy*, 4/3 (Autumn).

—— and Prendergast, R. (1997), 'Innovation and Competitive Advantage', in

J. Howells and J. Michie (eds.), *Technology, Innovation and Competitiveness*, Cheltenham: Edward Elgar.

Moss Kanter, R. (1994), 'Collaborative Advantage: The Art of Alliances', *Harvard Business Review* (July–Aug.), 96–108.

Oughton, C. and Whittam, G. (1996), 'Competitiveness, EU Industrial Strategy and Subsidiarity', in P. Devine, Y. Katsoulacos and R. Sugden (eds.), *Competitiveness, Subsidiarity and Industrial Policy*, London: Routledge, 58–103.

Richardson, G. B. (1972), 'The Organization of Industry', *Economic Journal*, 883–96; repr. in Buckley and Michie (eds.), *Firms, Organizations and Contracts*, 59–74.

SBRC (Small Business Research Centre) (1992), *The State of British Enterprise; Growth, Innovation and Competitive Advantage in Small and Medium-Sized Firms*, SBRC, University of Cambridge.

Schumpeter, J. A. (1947), *Capitalism, Socialism and Democracy*, 2nd edn., London: George Allen and Unwin.

—— (1961), *The Theory of Economic Development*, trans. R. Opie, Oxford: Oxford University Press.

6. The Determinants of Innovation in Small and Medium-Sized Enterprises

Eric Wood

1. INTRODUCTION

The role of small and medium enterprises (SMEs) in the innovation process has become an important component of the policy interest in small firms in the UK (see for example ACOST, 1990) and in the Europe Union as a whole (see European Commission, 1995). The reason for this appears to be the mounting evidence that SMEs, here defined to be firms with fewer than 500 employees, play a vital role in the innovation process. Cohen and Levin (1989) suggest that it is far from clear that large firms are now the most important source of innovations. Recent empirical studies have highlighted the important and growing contribution SMEs have made to total innovation output (Pavitt, Robson, and Townsend, 1987; Acs and Audretsch, 1988, 1991). Mueller (1988) argues that 'the small or newly-born firm is a primary source of new products and innovations' (p. 40).

Nevertheless, some doubt remains about the depth of technological capability within the SME sector. Bolton (1971) argues that 'small firms, in spite of relatively low expenditure on research and development by the sector as a whole, are an important source of innovation in products, techniques and services' (p. 84). More recently, Winter suggested that 'in a small firm, inward-looking (technological) search might better be typified by "a look in the suggestion box". Change then involves insightful solutions to recurring difficulties with the existing routines, fine-tuning of process parameters, better adaptation to the idiosyncratic strengths and weaknesses of the firm's personnel or equipment, or minor design improvements in process or product' (1984: 293).

Just what proportion of SMEs are characterized by a 'suggestion box' approach to innovation, what proportion are engaged in any R&D activity, and how R&D intensive are they, however, seem not to have received adequate attention. The aim here is twofold. In addition to evaluating the importance of key inputs to SME innovation including amongst others R&D activity, the chapter provides a detailed analysis of the patterns of innovative output from the UK SME sector. The reason for the latter is the growing evidence, discussed below, on the variety of different types of innovative strategy, both in terms of innovation input and output. It will be argued that identifying groups of firms with similar innovation output characteristics helps to distinguish which innovation inputs are important and to what kind of firm.

Section 2 provides an overview of the methods and findings of previous research in this area. Section 3 analyses innovation patterns in the UK SME sector using cluster analysis to identify different types of innovating firm according to their innovation output. Section 4 evaluates how the importance of different inputs to the innovation process varies across different types of SME innovator.

2. THE PATTERN AND DETERMINANTS OF INNOVATION: METHODOLOGICAL APPROACHES

2.1. *The development of research methodologies*

A major challenge facing researchers of innovation activity is to measure innovative activity in all its complexity and multiple dimensions. A large literature utilized R&D and patent data to analyse innovation patterns (for a review, see Cohen and Levin, 1989). Patel and Pavitt argued that the 'assumption that R&D expenditures measure "inputs" of innovative activities, and patents the resulting "outputs", has become increasingly fragile, as more has been understood empirically about the nature of innovative activities, and about the means that firms use to appropriate their results' (1992: 93–4). 'Inputs' into innovative activities include design, testing, production, and marketing, the relative importance of which varies significantly according to the firm's size and its principal sector of activity (see Mansfield *et al.*, 1971, quoted in Patel and Pavitt 1992: 94). The technology transfer process also consists of a complex mix of patenting, licensing, purchase of equipment, external R&D services, and formal and informal collaborative agreements.

In the past ten years, a number of large-scale company surveys in Europe and North America have provided an enormous variety of measures of both the inputs to and outputs from innovative activity. Having achieved this important step in measuring innovation, researchers have been presented with the new challenge of finding appropriate methods of analysing this breadth of information. After having to make do with one or two indicators of innovative activity, researchers working on these innovation surveys typically have well in excess of 100 variables measuring the importance of different aspects of the innovation process.

Broadly speaking, there are two alternative approaches to an analysis using a large number of variables on innovative activity. One alternative is a large number of separate, unrelated, or partially related runs with a small number of variables in each. This enables one to draw precise conclusions about particular aspects of the innovation process. It does, however, have the disadvantage of making it more difficult to obtain an overview of the innovation process. An alternative is a small number of runs with a large number of variables in each. The number of variables which can be included in standard regression models is limited by the problem of multicollinearity in the explanatory variables and by degrees of freedom. Two approaches have been adopted to cope with a large number of variables in a particular run. In one, information from a large number of variables is compressed into a smaller number of uncorrelated variables, typically using principal component analysis. In the other, information from a large number of variables is used to create a smaller number of groups of cases, using cluster analysis. The advantage of these latter approaches is that they provide an overview of a large amount of information, but they suffer from the disadvantages of reduced precision, limited robustness, and possibly also, difficulties in interpretation.

A large number of separate, mostly unrelated runs of the Centre for Business Research (CBR) innovation data on UK SMEs has already been carried out (see Cosh and Hughes, 1996). That analysis provided extremely detailed and precise information on how the extent and nature of the inputs to and outputs from innovation activity varied by, for example, firm size, firm age, broad industrial sector, and growth rate. We build on that analysis here by using a combination of the above two approaches on the same data to provide an overview of the patterns of innovation output as well as a univariate analysis of the importance of different inputs to innovation. The next section reviews previous research which has adopted this broad approach.

2.2. Recent empirical research on the patterns of innovation

Using the Science Policy Research Unit (SPRU) innovation data on major innovations in the UK between 1945 and 1983, Pavitt (1984) developed a taxonomy for classifying companies according to the precise emphasis of their innovation activities. This work identifies common features of the innovation activities in particular industries and then groups a large number of industries into a smaller number of groups each with similar features of the innovation activities. This procedure relies on a range of information on inputs to and outputs from the innovation activities in each industry. The four patterns of industry innovation are supplier dominated, specialized equipment suppliers, scale intensive, and science-based. The model was subsequently developed further by Pavitt, Robson, and Townsend (1989).

A similar methodology was adopted by Archibugi, Cesaratto, and Sirilli (1991) for business units contained in the Italian innovation database. Archibugi et al. used information on both inputs to and outputs from the innovation process. Regarding inputs to innovation, they used data on a range of internal and external sources of information and how prominent they were in the innovation process. As with Pavitt, Archibugi *et al.* (1991) group firms according to their industry innovation characteristics rather than the firms' own innovation characteristics. Their analysis identified five distinct groups of innovation types; producers of traditional consumer goods, suppliers of traditional intermediate goods, specialised suppliers of intermediate goods and equipment, mass-production assemblers, and R&D based.

Cesaratto, Mangano, and Massini (1995) used seventeen variables on inputs to and outputs from innovation to identify five main types of innovator. A difference between their work and the previous work is that Cesaratto *et al.* did not consider the specific industrial sector to which a firm belonged. This means that they classified a firm to a group in which its individual innovation characteristics match, rather than one which necessarily matches the innovation characteristics of its industry.

Figure 6.1 shows a comparison of the results of the clustering results of Pavitt, Robson, and Townsend (1987), Archibugi, Cesarotto, and Sirilli (1991), and Cesaratto, Mangano, and Massini (1995). The comparison was made on the basis of the characteristics of the different categories of innovator types as described by the different authors, chiefly the level of innovativeness of the different categories of innovator, the description of the primary inputs to their innovations, and the main industries which each category covered. The table indicates the similar categories identified by Pavitt *et al.* (1987) and Archibugi *et al.* (1991). The only substantive difference is that Archibugi *et al.* split the Pavitt *et al.* category of 'supplier dominated firms' into 'producers of traditional consumer goods' and 'suppliers of traditional intermediate goods'. Given the similarity of their approaches, the close match in their results is not entirely surprising.

The categories identified by Cesaratto *et al.* (1995), on the basis of a firm's own innovation characteristics, are rather different from the other categorizations. There is no simple one-to-one correspondence between the categories identified by Archibugi *et al.* and those identified by Cesaratto *et al.*: for example, the Cesaratto *et al.* category 'complex innovators' would appear to draw firms from 'suppliers of traditional intermediate goods', 'specialised suppliers of intermediate goods and equipment', 'mass production assemblers', and 'R&D based'. Given the differences in methodology between Cesaratto *et al.* and the others, the results of the comparison are consistent with each industrial sector containing a variety of different types of innovator. This suggests that it is not entirely appropriate to classify a firm to a particular innovation type simply on the basis of the industry in which the firm operates as the firm's innovation activity may be rather different from others in its industry.

A common feature of all of the above attempts to identify distinctive types of innovator is that information on both the inputs to and outputs from inno-

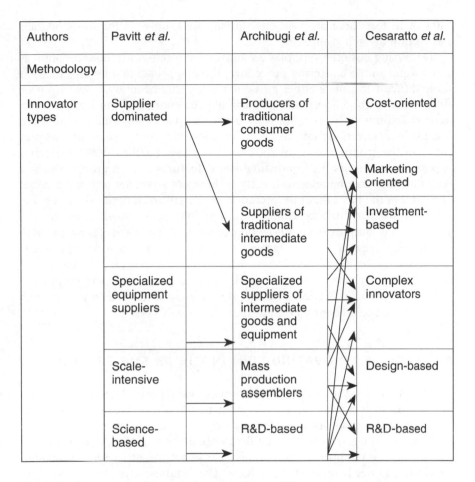

Authors	Pavitt *et al.*		Archibugi *et al.*		Cesaratto *et al.*
Methodology					
Innovator types	Supplier dominated		Producers of traditional consumer goods		Cost-oriented
					Marketing oriented
			Suppliers of traditional intermediate goods		Investment-based
	Specialized equipment suppliers		Specialized suppliers of intermediate goods and equipment		Complex innovators
	Scale-intensive		Mass production assemblers		Design-based
	Science-based		R&D-based		R&D-based

Fig. 6.1. Comparison of innovation types across different clustered sets

vation are used to group firms or industries. This makes it difficult to charac-
terize the strength of relationships between particular inputs and types of
innovation output. At best, one has to make deductions regarding such relationships; for example, it could be argued that there is a positive relationship
between the level of R&D expenditure and a firm's propensity to introduce a
product innovation or the probability that it will be a highly innovating business unit (see table 6 in Archibugi *et al.* 1991). A similar pattern is suggested
by Cesaratto *et al.*, who show that the categories in which R&D is a characteristic innovation source are more likely than others to produce 'absolute
product innovations', i.e. 'the number of products that business units
regarded as new for the world or the Italian market' (p. 122). However, it is

difficult to test these propositions statistically simply on the basis of their description of each group.

By utilizing both the variables on innovation inputs with those on innovation output in the clustering procedure, these approaches may also make it more difficult to isolate either particular categories of innovation output or differences in the importance of particular categories of innovation input across the different types of innovation output. In deciding which variables to include in a cluster analysis, a crucial question concerns the ease of interpretation of the groups created by the cluster analysis, i.e. the extent to which it is possible to identify the key distinguishing features of each group in such a way that they can be related directly to business strategies and managerial choices. On the basis that interpretation of the groups is easier the fewer the variables used in their creation, we adopt the approach of analysing the inputs to and outputs from innovation separately. The variables for innovation outputs are used to create groups of distinctive innovator types, whereas the variables for innovation inputs are used to create a smaller number of uncorrelated variables summarizing the key features of innovation input.

In the analysis in Section 3 below, cluster analysis is used to group firms according to the innovation output that they report.

3. TYPES OF INNOVATING FIRM IN THE UK SME SECTOR

The CBR database provides information on several aspects of a firm's innovation output including data on whether or not a firm introduced product (goods or services as appropriate) and process innovations, whether or not their innovations were new to the firm only or new to their industry or all industries, and the proportion of their sales which are made up of upgraded products and newly innovated products. The database provides information on whether or not firms introduced either product or process innovations both in the 1986–91 and 1992–5 periods. All of this information was used in the cluster analysis. The full list of variables used in the cluster analysis is shown in the first column of Table 6.1. Appendix 1 shows the questions that were used to generate these variables.

The main purpose of the cluster analysis is to see whether it is possible to identify distinctive types of innovating firm by the kind of innovation output which they report. To avoid making prejudgements about which firms are innovators and which are non-innovators, however, all firms for which there was a complete set of responses to the questions on innovation output were included in the analysis. In all, it was possible to include 600 firms. As will be seen below, the clustering procedure did identify a group which contains all the firms which could be considered non-innovators. A total of ninety-four firms had to be excluded owing to item non-response for one or more of the variables. It is important to note that the available innovation data for these firms suggests that they would not have been split evenly across the final cluster groups were it possible to include them. A significantly higher proportion of excluded cases (67 per cent) reported no innovations in the period 1992–5 by comparison with included cases (28 per cent) and are likely to have been classified to one of the six clusters which the analysis generated. Thus, the cases which are included in the cluster analysis cannot be said to be entirely representative of the sample. In addition, it should be noted that the entire sample of 694 which responded to the full questionnaire in the 1995 survey is itself not representative of the population. The reason for this is that there was no refreshing of the sample between the 1991 and 1995 surveys and, due to attrition, the 1995 sample contains a disproportionately high number of innovating firms as those firms that died were significantly less likely to have reported innovations in the period 1986–91 (see Bullock, Duncan, and Wood, 1996). Finally, it is worth noting that the original sample of firms included in the 1991 survey was stratified according to size, weighted towards larger SMEs (see SBRC, 1992). This has the effect of increasing the proportion of innovating firms in the sample, as smaller firms are less likely than larger ones to innovate (Cosh and Hughes, 1996).

Following Morrison (1967), principal component analysis was applied to the ten variables chosen for creating the groups of different types of innovator before conducting the cluster analysis. Using principal component analysis in this way helps to overcome the problem of 'double counting' whereby variables that are highly correlated carry excessive weight in a cluster analysis. An additional advantage of applying principal component analysis prior to the cluster analysis is that it makes it possible to include a combination of interval and binary variables which could otherwise not be used in the cluster analysis.

The four factors generated in the principal components analysis are shown in Appendix 2, together with the tests that were conducted on the ten variables to ensure that they were suitable for a principal component analysis. The four factors account for 67.5 per cent of the variance in the sample. In all but one variable, the four factors account for over 60 per cent of the variance. The only exception is the variable which measures the proportion of sales in 1995 made up of 'newly marketed products whose intended use, performance characteristics, technical construction, design, or use of materials and components was new or substantially changed in the last three years' for which the variance explained is only 24 per cent. The reason for this is not entirely clear. Despite the poor explanatory power of the four factors in the case of this variable, however, the cluster analysis was able to generate groups for which there were significant differences in the average values of this variable. The main features of the four factors shown in Appendix 2 could be summarized as follows:

(i) Factor 1: 'Novel product and process innovations and proportion of new products in total 1995 sales of primary importance'
(ii) Factor 2: 'Product innovation activity, mostly non-novel, of primary importance'
(iii) Factor 3: 'Process innovation activity, mostly non-novel, of primary importance'
(iv) Factor 4: 'Proportion of upgraded products in total 1995 sales dominant'

Appendix 3 shows the results of the cluster analysis which was applied to the above four factors and how the cluster centre values vary across the clusters and factors. Instead of identifying the distinctive features of the clusters in terms of their scores for the different factors, however, an easier way is to analyse the variation between the clusters with respect to the original ten variables which were used in the principal component analysis. Table 6.1 provides such an analysis for the six cluster groups, showing a measure of both the within- and between-groups distances. The within-groups distances are indicated by the standard deviation of the variables across the cases within each cluster. The between-groups distances are measured using the Bonferroni One Way ANOVA test. This is a multiple comparison procedure to determine which means are significantly different. The Bonferroni test adjusts the significance level to the number of comparisons one is making.

In general, the within-groups distances are relatively high, i.e. the standard deviations are large. Despite this, it is clear that there are significant differences between the groups. Table 6.1 shows that there are significant differences between different groups with respect to all variables. A different presentation of the same information on between-group distances as in Table 6.1 is shown in Table 6.2. The advantage of Table 6.2 is that it provides a better indication of the overall distance between groups. It can be seen from Table 6.2 that in all cases, significant between-group differences exist with respect to at least two variables and in most cases, significant differences exist with respect to at least 4 variables.

Firms in Cluster 1 can be distinguished from all others in that they are significantly more likely to have introduced both a novel product and a novel process innovation (novel meaning that the firm judged their innovation to be new either to their industry, or to all industries). Another distinctive feature of this group is that it has the highest average proportion of newly innovated products in its 1995 sales at 23.5 per cent. This group could be termed 'product and process originators'. Cluster 2 firms are also likely to have introduced novel product innovations, though less so than Cluster 1 firms. Unlike Cluster 1 firms, however, no Cluster 2 firms reported novel process innovations. It can be seen from Table 6.1 that Cluster 2 firms are less likely than most others to have introduced any process innovations, at least in the period 1992–5. Cluster 2 firms have a marginally but not significantly lower propor-

Table 6.1. Descriptive statistics of clusters of innovating and non-innovating firms

Variable name	Mean value (and standard deviation)						
	Cluster 1 (n=38) (a)	Cluster 2 (n=87) (b)	Cluster 3 (n=43) (c)	Cluster 4 (n=160) (d)	Cluster 5 (n=93) (e)	Cluster 6 (n=179) (f)	All firms (n=600)
Product innovation 1986–91	0.89^{cef} (0.31)	0.78^{ef} (0.42)	0.58^{f} (0.50)	0.89^{cef} (0.32)	0.37 (0.48)	0.34 (0.47)	0.60 (0.49)
Process innovation 1986–91	0.63^{ef} (0.49)	0.51^{ef} (0.50)	0.67^{ef} (0.47)	0.95^{abcef} (0.21)	0.03 (0.18)	0.30^{e} (0.46)	0.51 (0.50)
Product innovation 1992–5	1.0^{cdef} (0.0)	1.0^{cdef} (0.0)	0.40^{f} (0.49)	0.79^{cef} (0.41)	0.65^{cf} (0.48)	0.08 (0.28)	0.57 (0.50)
Process innovation 1992–5	1.0^{bdef} (0.0)	0.28^{f} (0.45)	1.0^{cdef} (0.0)	0.60^{bf} (0.47)	0.62^{bf} (0.49)	0.11 (0.32)	0.49 (0.50)
Product innovation 1992–5 (new to your industry)	0.95^{cdef} (0.23)	0.82^{cdef} (0.39)	0.09 (0.29)	0.11^{f} (0.31)	0.03 (0.18)	0.0 (0.0)	0.22 (0.41)
Product innovation 1992–5 (new to all industries	0.97^{bcdef} (0.16)	0.79^{cdef} (0.41)	0.12 (0.32)	0.06 (0.23)	0.10^{f} (0.30)	0.0 (0.0)	0.22 (0.41)
Process innovation 1992–5 (new to your industry)	0.89^{bcdef} (0.31)	0.0 (0.0)	0.72^{bdef} (0.45)	0.03 (0.17)	0.02 (0.15)	0.0 (0.0)	0.11 (0.31)
Process innovation 1992–5 (new to all industries	0.82^{bcdef} (0.39)	0.0 (0.0)	0.70^{bdef} (0.46)	0.01 (0.11)	0.01 (0.10)	0.0 (0.0)	0.12 (0.33)
Upgraded products as % 1995 sales	28.6^{f} (21.1)	19.2^{f} (20.5)	15.8^{f} (13.7)	29.7^{bcf} (25.8)	48.1^{abcdf} (28.9)	4.9 (8.7)	22.6 (25.4)
New products as % 1995 sales	23.5^{def} (21.4)	18.8^{ef} (19.8)	17.1^{f} (21.0)	15.0^{f} (16.2)	11.7^{f} (15.5)	2.7 (10.0)	12.0 (17.2)

Notes: 1. The superscripted letters indicate a significant difference in the mean value for a particular variable between two clusters. Significance is measured at the 5% level in all cases and was calculated using the Bonferroni One Way ANOVA test. A superscripted 'd' next to a mean value, for example, indicates that that mean value is significantly higher than the mean value in Cluster 4.

2. Cluster 1: 'product and process originators'; Cluster 2: 'product originators'; Cluster 3: 'process originators'; Cluster 4: 'product and process imitators'; Cluster 5: 'incremental product and process imitators'; Cluster 6: 'occasional imitators'.

tion of their 1995 sales made up of newly innovated products (18.8 per cent) by comparison with Cluster 1 firms. This group will be referred to as 'product originators'. Cluster 3 firms are likely to have introduced a novel process innovation, though less so than Cluster 1 firms. Only a small proportion of Cluster 3 firms introduced a novel product innovation. Cluster 3 firms have a similar proportion of their 1995 sales made up of newly innovated products (17.1 per cent) by comparison with Cluster 2 firms. Cluster 3 will be referred to as 'process originators'.

Table 6.2. The 'between-groups' distances between clusters

	Cluster 2	Cluster 3	Cluster 4	Cluster 5	Cluster 6
Cluster 1	-/-/-/x/-/x/-/-	x/-/x/-/x/x/-/-	-/x/x/x/x/x/-/x	x/x/x/x/x/x/x/x	x/x/x/x/x/x/x/x
Cluster 2		-/-/x/x/x/x/-/-	-/x/x/x/-/x/-	x/x/x/x/-/x/x	x/x/x/x/-/x/x
Cluster 3			-/x/x/x/-/x/x/-	-/x/x/-/x/x/-	x/x/x/x/-/x/x/x
Cluster 4				x/x/x/-/-/-/x/-	x/x/x/x/-/x/x
Cluster 5					-/x/x/x/-/-/x/x

Notes: 1. An 'x' indicates a significant difference between two cluster groups with respect to a particular variable. A '-' indicates that the difference between two cluster groups with respect to a particular variable is not significant. Each cell shows the significance of differences between two cluster groups with respect to eight variables, in the same order as they are presented in Table 6.1. Two variables were excluded from Table 6.2, namely 'Product innovation 1992–5 (new to all industries)' and 'Process innovation 1992–5 (new to all industries)' as the differences with respect to these variables were almost identical to 'Product innovation 1992–5 (new to your industry)' and 'Process innovation 1992–5 (new to your industry)', respectively.

2. Cluster 1: 'product and process originators'; Cluster 2: 'product originators'; Cluster 3: 'process originators'; Cluster 4: 'product and process imitators' Cluster 5: incremental product process imitators" Cluster 6: 'occasional imitators'.

Firms in Clusters 4 and 5 have a similarly low probability of having reported either novel product or novel process innovations. 11 per cent of firms in Cluster 4 report product innovations new to the firm's own industry, while 10 per cent of firms in Cluster 5 report product innovations new to all industries. (The latter appears contradictory as an innovation new to all industries by definition needs also to be new to the firm's own industry, yet only 3 per cent of firms in Cluster 5 report product innovations new to the firm's own industry). Despite the relatively low probability of novel innovations, more than 60 per cent of firms in both groups reported a product or process innovation (or both) in the period 1992–5. Cluster 4 firms reported a higher proportion of 1995 sales made up of newly innovated products (15.0 per cent) than those in Cluster 5 (11.7 per cent).

One feature which distinguishes these two groups is that Cluster 4 firms are significantly more likely than Cluster 5 ones to have introduced an innovation, particularly a process innovation, in the period 1986–91. (Firms in Cluster 5 are in fact less likely to have reported a process innovation in the period 1986–91 than those in Cluster 6 which, as will be seen below, appears to be the least innovative group by all other measures). This does not seem entirely in line with the relative probabilities of firms in these groups introducing such innovations in the period 1992–5. It is probable that the reason for the particularly low probability of process innovations in 1986–91 in Cluster 5 is partly due to differences in the way that the innovation questions were asked between the 1991 and 1995 surveys (see Appendix 1). We will return to a discussion of this point below. The pattern for product innovations is similar. Cluster 5 firms are slightly less likely than Cluster 4 firms to have introduced a product innovation in 1992–5 and dramatically less likely than Cluster 4 firms to have done so in 1986–91. Differences in the way the questions were asked in the 1991 and 1995 surveys may also account for this discrepancy, as will be seen below.

Another feature which distinguishes these two groups is the proportion of 1995 sales made up of 'upgraded products'. Cluster 5 firms reported a significantly higher proportion on average (48.1 per cent) than those in Cluster 4 (29.7 per cent) and in fact all of the other groups. On the basis that the primary difference between these groups is the proportion of 1995 sales made up of upgraded products, the following descriptions were chosen for these groups; 'incremental product and process imitators' for Cluster 5 and 'product and process imitators' for Cluster 4.

Firms in Cluster 6 are distinctive by almost every measure of innovativeness. No firms in this cluster reported a novel innovation. They are also significantly less likely to have reported either product or process innovations in 1992–5 than firms in all other groups and significantly less likely to have reported either product or process innovations in 1986–91 than those in most other groups. They report a significantly lower proportion (on average) of 1995 sales made up either of upgraded or newly innovated products (4.9 per cent and 2.7 per cent respectively) than all other groups. The term chosen to summarize this group is 'occasional imitators'.

Table 6.3 shows how this sample of 600 firms is split across the different cluster groups. As noted above, these 600 cases are not representative of the UK SME population due to a combination of stratification, attrition, and item non-response. Therefore, it is not possible on the basis of these results to draw conclusions about the pattern of innovation in the SME population as a whole. 30 per cent of this sample of SMEs appear to be 'occasional imitators', i.e. innovate only sporadically, producing no novel innovations and have a negligible proportion of their sales made up of recently improved or new products. The smallest group of consistently innovative firms is Cluster 1

Table 6.3. Proportion of sample across cluster (percentages)

	Cluster 1	Cluster 2	Cluster 3	Cluster 4	Cluster 5	Cluster 6	Total
Proportion of all firms	6.3	14.5	7.2	26.7	15.5	29.8	100
Proportion of firms in Clusters 1, 2, 3, 4, 5	9.0	20.7	10.2	38.0	22.1	[—]	100

Note: Cluster 1 'novel and process originators'; Cluster 2 'product originators'; Cluster 3 'process originators'; Cluster 4 'product and process imitators'; Cluster 5 'incremental product and process imitators'; Cluster 6 'occasional imitators'.

('product and process originators'), followed by Cluster 3 ('process originators'). Roughly half of firms in clusters which are typified by novel innovations are in Cluster 2 ('product originators'). The clusters which are typified
by novel innovations, namely Clusters 1, 2 and 3 account for around 40 per
cent of innovators in this sample. Clusters 4 and 5 which account for the
remaining 60 per cent of innovating firms, contain few firms which introduce
novel innovations. Cluster 4 is the largest of these, accounting for 38 per cent
of consistent innovators.

Table 6.4 provides a univariate analysis of the differences between the clusters across a number of other factors which have been shown to influence the
probability of innovation in SMEs (see Cosh and Hughes, 1996, Cosh,
Hughes, and Wood, 1997a,b). These variables include firm size in terms of
number of employees, age, whether or not the firm is in manufacturing or
business services, whether or not the firm is in a high-technology industry
(based on the Butchart (1987) definition), whether or not the firm exports and
finally, whether or not the firm reports serious overseas competitors. A more
detailed analysis of the industry classification of different cluster groups is
shown in Appendix 4.

One of the clearest features of Table 6.4 is the distinctiveness of Cluster 5,
'incremental product and process imitators'. Cluster 5 has a significantly
lower proportion of manufacturing firms (29 per cent) than all other clusters.
The differences in the proportion of manufacturing firms between the other
groups is only marginal and not significant in any cases.[1] Cluster 5 firms are
also the youngest on average and significantly so by comparison with firms in
Clusters 1, 3, and 4. Cluster 5 firms are also the smallest on average. Finally,
Cluster 5 firms are less likely on average to export than any other group.

The clear distinctiveness of Cluster 5 firms by comparison with the other
groups across these variables confirms that, despite some similarity between
firms in this group and those in Cluster 4 (as seen in Table 6.1), Cluster 5 contains a genuinely distinctive group of firms. The fact that Cluster 5 contains a
uniquely high proportion of business service firms appears to be key to understanding this group. It appears to provide part of the explanation for the
apparent anomaly of the low proportion of firms in this group reporting
either product or process innovations in the period 1986–91. As shown in
Appendix 1, the question in the 1991 survey asked firms whether or not they
had introduced any major innovations in several areas including 'production
processes', a category which would seem less applicable to business service
firms than manufacturing firms as the former are not normally engaged in

---

[1] A more detailed analysis of the industrial classification of firms in the different clusters is
shown in Appendix 4. It generally reinforces the view that most industries contain a wide variety
of innovator types.

Table 6.4. Univariate analysis of the characteristics of innovator types

	Mean value or percentage						
	Cluster 1 (n=32) (a)	Cluster 2 (n=80) (b)	Cluster 3 (n=41) (c)	Cluster 4 (n=144) (d)	Cluster 5 (n=84) (e)	Cluster 6 (n=145) (f)	All firms (n=526)
Average number of employees (1990)	120.8[bdef]	59.7	76.0	66.3	35.1	43.3	61.5
Average age	37.1[e]	27.4	36.9[e]	37.0[e]	18.3	29.9	30.1
% manufacturing (vs. business services)	59.5[e]	57.5[e]	60.5[e]	65.6[e]	29.0	57.3[e]	55.0
% high technology industry (vs. low-tech)	16.2	24.1[f]	9.3	20.6[f]	19.4	8.4	16.0
% firms exporting (1991)	74.5[cef]	54.9[ef]	40.5	48.7[f]	30.3	30.7	42.0
% firms with serious overseas competitors	48.7[f]	43.4[f]	23.8	35.7[f]	28.4	15.6	29.0

Notes: 1. The superscripted letters indicate a significant difference in the mean value for a particular variable between two clusters. Significance is measured at the 5% level in all cases and was calculated using the Bonferroni One Way ANOVA test. A superscripted 'd' next to a mean value, for example, indicates that that mean value is significantly higher than the mean value in Cluster 5.

2. Cluster 1: 'product and process originators'; Cluster 2 'product originators'; Cluster 3 'process originators'; Cluster 4 'product and process imitators'; Cluster 5 'incremental product and process imitators'; Cluster 6 'occasional imitators'.

activities which could be described as 'production'. Not surprisingly, a significantly lower proportion of business service firms reported 'production process' innovations than did manufacturing firms (SBRC 1992). The reason why the picture regarding process innovations is different for this group in 1992–5 is that the relevant question in the 1995 questionnaire referred simply to 'processes' rather than 'production processes' (see Appendix 1) and thus appears less likely to discourage respondents in business service firms from responding.

The fact that firms in this group report a significantly higher proportion of 1995 sales made up of 'upgraded products' than firms in all other groups suggests that business service firms which are innovative but do not introduce novel innovations regard a significantly larger proportion of their sales as consisting of upgraded products by comparison with firms in other clusters. If correct, then this would help to account for the low proportion of firms in Cluster 5 which reported product innovations in the period 1986–91. In 1991, firms were asked whether or not they had introduced any major innovations in products or services in the last 5 years. If, as it appears, product/service innovation in this group tends to be incremental in nature, then one would not expect a high proportion of these firms to report 'major innovations' in products or services.

Cluster 1 firms are distinctive in being larger on average than others and significantly so in all other groups except those in Cluster 3. They also have the highest proportion of firms which export and the highest proportion of firms with serious overseas competitors. Somewhat contrary to expectations, Cluster 1 firms are not the most likely to be in high technology industries, with only 16.2 per cent in these industries. Instead, Cluster 2 firms are most likely to be in high technology industries (24.1 per cent), followed by those in Clusters 4 (20.6 per cent) and 5 (19.4 per cent). Another distinctive feature of Cluster 2 firms is that on average they are the youngest and smallest of the novel innovating firms, i.e. those in Clusters 1, 2, and 3. Cluster 1 and 2 firms are roughly twice as likely as Cluster 3 firms to report serious overseas competitors and are also more likely than Cluster 3 firms to be exporters.

In summary then, it appears that the cluster analysis has identified groups which are distinctive not only with respect to the variables that were used in the cluster analysis, but also with respect to other variables which have been shown to be significant determinants of innovation. The next step is to evaluate the extent to which these groups rely on different types of input to their innovation activities.

4. INNOVATION INPUTS IN DIFFERENT TYPES OF SME INNOVATORS

This section investigates the extent to which the importance of key inputs to innovation activity varies across different types of innovating firm as defined by the cluster analysis of innovation output. Two types of variable on innovation inputs are included in the univariate analysis. First, there are variables which measure the capacity for technology development within the firm, as indicated both by the level of R&D activity and the level of technological skill. A primary indicator of whether or not the firm is engaged in R&D is whether or not they report staff engaged in R&D either full or part time in the financial year ending in 1995. Another binary variable, indicating whether or not a firm is engaged in R&D on a continuous as opposed to occasional basis provides a measure of the degree of formality in a firm's R&D activity. A firm engaged in R&D on a continuous basis, for example, is more likely than one which occasionally engages in R&D to have an established R&D department. R&D intensity is measured by the proportion of staff in full-time R&D and the proportion of turnover in the financial year ending in 1995 spent on R&D. Both measures are useful as there may not be a perfect correlation between them due, for example, to variation across industries in the proportion of R&D costs due to capital expenditure and to inter-firm variation in the use of external R&D services.

Three variables provide an indication of the technological skills within the firm, namely the proportion of staff who are technicians or lower professionals, the proportion of staff who are technologists, scientists, or higher professionals, and whether or not the firm entered into a formal or informal collaborative partnership in the period 1992–5. The first two measures are not without problems as indicators of technical skill. In addition to including occupations with formal technical qualifications such as technicians, technologists, and scientists, both variables also include occupations which do not necessarily involve technical qualifications, namely lower and higher professionals which might include sales personnel and managerial staff without technical qualifications. The reason for including the latter as an indicator of technological skill is that firms are only likely to enter into collaborative agreements if each participant believes that what they can contribute in terms of technical expertise can be at least matched by the other partners. It should be noted, however, that not all such collaborative agreements exist for the purpose of technology development. Nevertheless, around two-thirds of the collaborating firms in this sample report that expanding the range of expertise or products offered to customers was an important reason for their collaboration (Kitson and Wilkinson, 1996).

Archibugi et al. (1997) have demonstrated that in Italy, non-R&D innovation expenditures including design, tooling-up, and trial production and investment in new equipment tend to be of greater importance to innovation than R&D expenditure, particularly amongst smaller firms. Unfortunately, the questions on these aspects of innovation spending in the CBR survey suffer from high item non-response and were excluded from this analysis.

Secondly, the analysis includes variables which measure whether or not relationships with external organizations are made use of in the process of developing new products or processes. These are all binary variables arising from questions asked in the 1991 survey. The 1995 survey did include a question which asked respondents to rate the importance of information from external organizations on a Likert scale. In theory, the latter should provide more precise and up-to-date information on the importance of information from the different external sources than the 1991 binary variables. However, respondents which reported neither a product nor a process innovation in the 1995 survey were instructed not to answer the question on the use of information from external sources. Thus, if the Likert scale variables had been included, all non-innovating firms in the 1995 survey would have had to be excluded from the analysis. Even without the use of the Likert scale variables, missing values for one or more of the other variables on innovation inputs meant that 158 of the 600 firms which were included in the cluster analysis had to be excluded from the analysis of inputs, leaving a total of 442 firms that could be included.

Table 6.5 provides a univariate analysis of the importance of different innovation inputs across the clusters of innovator type. The table indicates significant differences in the importance of most of the innovation inputs across the categories of innovator type. A striking feature of the table is the distinctiveness of Cluster 6 firms. They are significantly less likely than firms in all other clusters to have any staff engaged in R&D and the probability of them having any staff engaged in R&D (18 per cent) is four times lower than the average for the other groups of firm (71 per cent). Cluster 6 firms are also significantly less likely than firms in all other groups to be engaged in R&D on a continuous basis, the probability (8 per cent) is more than six times below the average for firms in the other clusters (50 per cent). Moreover, firms in Cluster 6 are significantly less likely than firms in other groups to have entered collaborative agreements, the probability (17 per cent) more than three times lower than for all firms (57 per cent). In addition, Cluster 6 firms spend the lowest proportion, on average, of turnover on R&D (1.2 per cent as opposed to 3.4 per cent for firms in Clusters 1–5). Finally, Cluster 6 firms tend to have a lower proportion of technically skilled staff than firms in other clusters. Within the clusters which report substantial innovation output, Cluster 5 firms are something of an exception, with a significantly lower incidence and intensity of R&D activity.

While the low incidence and intensity of R&D activity as well as the below-average proportion of technically skilled staff amongst the Cluster 6 firms may not be entirely surprising, the results clearly indicate that firms which report substantial innovative output, i.e. those in Cluster 1–5, have a significantly greater capacity for technology development by comparison with Cluster 6 firms which report negligible innovation output. This finding challenges the view that small firm innovation can be characterized by 'a look in the suggestion box'.

An interesting question is whether there are identifiable differences between firms which produce original or novel innovations and those which simply imitate innovations developed elsewhere. In other words, are there clear differences between Clusters 1–3 and Clusters 4 and 5. As noted above, Cluster 5 appears to be significantly less R&D intensive than other innovating firms. This leaves the question of whether or not there are significant differences between Clusters 1–3 and Cluster 4. Within Clusters 1–4, the group which appears to be the least R&D intensive by most measures is Cluster 3, rather than Cluster 4. Although firms in Cluster 3 are not generally less likely than other innovating firms to have staff engaged in R&D, they tend to have a considerably lower proportion of staff engaged full time in R&D as well as a significantly lower proportion of staff who are higher professionals by comparison with those in Clusters 1, 2, 4, as well as those in Cluster 5. It appears, therefore, that firms

Table 6.5. Univariate analysis of innovation input factors across different innovator types

Survey year		Mean factor score						All firms (n=442)
		Cluster 1 (n=30) (a)	Cluster 2 (n=73) (b)	Cluster 3 (n=35) (c)	Cluster 4 (n=114) (d)	Cluster 5 (n=72) (e)	Cluster 6 (n=118) (f)	
1995	Firm engaged in continuous as opposed to occasional R&D	0.87[bcdef]	0.51[ef]	0.49[f]	0.54[ef]	0.29[f]	0.08	0.39
1995	Any staff engaged in R&D either full or part time	0.97[ef]	0.74[ef]	0.83[ef]	0.71[ef]	0.51[f]	0.18	0.57
1995	% staff in full-time R&D	3.97	3.5	0.8	2.6	2.1	0.9	2.2
1995	% staff who are technicians or lower professionals (full time)	9.1	10.9	11.2	13.3	13.3	6.9	10.7
1995	% staff who are technologists, scientists, or higher professionals (full time)	18.4[c]	16.2[cf]	2.9	10.3	13.8	7.1	11.0
1995	% of turnover in 1995 spend on R&D	4.0	4.3	2.1	3.8	2.2	1.2	2.8
1995	Firm entered formal or informal collaborative agreement	0.83[af]	0.59[f]	0.53[f]	0.56[f]	0.47[f]	0.17	0.46
	Make use of following external sources for innovation:							
1991	university/higher education	0.53[bcedef]	0.16	0.17	0.21[ef]	0.04	0.07	0.16
1991	private research institutions or consultants	0.47[ef]	0.33[f]	0.20	0.32[f]	0.10	0.19	0.25
1991	government research establishments	0.07	0.15	0.09	0.11	0.03	0.08	0.09
1991	suppliers or customers	0.47	0.51	0.49	0.72[ef]	0.38	0.39	0.50
1991	other firms	0.37	0.34[f]	0.20	0.27	0.15	0.13	0.23
1991	trade or professional journals	0.47	0.44	0.34	0.56[e]	0.31	0.39	0.43

Notes: 1. The supersripted letters indicate a significant difference in the mean value for a particular variable between two clusters. Significance is measured at the 5% level in all cases and was calculated using the Bonferroni One Way ANOVA test. A superscripted 'd' next to a mean value, for example, indicates that that mean value is significantly higher than the mean value in Cluster 5.

2. Cluster 1: 'product and process originators'; Cluster 2: 'product originators'; Cluster 3: 'process originators'; Cluster 4: 'product and process imitators'; Cluster 5: 'incremental product and process imitators'; Cluster 6: 'occasional imitators'.

which focus exclusively on novel process rather than novel product innovations are not more R&D-intensive than firms which introduce non-novel innovations. However, there is some evidence that firms introducing novel product innovations are associated with higher R&D intensity. Firms in Clusters 1 and 2 have a higher proportion of staff in full-time R&D, spend a higher proportion of turnover on R&D, and have a higher proportion of staff who are technologists, scientists, or higher professionals by comparison with those in Cluster 4.

Turning now to the use of information from outside organizations for the purposes of innovation, it can be seen that the use of information from universities is largely a feature of innovating firms. Amongst firms in Clusters 1–4, 23 per cent use information from universities in their innovative activity as opposed to 7 per cent in Cluster 6. Despite containing innovative firms, Cluster 5 is again an anomaly with only 4 per cent of firms in the group using information from universities. If, as seems likely, the use of information from universities is a distinguishing feature between innovative and non-innovative SMEs, then the suggestion that the links between universities and the SME sector as a whole have weakened over the last five years (see Moore, 1996) should be a matter of concern to policy-makers. Cluster 1 firms are significantly more likely than all others to rely on university links in their development of new products or processes with over 50 per cent of firms in this cluster using information from universities. Unlike firms in any other cluster, those in Cluster 1 are more likely to use information from universities than from any other source in developing new products or processes. As Cluster 2 firms are less likely than Cluster 4 firms to make use of information from universities, the use of information from universities does not appear to be a specific characteristic of novel product innovation.

In all other clusters than Cluster 1, the most important source of information for innovation is suppliers or customers. Cluster 4 firms are the most likely of any group to rely on information from suppliers and customers with over 70 per cent of firms in this group using information from these sources. In all other clusters, around 50 per cent or fewer of firms use information from suppliers or customers. Another important source of information for all groups is trade or professional journals and once again, firms in Cluster 4 are the most likely to use information from this source.

5. CONCLUSION

The most outstanding feature of the pattern of inputs to innovation in the SME sector is the sharp contrast between firms in Cluster 6 which report negligible innovation output and those which report substantial innovation output, i.e. those in Clusters 1–5. By comparison with firms reporting negligible innovation output, those with substantial innovation output are significantly different in their use of innovation inputs; the latter are significantly more likely than the former to have any staff engaged in R&D, to be engaged in R&D on a continuous as opposed to an occasional basis, and to enter into collaborative agreements. While fewer than 20 per cent of Cluster 6 firms report staff engaged in R&D, over 70 per cent of firms in Clusters 1–5 have staff engaged in R&D activity. And while 50 per cent of firms in Cluster 1–5 engage in R&D on a continuous basis, only 8 per cent of Cluster 6 firms do so. Cluster 6 firms spend 1.2 per cent of turnover on R&D on average by comparison with 3.4 per cent for the other clusters. Firms in Clusters 1–5 tend also to have a higher proportion of staff who are technically skilled than those in Cluster 6. Finally, it appears that Cluster 6 firms are significantly less likely than innovative firms to make use of information from outside sources including universities, as well as suppliers and customers, for the purposes of innovation. While this may simply reflect the fact that Cluster 6 firms are less likely to be engaged in innovation activity at all and hence that they are not seeking information for innovation, it could also mean that attempts to innovate in these firms are less likely to succeed due to the fact that they do not consult widely enough amongst external organizations. These results all point towards the conclusion that the innovation output reported by firms in Clusters 1–5 is not simply the result of 'a look in the suggestion box', but is rather the result of a considerable depth of costly innovative activity involving both internal and external searches for new technologies.

Amongst those SMEs which report substantial innovative output, there is considerable variation in the nature of innovative activity, both in terms of their characteristics and the inputs to and outputs from innovation. Cluster 5 is a distinctive group, containing a uniquely high proportion of business service firms. Innovation output in this group appears to be characterized by incremental innovation. Regarding inputs to innovation, Cluster 5 firms are less R&D-intensive and are less likely to make use of information from outside organizations by comparison with all other clusters of innovating firm. There also appear to be important differences between novel innovator firms, i.e. those which report novel product innovations, novel process innovations or both, and the main group of non-novel innovators, namely Cluster 4. In terms of their innovative output, novel innovators tend to report a higher proportion of sales consisting of new products and a lower proportion of sales consisting of upgraded products, though these differences are not generally significant. In terms of the inputs to innovation, novel innovators are less likely to rely on information from suppliers and customers, as well as from trade or professional journals, for their innovation than are non-novel innovators. Firms which introduce novel product innovations also tend to be more R&D-intensive than non-novel innovators, spending a higher proportion of turnover on R&D and having a significantly higher proportion of staff who are technologists, scientists, or higher professionals.

In terms of policy implications, it seems clear that policies which support the transfer of knowledge and skills to SMEs are likely to promote the incidence and extent of innovative activity in the sector. The Teaching Company Scheme, for example, which enables the employment of graduate engineers and scientists in SMEs is likely to have a positive impact on the capacity of SMEs to innovate. The evidence suggests that, by increasing the level of technical skill within a firm, this scheme would appear to have the potential to increase the probability either that the firm will innovate or that the firm will introduce a novel innovation. In addition, it is possible that the employment of people direct from university may promote the ongoing exchange of information and the transfer of technology between universities to firms which is also likely to promote SME innovation. In addition, measures that enable smaller firms to sustain adequate levels of R&D expenditure, such as those governing the rate of relief on capital expenditures for R&D (e.g. the Scientific Research Allowance) are likely to be important means to promote innovation in the SME sector. R&D appears to be a vital input to innovation not only in SMEs which introduce novel innovations. Even firms which do not report novel innovation are engaged in substantial R&D expenditure.

REFERENCES

ACOST (Advisory Council On Science and Technology) (1990), *The Enterprise Challenge: Overcoming Barriers to Growth in Small Firms*, London: HMSO.

Acs, Z. J. and Audretsch, D. B. (1988), Innovation in Large and Small Firms', *American Economic Review*, 78: 678–90.

—— —— (1991), 'Innovation and Size at the Firm Level', *Southern Economic Journal*, 57/3: 739–44.

Archibugi, D., Cesaratto, S., and Sirilli, G. (1991), 'Sources of Innovative Activities and Industrial Organization in Italy', *Research Policy*, 20: 299–313.

—— Evangelista, R., Perani, G., and Rapiti, F. (1997), 'Expenditure, Outcome and Nature of Innovation in Italy', Institute of Studies on Research and Scientific Documentation, and National Institute of Statistics, Italy, mimeo.

Baldwin, J. R. and Johnson, J. (1995), 'Human Capital Development and Innovation: The Case of Training in Small and Medium-Sized Firms', Micro-Economic Analysis Division, Statistics, Canada, mimeo.

Bolton, J. E. (1971), *Report of the Committee of Inquiry on Small Firms*, Cmnd. 4811, London: HMSO.

Bullock, A., Duncan, J., and Wood, E. (1996), 'The Survey Method, Sample Attrition and the SME Panel Database', in Cosh and Hughes (eds.), *The Changing State of British Enterprise*.

Butchart, R. L. (1987), 'A New UK Definition of High Technology Industries', *Economic Trends*, 400: 82–8.

Cesaratto, S., Mangano, S., and Massini, S. (1995), 'New Dimensions on Division of Labor: The case of Italy (1981–85)', in C. DeBresson (ed.), *Economic Interdependence and Innovative Activity: An Input-Output Analysis*, Aldershot: Edward Elgar.

Cohen, W. M. and Levin, R. C. (1989), 'Empirical Studies of Innovation and Market Structure', in R. Schmalensee and R. D. Willig (eds.), *Handbook of Industrial Organization*, II. 1060–1107.

Cosh, A. and Hughes, A. (eds.) (1996), *The Changing State of British Enterprise*, Cambridge: ESRC Centre for Business Research, University of Cambridge.

—— —— and Wood, E. (1997*a*), 'Innovation, International Competition and Export Performance in the British SME Sector', paper presented at the joint ESRC Centre for Business Research and Warwick Business School Conference on Innovation and Performance of Small and Medium-Sized Enterprises, Robinson College Cambridge, March.

—— —— —— (1997*b*), Innovation in UK SMEs: Causes and Consequences for Firm Failure and Acquisition in Z. J. Acs and B. Carlsson (eds.), *Entrepreneurship, SMEs and the Macro Economy*, Cambridge: Cambridge University Press.

European Commission (1995), 'Green Paper on Innovation', *Bulletin of the European Union*, suppl. 5/95.

Kitson, M. and Wilkinson, F. (1996), 'Markets and Competition', in Cosh and Hughes (eds.), *The Changing State of British Enterprise*.

Mansfield, E., Papoport, J., Schnee, S., Wagner, S., and Hamburger, M. (1971), *Research and Development in the Modern Corporation*, New York: Macmillan.

Moore, B. (1996), 'Sources of Innovation, Technology Transfer, and Diffusion', in Cosh and Hughes (eds.), *The Changing State of British Enterprise*.

Morrison, D. G. (1967), 'Measurement Problems in Cluster Analysis', *Management Science*, 13/12: B775–B780.

Mueller, D. C. (1988), 'The Corporate Life-Cycle', in S. Thompson and M. Wright (eds.), *Internal Organisation, Efficiency and Profit*, London: Phillip Allan, 38–64.

Nickell, S. and Nicolitsas, D. (1995), 'Does Doing Badly Encourage Management Innovation?', Paper prepared for the R&D, Innovation and Productivity Conference at the Institute of Fiscal Studies, London, May 15–16 1995.

Patel, P. and Pavitt, K. (1992), 'The Innovative Performance of the World's Largest Firms: Some New Evidence', *Economics of Innovation and New Technology*, 2: 91–102.

Pavitt, K. (1984), 'Sectoral Patterns of Technical Change: Towards a Taxonomy and a Theory', *Research Policy*, 13: 343–73.

—— Robson, M., and Townsend, J. (1987), 'The Size Distribution of Innovating Firms in the UK: 1945–1983', *Journal of Industrial Economics*, 35/3: 297–316.

—— —— —— (1989), 'Technological Accumulation, Diversification and Organisation in UK companies, 1945–1983', *Management Science*, 35: 81–99.

SBRC (Small Business Research Centre) (1992), *The State of British Enterprise: Growth, Innovation and Competitive Advantage in Small and Medium-Sized Firms*, Cambridge: SBRC.

Winter, S. G. (1984), 'Schumpetarian Competition in Alternative Technological Regimes', *Journal of Economic Behaviour and Organization*, 5 (Sept.–Dec.), 287–320.

APPENDIX 1. THE QUESTIONNAIRE
APPROACH TO INNOVATION

Innovation questions in the 1995 Survey

*In this section we would like you to tell us about your innovative activity. We are interested in innovation in products and processes which are **new to your firm.***

*In answering the questions in this section, please count innovation as occurring when a new or changed product is introduced to the market (product innovation) or when a new or significantly improved production method is used commercially (process innovation), and when **changes** in knowledge or skills, routines, competence, equipment, or engineering practices are required to make the new product or to introduce the new process.*

*Please do **not** count as product innovation, changes which are purely aesthetic (such as changes in colour or decoration), or which simply involve product differentiation (that is minor design or presentation changes which differentiate the product while leaving it technically unchanged in construction or performance).*

B1   Has your firm introduced any innovations in products (goods or services) or processes during the last three years which were new to your firm? (*Please tick only **one** box in **each** row*)

	Yes	No
Products		
Processes		

If you ticked No for *both* products and processes please skip B2–B6 and move onto question B7.

B2   If you introduced a product innovation, was it, to the best of your knowledge, already in use in other firms either in (a) your industry or (b) other industries? If you made more than one product innovation please answer with respect to your most important product innovation. (*Please tick only **one** box in **each** row*)

Product Innovation	Yes	No	Don't Know
(a) in use in your industry			
(b) in use in other industries			

B3   If you introduced a process innovation was it, to the best of your knowledge, already in use in other firms either in (a) your industry or (b) other industries? If you made more than one process innovation please answer with respect to your most important process innovation. (*Please tick only **one** box in **each** row*)

Product Innovation	Yes	No	Don't Know
(a) in use in your industry			
(b) in use in other industries			

B4 How were your firm's **total** sales in the last financial year distributed across the following types of products?

Products which were essentially technically unchanged in the last three years	%
Products whose technical characteristics have been enhanced or upgraded in the last three years	%
Newly-marketed products whose intended use, performance characteristics, technical construction, design, or use of materials and components was new or substantially changed in the last three years	%
Other products (Please specify):	%
Total sales last year	100%

Innovation question in the 1991 Survey

F1. Has your firm been successful in introducing any major innovations during the **last 5 years**? *tick as appropriate*

	Yes	No
In products or services		
In production processes		
In work practices, or workforce organisation		
In supply, storage or distribution systems		
In administration and office systems		

APPENDIX 2. TESTING THE SUITABILITY OF THE VARIABLES FOR THE PRE-CLUSTERING PRINCIPAL COMPONENT ANALYSIS

Explanation of variables used in the pre-clustering principal component analysis

Variable	Description	Values
PRCUSE31	Process innovation 1992–5 (new to your industry)	1 yes, 0 no
PRCUSE32	Process innovation 1992–5 (new to all industries)	1 yes, 0 no
PRCUSE31	Process innovation 1992–5 (new to your industry)	1 yes, 0 no
PRCUSE32	Process innovation 1992–5 (new to all industries)	1 yes, 0 no
PROC1C	Process innovation 1986–91	1 yes, 0 no
PROD1C	Process innovation 1986–91	1 yes, 0 no
PROC3	Process innovation 1992–5	1 yes, 0 no
PROD3	Process innovation 1992–5	1 yes, 0 no
SALPC32	Upgraded products as % 1995 sales	%
SALPC33	New products as % 1995 sales	%

Notes: 1. Kaiser-Meyer-Olkin Measure of Sampling Adequacy = .70659
2. Bartlett Test of Sphericity = 1365.8974, Significance = .00000

Factor matrix

	Factor 1	Factor 2	Factor 3	Factor 4
PRCUSE31	.59177	−.61075	.10417	−.12232
PRCUSE32	.55823	−.65927	.03896	−.08787
PRDUSE31	.69277	.16118	−.47345	−.08601
PRDUSE32	.68916	.09969	−.49902	−.05869
PROC1C	.39296	.35465	.53405	−.47711
PROD1C	.51683	.44299	.38103	−.23393
PROC3	.50743	−.33144	.43274	.24107
PROD3	.65533	.40533	−.13118	.19176
SALPC32	.29733	.20270	.28394	.77290
SALPC33	.47068	.04900	−.07719	.11061

Anti-image correlation matrix

	PRCUSE31	PRCUSE32	PRDUSE31	PRDUSE32	PROC1C	PROD1C	PROC3	PROD3	SALPC32	SALPC33
PRCUSE31	.65779									
PRCUSE32	-.53136	.63758								
PRDUSE31	-.22602	.09824	.71189							
PRDUSE32	.07045	-.25785	-.48290	.70672						
PROC1C	-.02062	.02465	.02377	.00600	.63599					
PROD1C	-.05005	.02106	-.09147	-.01634	-.39849	.71146				
PROC3	-.21030	-.17328	.06358	.05854	-.11959	-.03204	.75391			
PROD3	.08041	.08572	-.22134	-.23944	-.09892	-.11823	-.18575	.77613		
SALPC32	.01275	.01519	.02751	.00651	.09535	-.15213	-.14882	-.16172	.67284	
SALPC33	-.03208	-.07452	-.06610	-.02026	.00669	-.06856	-.04435	-.15398	-.00703	.88793

Note: Measures of Sampling Adequacy (MSA) are printed on the diagonal.

Final statistics

Variable	Communality	Factor	Eigenvalue	Pct of Var	Cum Pct
PRCUSE31	.74902	1	3.03511	30.4	30.4
PRCUSE32	.75550	2	1.48322	14.8	45.2
PRDUSE31	.73747	3	1.20700	12.1	57.3
PRDUSE32	.73735	4	1.02037	10.2	67.5
PROC1C	.79304				
PROD1C	.66326				
PROC3	.61272				
PROD3	.64772				
SALPC32	.80748				
SALPC33	.24213				

APPENDIX 3. RESULTS OF CLUSTER ANALYSIS USING 4 FACTORS IDENTIFIED IN APPENDIX 2

Final cluster centres

Cluster	FAC1_1	FAC2_1	FAC3_1	FAC4_1
1	1.6545	2.2389	.0089	−.2061
2	1.6851	−.7260	−.0151	−.3321
3	−.5932	2.2195	.1457	−.2737
4	−.3068	−.2074	.9909	.4969
5	−.2264	−.2335	−.8866	1.2430
6	−.6359	−.3489	−.4546	−.8191

Number of cases in each cluster

Cluster	Unweighted cases	Weighted cases
1	38.0	38.0
2	87.0	87.0
3	43.0	43.0
4	160.0	160.0
5	93.0	93.0
6	179.0	179.0
Missing	0	
Valid cases	600.0	600.0

APPENDIX 4. INNOVATOR TYPES BY INDUSTRY

Industry	Column percentages						
	Cluster 1 (n=37)	Cluster 2 (n=87)	Cluster 3 (n=43)	Cluster 4 (n=160)	Cluster 5 (n=93)	Cluster 6 (n=178)	All firms (n=598)
Metals	5.4	5.7	4.7	8.1	3.2	2.8	5.0
Chemicals	13.5	5.7	7.0	4.4	6.5	4.5	5.7
Mechanical engineering	27.0	18.4	16.3	20.0	10.8	17.4	17.7
Electrical engineering	8.1	11.5	4.7	9.4	3.2	2.8	6.4
Food processing	2.7	2.3	4.7	1.9	0.0	2.8	2.2
Textiles, clothing, footwear	0.0	5.7	11.6	5.0	2.2	9.0	6.0
Timber and furniture	0.0	2.3	4.7	6.9	1.1	6.7	4.7
Paper and pulp	2.7	5.7	7.0	10.0	2.2	11.2	7.9
All manufacturing	59.5	57.5	60.5	65.6	29.0	57.3	55.0
Management consulting and advertising	21.6	19.5	25.6	13.1	45.2	29.2	25.3
Technical and professional consulting	18.9	20.7	11.6	20.6	20.4	10.1	16.7
Other business services	0.0	2.3	2.3	0.6	5.4	3.4	2.5
All business services	40.5	42.5	39.5	34.4	71.0	42.7	45.0

Notes: Cluster 1: 'product and process originators'; Cluster 2: 'product originators'; Cluster 3: 'process origi-nators'; Cluster 4: 'product and process imitators'; Cluster 5: 'incremental product and process imitators'; Cluster 6: 'occasional imitators'.

7. Innovation Networks: The View from the Inside

Nick Oliver and Michelle Blakeborough*

Recent years have seen many claims that new models of industrial organization are emerging. These models encompass both operations and innovation, and have been variously labelled 'flexible specialisation' (Piore and Sabel, 1984) 'the Japanese model' (Schonberger, 1982) and 'lean production' (Womack, Jones, and Roos, 1990), to name but three. The basic tenets of these models vary, but they share certain common features. Of particular interest here are the *interfirm relationships* claimed by the new models.

Piore and Sabel's (1984) work alleges the demise of the large corporation as a major centre of production and innovation. Based on observations of 'industrial districts', Piore and Sabel argue for the supremacy of *networks* of relatively small firms, capable of rapidly configuring themselves to meet fragmenting and rapidly changing market demands. Piore and Sabel argue that this system provides the benefits of specialization previously thought to be the prerogative of very large corporations, without the inflexibility endemic to large-scale, hierarchically controlled structures. More recently, Sturgeon (1997) argues that debates about industrial competitiveness have shifted away from questions about the internal structures of corporations towards co-operative interactions between firms.

This shift has been driven partly by 'success' stories from a number of regions of the world. These include Japan (Dore, 1986; Kenney and Florida, 1993; Sako, 1992; Womack, Jones, and Roos, 1990) and Germany and Italy (Piore and Sabel, 1984). East Asia has attracted particular attention, with several authors arguing that an alternative form of 'network capitalism' has emerged, radically different in form and superior in performance to Anglo–American forms (Orru, Biggart, and Hamilton, 1997; Hampden Turner, 1997).

These claims have several threads to them. The Japanese model draws heavily on the example of the automotive industry and tends to focus on the role of suppliers and smaller firms in supporting *production*. However, the fact that first-tier Japanese automotive suppliers typically play a much greater

* The authors gratefully acknowledge the contribution of their colleagues on the ION project at the Universities of Bath, Brighton, and Cambridge, namely John Bessant, James Callaghan, Christine Harland, Marie Kenney, Thomas Johnson, Richard Lamming, and Jurong Zheng. This research is supported by EPSRC grant no. GR/L21617.

role in the development of new-product development has not gone unnoticed (Clark and Fujimoto, 1991; Nishiguchi, 1994). In other regions, *innovation* has received more attention than production, examples being the industrial districts of Northern Italy, the Baden-Württemburg region of Germany, and Silicon Valley in California.

Interest in these regions has been fuelled by the perception that these spatially concentrated, apparently co-operative networks of small to medium-sized firms typically out-perform more traditional models of industrial organization based on competitive relations between large, vertically integrated firms. The network model is characterized by individual firms who possess a restricted set of core competencies and who rely on a wider network of firms for other inputs. Clearly, such interdependencies create the need for different interfirm relations to the short-term competitive ones which have traditionally been the norm in many Western economies.

In this respect, Sako (1992) contrasts Japanese and British interfirm relations distinguishing between 'obligational' contracting relations in Japan, and traditional 'adversarial' relations in Britain. The former permit the sharing of experience, knowledge, and other resources, and facilitate learning and technology transfer within networks of firms. In addition, it is argued that network systems have the ability to readily reconfigure themselves to address changing requirements of existing markets and/or the emergence of new ones. Some commentators predict the rise of the 'virtual corporation', where international brand names front a myriad of independently owned firms engaged in the productive process. Bennetton is a commonly cited example of this.

The alleged benefits of partnerships and collaborations are not unique to small firms. The president of Procter and Gamble (Europe) recently outlined the benefits of the network model to P&G. These included greater access to resources, such as skills and expertise; greater access to markets via partnerships in retailing and distribution; the enhancement of image (as shown by P&G's latest strategy of partnering with leading-label clothing firms to advertise washing powders); and cost reduction (Einsmann, 1997).

NEW-PRODUCT DEVELOPMENT

Although the difficulties of developing collaborative supply chains in a Western context have received some attention (Lamming, 1993; Oliver and Wilkinson, 1992; Sako, 1992), the issues involved in *new-product development* within network structures have hitherto received less attention. This may be because there is less networked R&D than there is production; issues of commercial sensitivity are clearly significant where R&D is concerned, and firms may be reticent to co-operate with others because of this.

In addition, it is well recognized that new-product development, even within the individual firm, represents a major challenge. The reasons for this include the non-routine nature of new-product development, and the need to co-ordinate a range of specialist skills—typically inputs are needed from marketing, purchasing, industrial design, a variety of engineering disciplines, and production. This situation may generate acute integration problems within the individual firm due to the heightened interdependency between functions during the development process. Differences in orientation between disciplines with respect to time scales, structuring of activities, and other issues may all lead to tensions which the new-product development process may surface.

These problems are likely to be greatly exacerbated when multiple firms are involved in the new-product development process. In addition to the usual problems, there are issues of the ownership of intellectual property, ambiguity about authority relations between the players, and interfirm, as well as interfunctional, cultural differences. If the development process involves firms from different nations, then differences in national culture may represent a further complication.

INTERFIRM NETWORKS

Despite the above problems, successful systems of innovation are frequently characterized by well-established contacts with external sources, i.e. 'networks' of relationships. The identification of innovative regions such as Baden-Württemberg and Silicon Valley have led to a number of attempts to reproduce such conditions elsewhere, science parks being a prime example.

A number of definitions of networks exist. Social networks were first identified and studied in anthropological studies in the 1950s. The term 'network' was used to refer to a structural picture of a community which identified the relationships surrounding each individual, creating a model of the linkages in the whole population. 'Business' networks (Forsgren and Johanson 1992) refer to exchange relationships between actors controlling business activities. Jarillo's (1988) 'strategic' networks differ from business networks in that strategic networks are set up by a 'hub' firm which then actively manages the network in order to gain advantage over competitors. The terms 'strategic' and 'business' do not necessarily incorporate other relationships that may play an important part in an innovation system. For example, social-expressive relationships such as friends at the golf or Rotary club may play an informal role, perhaps by providing advice, assistance, or introductions.

When investigating innovation networks it is useful to consider two different types of network: collaborations *actively* set up by a firm in order to develop a new product; and the *backcloth* of multiple networks that surround the firm. Monsted (1993) distinguishes between three types of network: (1) networks for service and assistance—e.g. providing technical services and giving access to equipment to borrow; (2) networks for information and structuring—the collection of information, through formal as well as informal channels of information, and the evaluation of information received; (3) networks for entrepreneurship and product development.

Clearly, there are a large number of networks of which a firm can be a member. When technological change is advancing rapidly, firms must keep abreast of developments in order to stay competitive. It is therefore critical for innovative firms to be within networks that provide such intelligence. Lindquist (1996) found that in addition to 'harder' networks that were transactionally based, successful businesses also regarded 'softer' networks as important. These included:

- informal relationships—industry forums, conferences, and other soft networks for information sharing;
- links with staff from customers and suppliers;
- community involvement—sponsorship of local activities;
- community networks.

Firms may thus need not only to manage their strategic networks, but also to place themselves strategically in others, and it is reasonable to suppose that any given firm will have a network configuration appropriate to its particular needs. Lindquist cites the following motives for firms becoming involved in the collaborative relationships that underpin interfirm networks:

- the need for complementary technologies;
- cost or risk sharing;
- access to new markets.

Lack of trust often lies behind the reluctance of firms to enter into collaborative relationships. Powell, Koput, and Smith-Doerr (1996) identify several issues including an unwillingness to relinquish control, the complexity of joint projects, and differential abilities to learn new skills. Additional worries concern commercial sensitivity, leakage of information, and possible conflicts over intellectual property rights. On the other hand, the need to move into global, quickly changing markets, and the increasing requirements for diverse ranges of knowledge are intensifying the pressure on firms to work together. This is particularly true in new product development. R&D is an expensive resource and complex products that cross organizational boundaries of expertise necessitate large investments, making it more practical either to contract out parts of the process or to conduct joint developments with partners.

NETWORKS AND INNOVATION

A supportive local environment has been identified as one requirement for successful innovation, particularly for small to medium-sized enterprises. In his study of three Swedish firms Lindquist (1996) noted that the degree of interaction with other firms is dependent on the *stage* of the innovation process in question. Lindquist uses the model of innovation developed by Ghoshal and Bartlett (1988), who divide the innovation process into three stages:

Stage 1: sensing (i.e. the development of ideas);
Stage 2: response (development of product and processes);
Stage 3: implementation (exploitation).

Lindquist argues that broad, geographically dispersed networks consisting of many players are required in the 'sensing' and 'implementation' phases of the innovative process, but that a smaller, narrower network is more common during the 'response' stage, giving the number of players involved in the process over time an 'hour-glass' shape (i.e. relatively high at the beginning and end of the process, and relatively low in the middle).

Many of the initiatives to encourage innovation networks fall into the sensing stage of innovation (Solvell and Bresman, 1995). In many countries 'technopolitan strategies' such as the development of science parks and specialized research centres have been seen as ways of encouraging industry–university and other ties at a regional level (Chorda, 1995), in order to develop a 'technology culture' (Gwynne, 1996). In some countries governments have introduced public policies to encourage co-operation between firms with varying levels of success, highlighting cultural differences. Centres set up in Italy with government support, for example, strengthened existing ties and co-operation. In Denmark, policies to encourage networks were introduced in the hope that firms would become more open to working together in the long-term if initially encouraged to do so by government financial support. In the USA, both models have been used: the Danish model of network facilitators and grants to three or more firms involved in collaborative activity; and the Italian model of giving money to regional trade associations to play a proactive role in encouraging collaboration between their members (Rosenfeld, 1996).

Multifirm new-product development tends to be more common in sectors such as high-technology products and pharmaceuticals, industries in which small firms are able to react more quickly to technological changes than their larger counterparts (Pearson and Powell, 1996). In Hagedoorn's (1995) study of trends in strategic technology partnering he observes that 70 per cent of collaborations are in the sectors of IT, biotechnology, and new materials. From these collaborations large firms gain access to knowledge, and small firms access to finance to bring them to market. However, there are many possible types of relationship. The forms these may take include information exchange, collaboration to reduce risk or cost, transfer of technology, industry forums, and strategic alliances.

Although there have been policies to encourage firms to develop collaborative relationships, little has been done to find ways to help them to tailor the network structure to their own requirements, or to manage these relationships. It is likely that factors such as location, industrial sector, size of firm, and geographical dispersion of the network will all affect the character of the network. The rest of this chapter presents the findings of a preliminary study of networks of firms involved in new product development in the UK, and draws out some of the key issues in this area. Specifically, the chapter addresses five questions:

1. What are the characteristics of interfirm networks across a range of new-product development projects?
2. Why do firms choose to develop new products using a network, rather than developing products in-house?
3. What are the issues involved in setting up a new-product development network?
4. What are the main operational issues which emerge in networked development projects?
5. What are the main factors which appear to facilitate or impede the success of such projects?

The approach used to address these questions is described in the section which follows.

RESEARCH METHODS

In the first stage of the study, personnel from five UK technology consulting firms, all of whom were involved in multifirm new-product development, were interviewed in a semi-structured manner. The purpose of this was to gain an overview of the area, and identify recently completed multifirm new-product development projects.

Next, seven recently completed new-product development projects involving several firms were identified, and interviews conducted with one or two individuals involved with the project, typically (but not exclusively) the project leaders in the 'core' firm. The interviews followed a semi-structured format. All the 'core' firms were located in the UK as, it transpired, were the majority of other players in each network.

RESULTS

The characteristics of the companies and projects are shown in Table 7.1.

Table 7.1. Project and company characteristics

Network	Size of main player	Time scale of project (months)	Number of players
A	Large	12	7
B	Large	72	6
C	Small	60	5
D	Small	3	6
E	Small	26	5
F	Large	18	8
G	Large	36	13

As Table 7.1 shows, the projects were of a similar size in terms of the number of players, varying from five to thirteen firms, but varied considerably in terms of the time scale of project—from three months up to six years. Size of main player was a little difficult to assess, as some of the main players were divisions of very large multinational firms, although effectively only the division was the main player in most cases. The differences in project time scales are partly due to the nature of the product itself. As Table 7.2 shows, some of the products involved medical applications and for these there was a lengthy process of testing and approval before the products could be launched.

The nature of the research design meant that some products were excluded from the study. Specifically, very simple products requiring a limited range of expertise to develop them, or reliant on one or two similar technologies, could

Table 7.2. Products covered by the study

Network	Product
A	Beer widget
B	Medical monitoring
C	Anesthetic
D	Scientific instrument I
E	Scientific instrument II
F	Printer
G	Chemical labelling system

not be selected for the study as they were unlikely to have required a network of firms for their development.

Table 7.3 shows the players in two of the networks studied in more detail, one producing the 'widget' to go inside a beer can to produce a head on the beer, the other a scientific instrument.

Table 7.3. Players in two networks

Network A	Network B
Brewery	Biological analysis company
Technology consultants	University laboratory
Can manufacturer	Electronics company
Metal component manufacturer	Software company
Electrocoating company	Computer company
Glue manufacturer	Printer supplier
Plastic insert manufacturer	

Why a network approach?

The main reasons cited by the respondents for using a network of firms to develop a product, rather than doing all the work in-house, included:

- the time available to carry out the development;
- a need for expertise which was not possessed by the company who had the idea in the first place;
- the use of external services because they were cheaper;
- scale of project, which was seen to be beyond the resources of some of the smaller firms.

Interestingly, the majority of firms reported that if they could have developed the product themselves, they would have done. Only a minority of firms actively and positively chose the network form of product development, a point to which we return below.

The choice of network partners was made in a variety of ways. Some firms went for a relatively 'hands-off' and formal approach, soliciting price quotations from a number of firms, sometimes after drawing up formal search criteria and conducting a mail shot to would-be partners. Despite the rhetoric of long-term collaboration and partnership common in the literature, this process often came over as 'arms-length' and focused very much on the specific transaction. In a telling piece of imagery, one firm likened the selection of partners to the purchase of a second-hand car, with the would-be purchaser walking round 'kicking the tyres'. The ritualistic nature of the exercise is also of interest; kicking the tyres actually tells one very little about what one is purchasing, but may be done more for the benefit of onlookers.

Personal referrals and contacts also figured quite highly in the selection process and became more significant as time pressure on projects mounted. For example, it was not uncommon for a firm initially selected by formal means to fail to deliver, whereupon there would be a frantic search for a replacement. Under such circumstances, informal methods of selection and personal contacts became much more significant. Firms with less experience in working collaboratively frequently underestimated the difficulty in picking partners.

If they are ignorant of [outsourcing] they tend to think its simple . . . just get someone in for nine months to do it.

Setting up the network

During the establishment of these networks a number of issues arose. Somewhat counterintuitively, one of the firms argued that it was important to have the basic skills needed in-house before one even contemplated outsourcing them. The rationale behind this was that unless one had the ability to assess how a partner was doing, it was very difficult to know if they were capable of the job, or indeed to monitor their progress. This suggests that network partners should be enhancements to the skills of existing players, rather than simple substitutes for them. Another firm stressed the importance of complementarity of skills (and agendas) between the partners. In situations where the partners were too similar (or when one had entered into the collaboration specifically to learn enough from the other to be able to do it themselves next time) territorial issues and defensive routines were a risk.

The establishment of contracts varied considerably from network to network, and varied partly, as one might expect, according to the length that the network had been established, and the frequency with which the various partners had worked with each other before. Here competing forces were apparent. On one hand, the establishment of formal contracts served to reduce uncertainty, and to set out the rules of the game in a reasonably unambiguous way to the various players. On the other hand, the need to get the projects moving quickly militated against lengthy contract negotiations and could introduce a degree of formality and awkwardness to the relationship at an early stage, with one patent attorney likening contracts to 'pre-nuptial agreements'. The patent attorney argued that if there were more 'pre-nuptuals' there may be fewer collaborations *per se*, but especially fewer unsuccessful ones. The problem of partner selection was clearly aggravated by the fact that some of the firms contracted work out only when they did not have time to carry out the development themselves, which also meant that there was little time to devote to search and selection.

Relationships

Three main types of relationship were observed; a relatively formal, contractual approach; partnerships based on a shared-risk model; and a model whose main purpose was to generate intellectual property to be exploited via licences or royalties by the core players, but where the product would ultimately be produced by spin-off companies. The first model was most apparent where the core player was a relatively large and powerful firm who wanted to ensure its unequivocal ownership of the product and the process, or when some of the players (for example some of the consulting firms) wished to minimize their exposure to risk. As one firm put it:

'Clean relationships are the ones we like—not ones where the work comes in dribs and drabs . . . We want to get in and get out.'

'So much of the process is outside our control; we'd really have to trust so many people . . . fixed prices or royalties are too risky.'

Most companies preferred partners located in the same country, and as Table 7.4 shows this is what most of them chose. Those partners that tended to be outside the UK were typically involved in marketing and distribution, although in two cases manufacturing occurred outside the UK.

The main advantage of UK partners reported by the firms was the greater ease of problem-solving compared to overseas partners. Consequently, project management was much easier, particularly when time scales were short, and when there was process as well as product innovation:

Table 7.4. Number of players by country of location

Country	A	B	C	D	E	F	G
UK	7	5	3	5	3	4	10
Austria		1					
Germany			1				2
USA			1	2	1		
Holland					1		
Sweden						2	
Estonia						1	
Ireland						1	
Japan							1
TOTAL	7	6	5	7	5	8	13

The bit that everyone forgets is that you have a new process . . . [you should develop] the process close to home until it is a turnkey process.

However, some firms reported that it was much more important to ensure that the partner had the relevant expertise than for them to be located nearby. In addition, apparently minor factors (such as time differences and differences between US and Imperial measures) proved to be surprisingly troublesome.

Language and cultural differences frequently emerged as issues, with two firms reporting difficulties in dealing with French and German partners. For one firm, one of the cultural differences with Germany was epitomized by a comment made by their German partner during a discussion about trust at an early stage of their collaboration:

To trust is good, but to control is better.

Facilitating the network

There were clear differences in approaches to project management by large and small firms. In general, larger firms operating within tighter time scales, and on projects necessitating close interaction between players advocated transparent management techniques. Such transparency typically took the form of practices such as involving all of the players at an early stage to try to establish shared goals and ownership of the project. Smaller firms, in contrast, either had longer-term, more open relationships, or brought in players on an *ad hoc* basis, as and when needed. The main reason for this difference seemed to be that larger companies tended to consider themselves to be the 'hub' of the network and assumed ownership of the project, whereas the smaller firms saw their relationships with other players in terms of partnerships. Another factor was the product itself. Those projects with clear management processes were characterized by combinations of expertise that needed to be dovetailed together, in contrast to projects of a linear nature or those which could easily be broken into modules with less need for interaction.

Problem areas

A number of the firms were less than happy with the new-product development process in their networked projects. In all cases the projects went through to launch, and the products enjoyed success in the market place. However, most observers felt that the process had been beset by frustrations and inefficiencies. Our overwhelming impression was that most firms (although not all) had adopted the multifirm product development model because they were unable to develop the product themselves, or because short time scales meant that they had insufficient time to do so. It may be overstating it to say that all outsourced product development was a 'distress purchase', but there certainly was an element of this in many cases. A number of respondents commented that if they could have carried out the development themselves they would have done, and that for them the complexities and difficulties of the dispersed model far outweighed stand-alone new-product development.

In addition to the problems of project management, another area of complexity in a network concerns ownership of intellectual property. It was striking that in those networks where more than one player was interviewed, everyone seemed to regard their firm as the most important player in the project. This was a particular problem for some of the technology consultancies, who on the one hand needed to demonstrate the importance of their contribution to other potential clients, yet at the same time had to keep their existing clientele happy As one commented:

Its very easy to get a large amount of publicity and completely piss-off the client . . . You get the publicity but screw up the relationship—which is the more valuable?

Interfirm relations seemed to be less problematic when the network comprised firms of approximately equal size. Where relatively small firms were dealing with a relatively large one, sensitivities were much higher and the smaller firms lived in constant fear of having their intellectual property expropriated by the larger:

Problems arise when relationships are unequal, or when Company A claims something from the relationship that's not there.

Another interviewee described large firm/small firm collaborations as 'unnatural matings' with all the dangers of 'accidental squashings' when one of the parties was vastly larger than the other.

Although three different models of benefit and risk-sharing could be seen, these were rarely articulated explicitly. The predominant mechanism was the arm's-length, contractual arrangement, albeit one which was increasingly mediated by personal contacts as time pressures bore down on the projects. Here a certain degree of schizophrenia was apparent on the part of some of the players, particularly some of the consultancies. There was a basic conflict between a desire for greater ownership and benefit-sharing on the one hand, but a fear of risk exposure in a situation where the final outcome was dependent on the efforts of many players whom one could not control.

The sharing of benefits via royalties was unusual, and was a particular concern to small firms interacting with large ones. For small firms with an innovative idea, entering into a licensing or royalty agreement with a large one could spell disaster if the large firm subsequently decided not to pursue the innovation. We came across patent attorneys moving into high-tech areas, specifically to pick up business dealing with such issues. Similarly, despite the rhetoric of collaboration, in some cases the reality fell short of this. When one of our firms asked one of its collaborators about cost transparency, they were told:

Of course its open, we tell you what the total costs are.

CONCLUSION

This chapter has presented the preliminary findings of a study into multifirm product development. Clearly, many of these findings are inevitably impressionistic, but they do give a flavour of the reality of innovation networks as seen from the inside. The motivations of the players in the collaborations covered by this study varied considerably. Smaller firms tended to look to larger firms in terms of market access and, occasionally, finance. The larger firms looked to collaborative projects when time scales were short and they did not have time to do the development themselves, or when they needed access to a knowledge base which could be best brought in from outside.

When time was not too short a semi-rational approach to search and development could be seen; as time pressures mounted, informal, personal contacts were increasingly used. Larger firms tended to set up networks on a project-by-project basis, and also favoured the semi-rational methods of search and selection described earlier. Smaller firms typically preferred personal contacts, and some sustained these even when no major development was underway. This allowed some to pursue what may be termed the 'moving train' model of development. Under this model, firms constantly interact and exchange information, even in the absence of a major project. This has the benefit of establishing a 'relationship infrastructure', which can then greatly facilitate the execution of major projects when they arise. The 'bottle of whisky at Christmas' syndrome is one example of this. Some firms reported that they never worked with a partner firm on a large project until they had worked with that firm on a number of small projects.

A further issue was the difficulty of conflict resolution in a networked project. Although in-house projects with major divisions between functions are not immune from this, the absence of an authority structure in a network can seriously impede recovery from unforeseen problems. Without recourse to a higher body to resolve the issue, buck-passing was often the result. There were a number of ways in which this issue was addressed. The establishment of clear roles and responsibilities at the start of a project was one tactic, and setting up management structures (such as steering committees who review progress on a regular basis) was another.

Contrary to popular opinion, this study found little evidence of the rise of the 'virtual product development' team. Although a variety of IT and other communication tools exist to facilitate interaction between geographically dispersed players, the companies in this study showed a clear preference for spatial concentration. Some activities, in particular problem-solving in the later stages of a project, proved notoriously difficult to execute other than on a face-to-face basis. Thus, although some companies were clearly more IT-literate than others, and therefore better able to deal with the problem of geographical dispersion, the face-to-face meeting, with all that it implies for how networks operate and are co-ordinated seems set to be a feature of multifirm product development projects for the foreseeable future.

REFERENCES

Chorda, I. S. (1995), Technopolitan Strategies: At the Edge of an Innovation-Driven Territorial Approach, *International Journal of Technology Management*, 10/7–8: 894–906.

Clark, K. B. and Fujimoto, T. (1991), *Product Development Performance*, Boston: Harvard Business School Press.

Dore, R. (1986), *Flexible Rigidities*, London: Athlone.

Einsmann, H. (1997), 'Creating Winning Relationships between Companies', The Arthur Andersen Lecture, University of Cambridge, 19 March.

Forsgren, M. and Johanson, J. (1992), 'Managing Internationalization in Business Networks', in M. Forsgren and J. Johanson (eds.), *Managing Networks in International Business*, Philadelphia: Gordon and Breach, 1–16.

Ghoshal, S. and Bartlett, C. A. (1988), 'Innovation Processes in Multinational Corporations', in M. L. Tushman and W. L. Moore (eds.), *Readings in the Management of Innovation*, Cambridge, Mass.: Ballinger Publishing Company.

Gwynne, P. (1996), 'Brittany Positions Itself to Attract Telecom R&D', *R&D Magazine* (Aug.) 34–5.

Hagedoorn, J. (1995), 'Strategic Technology Partnering During the 1980s: Trends, Networks and Corporate Patterns in Non-Core Technologies', *Research Biology*, 24: 207–31.

Hampden Turner, C., *Masters of the Infinite Game*, Oxford: Capstone.

Jarillo, J. C. (1988), 'On Strategic Networks', *Strategic Management Journal*, 9: 31–41.

Kenney, M. and Florida, R. (1993), *Beyond Mass Production: The Japanese System and its Transfer to the US*, Oxford: Oxford University Press.

Lamming, R. (1993), *Beyond Partnership: Strategies for Innovation and Lean Supply*, New York: Prentice Hall.

Lindquist, M. (1996), 'Innovation Networks Among Small Firms', *41st ICSB Conference Proceedings*, Stockholm, June 17–19.

Mönsted, M. (1993), 'Regional Network Processes: Networks for Service Sector or Development of Entrepreneurs? in C. Karlsson, B. Johannisson, and D. Storey (eds.), *Small Business Dynamics: International, National and Regional Perspectives*, London and New York: Routledge.

Nishiguchi, T. (1994), *Strategic Industrial Sourcing: The Japanese Advantage*, New York and Oxford: Oxford University Press.

Oliver, N. and Wilkinson, B. (1992), *The Japanization of British Industry: Developments in the 1990s*, Oxford: Blackwell.

Orru, M., Biggart, N., and Hamilton, G. G. (1997), *The Economic Organization of East Asian Capitalism*, Thousand Oaks, Calif. and London: Sage.

Pearson, A. and Powell, C. (1996), 'Innovation Management: Inter-firm Relationships', *41st ICSB Conference Proceedings*. Stockholm, June 17–19.

Piore, M. and Sabel, C. (1984), *The Second Industrial Divide*, New York: Basic Books.

Powell, W. W., Koput, K. W., and Smith-Doerr, L. (1996), 'Interorganisational Collaboration and the Locus of Innovation: Networks of Learning in Biotechnology', *Administrative Science Quarterly*, 41: 116–45.

Rosenfeld, S. A. (1996), 'Does Co-operation Enhance Competitiveness? Assessing the Impacts of Inter-firm Collaboration', *Research Policy*, 25: 247–63.

Sako, M. (1992), *Prices, Quality and Trust: Inter-firm Relations in Britain and Japan*, Cambridge: Cambridge University Press.

Schonberger, R. (1982), *Japanese Manufacturing Techniques*, New York: Free Press.

Solvell, O. and Bresman, H. (1995), 'Hour-Glass Innovation in the Multinational Enterprise: Between Heterarchy and Home Base', Presented at 21st EIBA Annual Conference, Italy, Dec.

Sturgeon, T. J. (1997), 'Turnkey Production Networks: The Organizational Delinking of Production from Innovation', International Conference on New Product Development and Production Networks, Berlin, 20–22 Mar.

Womack, J. P., Jones D. T., and Roos, D. (1990), *The Machine that Changed the World: The Triumph of Lean Production*, New York: Rawson Macmillan.

8. Innovation in Consumption and Economic Growth*

G. M. Peter Swann

1. INTRODUCTION

Economic analysis of the effects of innovation on economic growth has focused almost exclusively on the supply side. Most of the literature examines the effects of innovative activity by producers, whether in the form of process innovations or product innovations. How do process innovations impact on productivity? What is the value of product innovations? But we argue in this chapter that the consumer is also an innovator, and we need to have an understanding of how innovation in consumption impacts on economic growth. While the traditional literature looks at innovation and the production function, the aim of this chapter is to take a very preliminary look at the effects on innovation on the utility function. While there are some pioneering analyses of consumer innovation in the literature, this chapter is written in the spirit that these need to be gathered into a more coherent theory of innovation in consumption.[1]

It is helpful to distinguish three sorts of innovation. First, the pure producer innovation, for which there is already a ready market. This comprises, for example, the new improved version of an existing product or a cheaper version of an existing product which does not compromise quality. For such an innovation to find a market calls for little if any innovation on the part of the consumer. The consumer simply buys the new good, reads the instructions, and follows them. At the other extreme is the pure consumer innovation. One example of this is the new original recipe. A consumer (as cook) turns ordinary foodstuffs into a new dish by combining them in a new and original way. Another example is where the consumer uses a piece of software in a new way that was not envisaged by the producer. In both these cases, it is fair to say that the consumer is being innovative. The consumer does *not* simply read the instructions; he or she does things that aren't written down in the instructions.

---

* This chapter draws on work carried out with Robin and Bill Cowan, described in Cowan, Cowan, and Swann (1997), but neither of those co-authors is responsible for any errors here.

[1] Notably the work of Becker, summarized in Becker (1996), and encompassing household production theory. A slightly different strand of work—notably von Hippel (1988)—recognizes that consumers are an important source of innovative ideas for producers. Barnett (1953) is a classic anthropological study of innovation.

An intermediate, or mixed case is where both producers and consumers are being innovative. One example of this is the sort of producer innovation for which there will only be a market if consumption patterns evolve. A radically new fashion will only find a market if the consumer chooses to alter his or her taste in dress. This may happen because of a desire for distinction or variety. In this case, the consumer is innovative in the sense that he or she is a consumer of innovations—but *not* a creator of innovations. There is an analogy here with technology transfer in production. In that context the producer adopts a technology that is new to the firm, but has been developed elsewhere. In this context, the consumer adopts an innovation that is new to him or her, but has been developed elsewhere.

Section 2 of the chapter summarizes the main ways in which innovation is analysed in the production literature. Section 3 sets out the first part of a simple framework for analysing the effect of innovation in consumption on the utility function. Section 4 looks at one path of innovation in consumption, recognized by Marshall. Section 5 looks at a similar but more general path of innovative activity—related to the four forces of sustenance, association, distinction and aspiration in consumption behaviour. Section 6 sets out the second part of the framework for analysing the effects of innovation in consumption on the utility function. Sections 7 and 8 examine the macroeconomic significance of these innovations. Section 7 looks at the effect of innovation in consumption upon economic growth. Section 8 looks at the effects of innovation in consumption on inflation. Section 9 concludes.

2. INNOVATION AND PRODUCTION

In the economic and management literature, almost all analysis of the effects of innovation have focused on the supply side. Various strands of analysis have been pursued:

- analysis of production function residuals as a measure of technical change;
- analysis of R&D as an input to the production function;
- micro or engineering analyses of how process innovations shift production isoquants;
- micro analyses of the benefits of new products;
- econometric demand analyses that value new or improved products.

The analyses of process innovations can be summarized as follows, using a conventional cost function approach:

$$\text{Effect of process innovation} = c_1(x\ ;\ r) - c_0(x\ ;\ r),$$

where $c_0(.)$ and $c_1(.)$ are the production functions before and after the process innovation, x is a given (target) level of output and r is a vector of factor prices. The effect of the process innovation is measured as the reduction in the cost of producing output x at factor prices r.

In the case of new products, the approach is slightly different. Here we measure not so much the cost of production but compare the value of the new product (z_1) and the old (z_0) from the perspective of a representative consumer:

$$\text{Effect of product innovation} = g(u,p\ ;\ z_1) - g(u,p\ ;\ z_0),$$

where $g(.)$ is the consumer's conditional cost function, u is a target level of utility, p is a vector of product prices, and the vectors z_0 and z_1 describe the characteristics of the old and new products, respectively. The value of the product innovation is measured here as the extent to which it reduces the cost of reaching utility u.

The first case looks at innovations in the producer cost function; the second looks at the effect of product changes on a given consumer cost function.

3. INNOVATION IN CONSUMPTION: PART 1

Moving to the consumer context, the equivalent of the process innovation is easy to describe in abstract terms, as this section demonstrates. At first sight, however, there does not seem to be an equivalent to the product innovation: after all, from the perspective of modern economic consumption theory, the consumer produces one output only—utility. But on reflection, and looking forward to some of the key Marshallian concepts about consumption (in Sections 4 and 5), we can find an equivalent to the product innovation (Section 6).

What we are concerned about in this section is the effect of innovation on the utility function or the consumer cost function. The effect of consumer innovation could—in principle at least—be measured as:

$$\text{Effect of innovation by consumer} = g_1(u\ ;\ p) - g_0(u\ ;\ p)$$

where, as above, $g(.)$ is the consumer's cost function, u is a target level of utility, and p is a vector of product prices. The equation measures the extent to which innovation in consumption reduces the cost of achieving utility u. There is one potential difficulty here. Given that target utility u is normally treated as an ordinal index of indifference, and not a cardinal measure of welfare, there would appear to be some problems in comparing u scores before and after innovation. We can get around these problems, however, if we think of u as a target level of enjoyment—for example: a nourishing and enjoyable meal for two parents and two children. A new recipe which reduces the cost of preparing such a meal would count as a consumer innovation.

This example of a new recipe leads us naturally into the theory of household production, one of the main attempts within economics to analyse consumer innovation. Here the household combines goods and services with family labour to produce enjoyment. Indeed, by treating consumption as a production activity, we could use the measures of Section 2 above to analyse the effects of those process and product innovations introduced by the household.

But are such consumer innovations actually all that common? We would argue that the following examples could all be couched in terms of this framework. When consumers collect stamps, they take items that are often of modest value, combine them in an original and interesting way, and create a stamp collection of some value. The same logic applies to other forms of collecting, where the aim is to create a whole which is worth more than the sum of its parts. This would include collections of books, coins, antiques, memorabilia, and so on. Indeed, in some cases, such as train-spotting, the 'items' that are collected are of almost no value in themselves, while the collection is all.

Another group of examples are where the consumer turns objects of no value (often waste objects) into something of value in use—even if not of market value. Thus children can often create new games by combining old toys and other objects in a new and innovative way. The gardener uses plastic PET bottles as miniature cloches in which to grow cuttings. Some resourceful householders have made original furniture from waste items of wood, metal, and even glass bottles. Some rather stark examples of this are found in the study of subcultures. As described by Hebdige (1979), the aim of style innovation is to use everyday objects in a new and original way, and to imbue these objects with a new meaning. Members of the subculture use style innovation to reinforce their membership of the group.[2]

In all of these cases, the consumer is being innovative by creating enjoyment or added value by combining objects in a new way. The objects may or may not have some value on their own, but the value of the whole is greater than the sum of its parts. The parent manages to keep the family happy at low cost. The collector creates a collection of value from items that are unremarkable on their own. The fashionable youth achieves a style to impress his or her peer group at low cost. Looking at these from a cost function perspective, all these forms of innovation offer cheaper ways of reaching u from a given price list, and as such are analogous to the process innovation. But the consumer is also capable of the equivalent of product innovation. To understand this we need first to revisit Marshall's concept of a consumer.

---

[2] The anthropologist Mary Douglas has said that 'the real moment of choosing is . . . choice of comrades and their way of life' (quoted in Becker, 1996). Frank's (1985) study of *Choosing the Right Pond* can be seen in the same vein. From this perspective, consumption of goods is a way of associating with 'comrades' (or peers). An innovation in consumption is, then, a new way of using commodities to cement social relationships.

4. THE MARSHALLIAN CONSUMER

The average consumer in a developed society would expect u to rise over time. So while the aim is still to achieve u at least cost, the target is rising. A more important observation is that the ways of achieving increased u may change significantly as the target rises. Marshall recognized this in an important passage about the consumer:[3]

every step in his progress upwards increases the variety of his needs together with the variety in his methods of satisfying them. He desires not merely larger *quantities* of the things he has been accustomed to consume, but better qualities of those things; he desires a greater choice of things, and things that will satisfy new wants growing up in him.

and Marshall quotes Senior:[4]

Strong as is the desire for variety, it is weak compared with the demand for distinction, a feeling which . . . may be pronounced to be the most powerful of human passions.

These insights are important not simply because they highlight the social character of consumption, but because they emphasize that the way in which higher levels of u are achieved differs materially from the way in which base subsistence is achieved. It is useful to develop these observations into a very simple Marshallian *ladder* of consumption. This probably reads more into Marshall than he himself implies, but it is useful for the argument that follows. The ladder has five stages:

   I   increased quantity
  II   increased quality
 III   increased variety
 IV   satisfying new wants
  V   demand for distinction

At the simplest level, any consumer would progress from one stage to the next. Each of these stages would follow an r-shaped curve over time. When the consumer has reached satiation in terms of quantity, he or she progresses along the quality dimension. When he is satiated in terms of quality, he pursues variety, and so on. At the simplest, the consumer only embarks on the next stage when preceding wants are satisfied.

Different consumers would be at different stages on this progression. While these five different stages each represent a 'well-trodden path', followed by generations of earlier consumers, nevertheless for the individual consumer it seems like a major innovation to progress from one to the next. From this Marshallian perspective, innovation in consumption relates to reaching

---

[3] Marshall (1920, Book 3, ch. 2, sect. 1, para. 1).
[4] Marshall (1920, Book 3, ch. 2, sect. 1, para. 4).

higher levels of utility through more refined approaches to consumption. When it comes to satisfying the demand for distinction, the innovative consumer can in principle find an infinity of ways in which to distinguish him or herself (at least horizontally) from the rest.

From the perspective of this *ladder*, innovation in consumption is really akin to technology transfer from a more sophisticated neighbour. We saw in the previous section that consumers are capable of being more innovative than that. Nevertheless, in macroeconomic terms, this sort of evolution in consumption is important. The next section recasts the Marshallian ladder into a slightly more flexible model of evolution in consumption.

5. SUSTENANCE, ASSOCIATION, DISTINCTION, AND ASPIRATION

The concepts in Marshall and Senior can be used to underpin a slightly different, and perhaps more flexible approach to a theory of innovation in consumption. This approach—and the literature that underpins it—is set out in detail in Cowan, Cowan, and Swann (1997), and here we simply summarise the main components. We assume that there are four generic forces driving consumption: sustenance; association or repetition; distinction or variety; and aspiration. Each of these may be defined relative to the consumption activity of others (the social aspect to consumption), or relative to the consumer's own past history of consumption (the auto-referential aspect to consumption).

At its simplest, sustenance appears to be a non-social activity. It is about the satisfaction of the most basic needs. But, of course, the analysis of poverty has shown us that it is a relative and not an absolute concept. So sustenance is a social activity as well, and some consumption required to reach sustenance is associative in the sense described below. Equally, the level of consumption required to reach sustenance is auto-referential, in the sense that it depends on the consumer's previous history of consumption.

Association is the desire to consume what your peer group consumes. Repetition is the desire to repeat consumption that has been enjoyed in the past—whether by habit, or by accumulation of intellectual capital. While they

Table 8.1. Interdependencies in consumption

	Direction	Social	Auto-referential
1.	Positive	Association	Repetition/Habit
2.	Negative	Distinction	Variety
3.	Positive	Aspiration	Nostalgia

appear different, they are in fact different aspects of the same phenomenon. The first is a positive *social* correlation in consumption; the second is positive *auto-correlation* in consumption.

Distinction is the desire to consume in a fashion that is distinguished— often from an earlier, and now rejected peer group. Variety is the desire to change consumption from day to day or week to week. Again, they are equivalent concepts: the first social, the second auto-referential. Desire for distinction is negative social correlation in consumption; the desire for variety is negative auto-correlation in consumption.

Aspiration is the drive to join a higher social group, and this can sometimes be achieved by the right sort of consumption.[5] The auto-referential counterpart to this is a little less clear. It could arise if consumption today is shaped by consumption tomorrow, but consumption tomorrow is rarely an exogenous effect on behaviour today. Instead, it is anticipated rather than actual, and these plans are usually determined endogenously in the light of today's circumstances. However, the nostalgic consumer may aspire to achieve the consumption patterns of the past.

Some consumers may progress in a linear path from sustenance to association to distinction and aspiration. The majority of consumers who have progressed beyond sustenance, however, will be associating, distinguishing, and aspiring at the same time, but with reference to different groups. The new undergraduate may associate with his or her new peers, seek to distinguish themselves from old school-friends, and aspire to be a well-paid employee on graduation. Moreover, one individual may experience each of these three different sentiments to a particular group at different times in his or her lifetime. The sixth-former aspires to be a student; then having made it to university, associates with fellow students; then after graduation, seeks to show that they are no longer a student.

Again these cycles in preferences represent a 'well-trodden path'. To graduate from aspiration to association and then to the desire for distinction is not a new historical experience. But it is a new experience for the maturing consumer, and is a powerful force behind the variation of tastes and apparently innovative consumption behaviour. And indeed, the desire for distinction is often innovative in character. Some admittedly seek distinction through a Ferrari or Rolls-Royce—artefacts that have been owned by others before them to affirm their distinction. But others seek distinction through doing things that are new and different.

In the rest of this chapter it is useful therefore to recognize the difference between *vertical* distinction, which is to consume the best, and *horizontal* distinction, which is to consume in a way that is idiosyncratic and original, though not necessarily better. This use of vertical and horizontal follows the

---

[5] Though as Lewis (1955) notes, it is only in a minority of societies that status can be conferred by material wealth.

accepted use of these terms in the economic analysis of product differentiation.

6. INNOVATION IN CONSUMPTION: PART 2

It is instructive to return to the analysis of Section 3 armed with the concepts of the last section. The effect of the innovation in the cost function could, for example, be decomposed into three or more parts: innovation in means of achieving sustenance (S); innovation in means of achieving association (A); innovation in means of achieving distinction (D). If:

$$u = v (S, A, D).$$

Then the cost function representation of innovation in consumption can be written as:

$$[g_{1S}\{S,p\} + g_{1A}\{A,p\} + g_{1D}\{D,p\}] - [g_{0S}\{S,p\} + g_{0A}\{A,p\} + g_{0D}\{D,p\}],$$

where the $g(.)$ functions describe the cost of achieving S, A, or D at given prices, p. Innovations in g_S represent new, cheaper means of achieving sustenance. Innovations in g_A represent new, cheaper ways of achieving association, or sharing consumption activities with a peer group. Innovations in g_D represent new, cheaper ways of achieving distinction. So, for example, the new recipe represents a change to g_S. The new children's game or the new collection hobby represents a change in g_A. The style innovation can be an innovation in g_A and/or g_D. A stream of such innovations over time means that the consumer will make up u from different combinations of S, A, and D.

We can now proceed to examine the second sort of innovation in consumption—or perhaps we should say *evolution of* consumption—that emerges when consumers step up a Marshallian *ladder*. Here, we compare the ways consumers achieve u_1 with the way they used to achieve u_0:

$$g(u_1; p) - g(u_0 ; p),$$

where:

$$u_1 = v (S_1, A_1, D_1)$$
$$u_0 = v (S_0, A_0, D_0),$$

and where, probably:

$$A_1 - A_0 > S_1 - S_0$$
$$D_1 - D_0 > S_1 - S_0.$$

Indeed, for the more sophisticated consumers:

$$D_1 - D_0 > A_1 - A_0$$

That is, as the consumer progresses upwards, they add most to their budget for distinction and least to their budget for sustenance. Thus we have seen two distinct examples of innovation (or evolution) in consumption. The first is the innovation in g(.)—which can be broken down into innovations in ways of creating sustenance, association and distinction. The second is a changing balance between sustenance, association, and distinction as the consumer progresses up the Marshallian ladder.

7. INNOVATION IN CONSUMPTION AND GROWTH

We have seen that the consumer can be a consumer of innovations or someone who does the innovation themselves. For the rest of this chapter, this distinction is less important than the fact that demand for different types of products changes over time, and that the causes are endogenous rather than random. The focus of this book is on innovation and growth. What is the significance of this analysis of consumption for economic growth?

Consumption—to repeat the obvious—is the sole end and object of all economic activity. Opportunities for employment are necessarily limited by the extent of aggregate demand.   (Keynes, 1936, 104)

If consumption were non-social, and if there were little demand for variety and limited aspiration, then it is easy to see how satiation would readily set in—and hence in Keynes's words, opportunities for employment are limited. Innovations in consumption create demand for new product and services. So when aspiration and the desire for association, distinction, and variety are powerful forces, then opportunities for employment appear to expand. But do they? Using the categories of the last section, we shall argue that the effects of consumption on growth depend on which forces are driving consumption.

The desire for association in consumption leads to a growth in demand for products owned by our peers: televisions, radios, video recorders, mobile phones, and so on. Such products are often in competitive and elastic supply, so the increase in aggregate demand leads to growth in supply.

The desire for distinction, on the other hand, leads to a growth in demand for products that others do not consume. The effects on growth, however, depend on what sort of distinction is sought. *Vertical* distinction, or superiority, is sometimes sought by consuming positional goods that are in limited supply. Indeed, the value of the positional good stems from the fact that it is a limited edition, even if it is technically feasible to expand supply. Part of the distinction of the Ferrari or Rolls-Royce is that it is a comparative rarity. More could be produced, but if too many were produced they would lose their exclusivity. Sometimes, of course, consumers seek distinction by consuming goods that are inherently in limited supply (old master paintings, Stradivarius violins, old houses, and so on). Some of these indeed could be described as 'chain' goods, in that supply is fixed, so the act of consumption by one means the end of consumption by another, as the good is passed along the 'chain'. Either way, supply of positional goods offering vertical distinction is inelastic and uncompetitive. This means that growth in demand may only have a limited effect on growth of supply.

When we turn to *horizontal* distinction—the desire to be different, though not necessarily superior—then innovation in consumption can generate a growth in supply. The consumer seeking horizontal distinction may not be able to afford consumption goods that are in inelastic supply. So they consume goods that are not of necessity scarce, but are simply unfashionable at present. If they are lucky, they will be able to continue such consumption in privacy for some time. If not, and if their consumption space is invaded as others copy, then they will experience a continuing drive for innovation in consumption. If goods sought for horizontal distinction are in competitive and elastic supply, then this source of demand will generate a growth in supply.

In a celebrated paper, Johnson (1952) studied the effects of income redistribution on aggregate consumption when consumer preferences are interdependent. We can do the same using the perspective developed above. First, consider pure redistribution of income from those at the top of the income spectrum to those towards the bottom. This looks like redistribution from those who may seek distinction from positional goods in inelastic supply to those who seek sustenance or associative goods in competitive and elastic supply. That would have a positive effect on supply, and a negative effect on the price of positional goods.

Second, consider income re-ranking—that is, where the points on the income league table remain unchanged, but where some move up in rank and where others move down. This re-ranking means that some find themselves above the station to which they are familiar, while others find themselves below. If this re-ranking is transitory, it may have little effect on consumption. But suppose that consumers expect it to be more permanent than that. How do they react? Take the *nouveau riche* consumer: he or she is traditionally seen as one most likely to need to confirm their status with conspicuous consumption.[6] Hence there is an increase in demand for distinction goods in inelastic supply. And what of the fallen aristocrat? He or she is liable to dig in, to hold onto their positional goods against all odds, but to reduce their consumption of everyday items in competitive and elastic supply. That is, they will wear old clothes, worn-out shoes, and drive an old car.

And what, finally, if the distribution of income remains constant for a long period of time? If the distribution does not change, and each person's rank in

---

[6] Notably by Veblen (1899).

that distribution does not change either, then there is no need (or opportunity) to affirm new wealth, and no desperate attempts to 'cling on' to old wealth. Innovation in consumption driven by the desire for distinction will mainly be limited to demand for horizontal distinction.

8. CONSUMPTION AND INFLATION

This section is really just a corollary to the last. The last section argued that the effect of consumption on growth depended on what type of consumption it was—following the categories introduced earlier in the chapter. Here we draw out the effects of consumption growth for inflation. In doing so we make an important assumption.

Assumption: consumption growth is not inflationary when it increases aggregate demand for a product in competitive and elastic supply,[7] but is inflationary when it increases aggregate demand for products in non-competitive and/or inelastic supply.

The justification for this assumption comes from simple supply and demand analysis—under competitive or monopolistic conditions. Under this assumption, the effect of consumption growth on inflation is the reverse of its effect on aggregate supply. An increase in demand for associative goods, mostly in elastic supply, is non-inflationary.[8] Likewise a demand for horizontal distinction need not be inflationary if these are goods in competitive and elastic supply. Sometimes, of course there may be a local monopoly in the supply of goods for horizontal distinction; but in other cases, horizontal distinction is obtained by 'style innovation'—creating distinction from the novel use of ordinary objects. By contrast, consumption growth that stems from a desire for vertical distinction is likely to be inflationary.[9] This is a demand for goods in inelastic and/or monopoly supply.

We can also use this assumption to explore the effects of income redistribution and re-ranking. Relative to a status quo of holding the distribution of income fixed, the redistribution of income described in the last section is non-inflationary—indeed, it is counter-inflationary—because there is a reduced demand for positional goods in inelastic supply and increased demand for goods in elastic supply. And relative to this status quo, re-ranking is inflationary, because there is an increase in the demand for positional goods in

---

[7] Strictly, we need to assume that these are in competitive, elastic *and domestic* supply.

[8] This ties in neatly with the Farrell and Saloner (1985) view that when network externalities are important, there are economies of scale in consumption.

[9] This is similar to the argument that product innovation in defence technologies is (or at least, was) inflationary. The cost of an item of given performance level may decline over time, but the cost of the best tends to keep rising. And to be fully defended you have to have the best, so the cost of providing secure defence continues to spiral.

Table 8.2. Consumption, income redistribution, and their effects on growth and inflation

	Growth	Inflation
Association	+	o
Horizontal distinction	(+)	o
Vertical distinction	o	+
Redistribution (greater equity)	+	o
Re-ranking	–	+

inelastic supply and a reduced demand for goods in elastic supply. Table 8.2 summarizes the predictions of Sections 8 and 9.

We should note, of course, that the index of inflation we are using here is one that encompasses the consumption activities of all consumers. In practice, the RPI is focused on the consumption activities of a lower middle-class family. Some positional goods may not show up in this index, and for that reason the rates of inflation measured by the RPI may not accord with these predictions.

9. CONCLUSION

We have argued in this chapter that the consumer can be innovative, for as Marshall put it, he seeks new methods of satisfying his growing needs. We distinguished two sorts of innovation in consumption. In one case the consumer is the creator of the innovation. In the other, he or she is a consumer of the innovations of others. But even in this second case, the consumer must be willing to change consumption patterns—perhaps from a desire for variety or distinction. The Marshallian ladder of consumption suggests that the consumer's motive changes as he or she climbs the ladder, and that will translate into a desire for different types of consumption. We have argued that consumption driven by a desire for association will often translate into a demand for goods in competitive and/or elastic supply. In contrast, consumption driven by a desire for vertical distinction will often translate into a demand for goods in inelastic and/or monopolized supply. The former demand will have a greater effect on economic growth; the latter will have a greater effect on inflation.

REFERENCES

Barnett, H. G. (1953), *Innovation: The Basis of Cultural Change*, New York: McGraw-Hill.

Becker, G. S. (1996), *Accounting for Tastes*, Cambridge, Mass.: Harvard University Press.

Cowan, R., Cowan, W., and Swann, G. M. P. (1997), 'A Model of Demand with Interaction Among Consumers', *International Journal of Industrial Organisation*, 15: 711–32.

Farrell, J. R. and Saloner, G. (1985), 'Standardisation, Compatibility and Innovation', *RAND Journal of Economics*, 16: 70–82.

Frank, R. H. (1985), *Choosing the Right Pond: Human Behaviour and the Quest for Status*, New York: Oxford University Press.

Hebdige, D. (1979), *Subculture: The Meaning of Style*, London: Methuen.

Hippel, E. von (1988), *The Sources of Innovation*, Oxford: Oxford University Press.

Johnson, H. G. (1952), 'The Effect of Income Redistribution on Aggregate Consumption with Interdependence of Consumers' Preferences', *Economica*, 19: 131–47.

Keynes, J. M. (1936), *The General Theory of Employment, Interest and Money*, London: Macmillan.

Lewis, W. A. (1955), *The Theory of Economic Growth*, London: Allen and Unwin.

Marshall, A. (1920), *Principles of Economics*, 8th edn., London. Macmillan.

Veblen, T. (1899), *The Theory of the Leisure Class: An Economic Study of Institutions*, New York: Macmillan.

Part III

Governance, Business Performance, and Public Policy

9.   Innovation and Corporate Structures: USA and Japan

Ronald Dore

The 1980s was a decade of burgeoning Japanese self-confidence. Especially after the Plaza agreement made it cheaper for Japanese companies to register patents in the USA, their share of total US-registered patents rose steadily to over 20 per cent. Technological performance became a hot academic subject and numerous attempts to count national contributions to scientific journals, to use citations to measure the quality of contributions and the importance of patents, to conduct Delphi studies on 'who's ahead' in a given number of fields of science and technology, concluded—in Japan with glee, and in the USA with alarm—that Japan was catching up fast and destined in many fields soon to overtake the USA. Particularly disturbing for Americans was the fact that some of their smartest weaponry depended on bought-in Japanese components. The effect of the technological news was magnified by the economic news. The Japanese economy was booming in the second half of the 1980s; the USA was a byword for productivity stagnation and the triple deficit.

In the 1990s the situation is very different. It is now America which has the dynamic economy; the solidity of Japan's recovery from its post-bubble stagnation seems still uncertain. And confidence and optimism have migrated along with economic dynamism. Citation studies and Delphic assessments of relative technological achievement have lost their interest in both countries; Americans do not need reassuring that they are still ahead, and Japanese fear to discover that their hopes of catch-up and overtake were somewhat inflated. And although the numbers—patent shares and the various science and technology indicators used by the OECD—do not suggest much falling-off of Japanese technological progress, the popular perception is that in many fields, but most noticeably in electronics, computers and software, and biotechnology, the American superiority is now increasing rather than being eroded.

The Japanese media, and the publicists speaking at business forums in Japan, are apt to interpret this in terms of business structures. Silicon Valley is seen as the symbol of what America has, and Japan lacks; the combination of individual technological brilliance, business entrepreneurship and venture-capital financing. There does, indeed, seem to be a big difference in the dominant innovation paradigms, as between the two countries. The sources of creativity remain elusive, but clearly the originality needed to make either breakthroughs or incremental improvements has to be combined with the high-grade learning ability needed to get rapidly to the frontiers of existing knowledge, in short, with high IQ. In the United States a high proportion of people with such talent get into the graduate schools of the major research universities. It is they, perhaps after a spell in an academic post, who provide one source of the entrepreneurial firms on Route 128 and the equivalent industrial parks elsewhere. Another source is provided by the corporate research laboratories from which people 'spin out', often giving rise to charges that in spinning out they have taken commercial secrets with them and thus providing lawyers with much lucrative business. The necessary capital is provided by venture-capital firms which specialize in taking high risks for the prospects of high returns.

In Japan, by contrast, men and women with comparable levels of IQ stay in graduate school only for a taught Master's degree which is nowadays seen as a part of basic training, a necessary supplement to what is usually no more than two years of specialist disciplinary study in the undergraduate degree. But, typically, they then go immediately, in their mid-20s, into the research lab of a major corporation. They may subsequently be sent abroad for a spell to an American graduate school, or they may do a part-time Ph.D. at a Japanese university—nowadays a major form of collaboration between universities and corporations—but the majority, even of the very brightest, remain committed to the firm they have joined and expect to make their career within it, not necessarily exclusively in research. Much of their work is done in teams, collaborating with colleagues with whom they have built up co-operative relationships over a period of years. Much of their work ends up, after considerable expense, with no commercially viable product; it is a high-risk activity. So is the launching of new products through the corporation's own procedures for entrepreneurial initiatives, integrating research, design, production planning, and marketing. Finance for the whole risky process is found from the corporation's own deep pockets.

Doubtless, a careful count would probably show that in the United States too, the corporate research, corporate finance, corporate commercialization recipe, quantitatively dominates by a clear margin over the graduate school whiz-kid, individual entrepreneur, venture-capitalist recipe. But that the latter recipe does play a substantial part in the American pattern of innovation, and a very small part in that of Japan, seems obviously true, though with variation among industrial sectors. Innovation in pharmaceuticals is more likely to follow the same predominantly corporate pattern in both countries than innovation in electronics.

The outcome of technological rivalry between Japan and the United States will probably in large part depend on the relative efficacy of these two recipes for transforming brainpower into commercially successful product innovation. Another major factor, of course, is how much brainpower the two societies dispose of in the first place. The relative importance of the recipes is not irrelevant to this either, since the high-powered university graduate schools which play such an important role in the US recipe are one factor—together with the English language, the openness of American society and America's general cultural hegemony—which explains the migration of a great deal of scientific talent to the United States. Look through any list of leading American scientists and engineers, and you will find a very considerable number from Asia, Europe, and Latin America, with first degrees from their native country. A good proportion of them came to do graduate work in the USA and subsequently settled down. Japan as a country, and lifetime-employing Japanese corporations as work environments, are far less attractive to in-migrants. Japan seeks to compensate for this to some extent by setting up R&D establishments in Europe, the United States. and, probably increasingly in future, in China (there are over 100 such establishments in Britain already) but its capture of foreign brainpower is obviously on a much more restricted scale than that of the USA.

In that context—and in so far as the abundance of native talent is an important factor in determining technological leadership—it is worth remembering, as China increasingly widens the catchment area for the meritocratic ladders which lead to its top universities, that for every Japanese who scores three standard deviations above the mean on IQ tests, there are ten Chinese; six Chinese for every American.

10. Sustainable Prosperity, Corporate Governance, and Innovation in Europe

Mary O'Sullivan

1. INTRODUCTION

The extent to which, and the manner in which, innovation occurs in an economy depends on decisions about the allocation of resources; that is, on investment decisions or strategies.[1] In particular, an economy's capacity to achieve sustainable prosperity—by which I mean a progressive spreading of the benefits of economic growth to more and more people over a prolonged period of time—is closely related to the process through which corporate revenues are allocated. Corporate strategists control substantial financial and productive resources that permit them to make strategic choices in the allocation of resources. Retained earnings—undistributed profits and capital consumption allowances—have always provided, and continue to provide, the financial resources that are the foundation of investments in productive capabilities that can make innovation and economic development possible.[2] The strategic choices of corporate decision-makers can thus have profound effects on the availability and viability of stable and remunerative employment opportunities. To understand what has happened and what will happen to employment opportunities and income levels, we have to understand strategic decision-making within major corporations, and how and why that process changes over time.

The strategic investment process that shapes an enterprise's innovative capabilities is influenced by a combination of institutionalized practices generated by the unique organizational history of an enterprise and the social and political history of the economy in which it has grown and continues to

---

[1] Joseph A. Schumpeter (1934), *The Theory of Economic Development*, Cambridge, Mass.: Harvard University Press.

[2] The contribution of internal funds to net sources of finance of non-financial enterprises during the period 1970–1989 has recently been estimated as 80.6% for Germany, 69.3% for Japan, 97.3% for the UK, and 91.3% for the USA; see Jenny Corbett and Tim Jenkinson (1996), 'The Financing of Industry, 1970–1989: An International Comparison', *Journal of the Japanese and International Economies*, 10: 71–96.

operate.[3] The social institutions that influence the process of strategic investment in corporate enterprises—*who makes investment decisions in corporate
enterprises, what types of investments they make, and how returns from successful investments are distributed*—can be characterized as a system of corporate governance.

How corporations are governed is a matter of European concern. Yet,
despite its importance to the sustainability of prosperity in Europe, the governance of corporations has not been a central element in the debates about
European integration. Even with respect to the dimensions of the integration
process that have direct implications for corporate governance, such as financial market regulation, corporate law, and industrial relations, a systematic
analysis of their impact on corporate governance has been lacking in policy
discussions.

If corporate governance has been largely neglected on the European continent, in contrast, in the United States and in Britain, corporate governance
has, for the last two decades, been widely discussed. To the extent that corporate governance is commanding increased, albeit as yet limited, attention
on the Continent, the issues are currently being framed in terms that are
largely derivative of the Anglo-American debates. Unfortunately, the concepts of economic performance on which these debates rely are devoid of any
systematic conception of innovation and the central role that business organizations play in that process.

2. A FRAMEWORK FOR ANALYSING DEVELOPMENTAL GOVERNANCE

The process of innovation is, however, central to the dynamic through which
successful enterprises and economies improve their performance relative to
each other as well as over time. Drawing on what is now an extensive body of
historical and theoretical research on the economics of innovation,[4] I set out

---

[3] The expression 'social institutions' is used herein to connote the shared schemes of percep-
tion, thought and action generated through the experience of a common history; see Pierre
Bourdieu (1990), *The Logic of Practice*, trans. Richard Nice, Stanford: Stanford University
Press, 52–65.

[4] See, for example, Michael Best (1990), *The New Competition*, Cambridge, Mass.: Harvard
University Press; Giovanni Dosi, C. Freeman, R. Nelson, G. Silverberg, and Luc Soete (1988)
(eds.), *Technical Change and Economic Theory*, New York: Pinter Publishers; Christopher
Freeman (1974), *The Economics of Industrial Innovation*, Harmondsworth: Penguin; Gene
Grossman and Elhanan Helpman (1991), *Innovation and Growth in the Global Economy*,
Cambridge, Mass.: MIT Press; Robert Lucas (1988), 'On the Mechanics of Economic
Development', *Journal of Monetary Economics*, 22: 3–42; Richard Nelson (1993) (ed.), *National
Innovation Systems: A Comparative Analysis*, New York: Oxford University Press; Keith Pavitt
(1991), 'Key Characteristics of the Large Innovating Firm', *British Journal of Management*, 2:
41–50; Edith Penrose (1995), *The Theory of the Growth of the Firm*, Oxford: Oxford University
Press ; Paul Romer (1986), 'Increasing Returns and Long Run Growth', *Journal of Political*

a perspective on innovative enterprise and then illustrate how an understanding of the who, what, and how of innovative investment can be used to illuminate the economic and political challenges that corporate governance poses.

2.1. Learning and business organization[5]

By definition, underlying the innovation process is a learning process; if we already knew how to generate higher quality, lower-cost products then the act of doing so would not require innovation. How the economist conceives of knowledge, the way it is acquired through learning, and its use in the decisions that shape the learning process has an important influence on his understanding of the economics of innovation. Basic to my analysis is the argument, already empirically supported, that increasingly across nations and over time, industrial development depends on learning that occurs through a process that is both collective and cumulative—or organizational—rather than individual and discrete.[6]

The way work is organized—how it is divided and integrated—within an enterprise shapes the extent to which, and the manner in which, knowledge is generated in the enterprise. Learning is influenced by what a person does—his experience—as well as the creativity with which that experience is shaped through the specification of the problems that he attempts to solve. How work is divided influences the scope that individuals have to learn because it shapes what they do and the autonomy that they have in doing it. People learn not only from their own experience and creativity but also from the experience and creativity of others on the basis of social relations that allow them to transmit and transform knowledge in a process of collective learning. Thus, the integration of work, as well as its division, affects the generation of knowledge in the organization because it influences the way people interact with each other in the performance of their work, the relationships that they establish, and thus the possibilities for collective learning.

Economy, 94/5: 1002–37; id. (1990), 'Endogenous Technical Change', *Journal of Political Economy*, 98/5, S72–102; Nathan Rosenberg (1976), *Perspectives on Technology*, Cambridge: Cambridge University Press; id. (1982), *Inside the Black Box*, Cambridge: Cambridge University Press.

  [5] Mary A. O'Sullivan (1996), 'Knowledge, Learning, and Innovation,' ch. 1 in 'Innovation, Industrial Development, and Corporate Governance,' Ph.D. diss., Harvard University.

  [6] My analysis of the learning process is based primarily on Penrose (1995); Michael Polanyi (1966), *The Tacit Dimension*, Garden City, NY: Doubleday and Company; id. (1962), *Personal Knowledge: Towards a Post-Critical Philosophy*, Chicago: University of Chicago Press; Bourdieu (1990); Thorstein Veblen (1904), *The Theory of Business Enterprise*, New York: C. Scribner & Sons; Peter Berger and Thomas Luckmann (1966), *The Social Construction of Reality*, Garden City, NY: Doubleday and Company; for an extended discussion, see O'Sullivan, 'Knowledge, Learning, and Innovation'.

How work is organized thus determines the identity of the insiders—those whose experience and creativity is integrated into a process of collective learning in the enterprise, and the identity of the outsiders—those who supply their effort to the enterprise but whose creativity and experience are dispensable to it. A common organizational characteristic of business enterprises is the distinction between managers and workers. The division of labour between them has exerted an important influence on the learning of both groups. An extreme view of this division is that managers are insiders and workers are outsiders, a characterization that is not an unreasonable approximation of the organization of work in mass-production industries during the Fordist era. However, an analysis of the organization of business enterprises in comparative-historical perspective shows that the concentration of learning in a narrow insider group is neither necessary for the development and utilization of technology, nor always competitive as a basis for the generation of innovation.

The effects of the hierarchical division and integration of labour on organizational learning is, however, only one aspect of the much broader phenomenon of the influence of the structure of work on the knowledge generated through the experience of performing it. For example, the specialization and integration of functions that cut across hierarchical divisions also exercises an important influence on the scope for organizational learning within enterprises. Studies by industrial sociologists provide a rich body of evidence that shows how the narrow specialization of functions, and a lack of integration among them, can stymie the development and utilization of technology within a business enterprise. Research on the organization of work on the shop floor, for example, has shown how the hermetic separation of tasks like machine maintenance and quality control from the operation of machines undermines shop-floor workers' abilities and incentives to overcome production problems and to contribute to product and process innovation.[7] There is also an extensive literature on the management of technology that emphasizes the dangers of functional segmentation in the development of new products and processes.[8]

---

[7] See, for example, Marc Maurice, Francois Sellier, and Jean-Jacques Silvestre (1986), *The Social Foundations of Industrial Power*, trans. Arthur Goldhammer, Cambridge, Mass.: MIT Press; Christel Lane (1989), *Management and Workers in Europe*, Aldershot: Edward Elgar.

[8] See, for example, K. B. Clark and T. Fujimoto (1991), *Product Development Performance: Strategy, Organisation, and Management in the World Auto Industry*, Cambridge, Mass.: Harvard Business School Press; Jeffrey Funk (1992), *The Teamwork Advantage: An Inside Look at Japanese Product and Technology Development*, Cambridge, Mass.: Productivity Press; R. M. Henderson and K. B. Clark (1990), 'Architectural Innovation: The Reconfiguration of Existing Product Technologies and the Failure of Established Firms', *Administrative Science Quarterly* (March), 9–30; G. I. Susman (1992) (ed.), *Integrating Design and Manufacturing for Competitive Advantage*, Oxford: Oxford University Press; Robert J. Thomas (1994), *What Machines Can't Do: Politics and Technology in the Industrial Enterprise*, Berkeley: University of California Press; D. E. Whitney (1988), 'Manufacturing by Design', *Harvard Business Review* (July–Aug.), 83–91.

2.2. *Strategy and business organization*

If the organization of work shapes the extent to which, and the manner in which, knowledge is generated in the business enterprise, then what influences how work is organized? The decisions or strategies that influence who is permitted to learn, and the extent to which they learn, in a business enterprise are decisions about the allocation of resources. In other words, a strategy that shapes an enterprise learning process is an investment strategy. To permit a group of people to engage in organizational learning, investments must be made in the development of the abilities and learning of the participants. Resources must also be committed to give them incentives to devote their effort, experience, and creativity to the learning process and to maintain access to their labour services over sustained periods of time. Finally, resources must be invested to make available the materials and machines with which people work and learn.

Reflecting its developmental character, during the learning process resources are expended without a return of revenues. To commit resources to innovation means forgoing their exchange while the developmental process is underway. The withdrawal of some of the learners or physical resources from the organizational learning process before it is complete may endanger the success of the entire undertaking. Thus the scale of innovative investment depends not only on the size of the investment in productive resources, and in the abilities and incentives of insiders, but also on the duration of the investment necessary to sustain that process over the developmental period during which learning occurs.[9]

Because innovation entails a learning process, the returns to these innovative investments are highly uncertain. Given macroeconomic conditions, an enterprise that invests in innovation confronts two types of uncertainty: productive uncertainty and competitive uncertainty. Productive uncertainty exists because business enterprises that undertake innovative strategies have to develop the productive capabilities of the resources in which they have invested before these resources can generate returns. The learning process may not be successful. Competitive uncertainty exists because even when a business enterprise is successful in generating a product that is higher quality and/or lower cost than it had previously been capable of producing, it may not gain competitive advantage and generate returns because a competitor, pursuing its own investment strategy, is even more successful at doing so. Even an innovative enterprise can be outcompeted.[10]

---

[9] William Lazonick and Mary O'Sullivan (1996), 'Organization, Finance, and International Competition', *Industrial and Corporate Change*, 5/1.

[10] For a discussion of different types of uncertainty that must be confronted in the innovation process, see Freeman (1974); Rosenberg (1982); William Lazonick (1991), *Business Organization and the Myth of the Market Economy*, New York: Cambridge University Press.

2.3. *The elements of the investment process*

From the characteristics of the organizational learning process flow an understanding of the nature of the investment process in the developmental enterprise. The core of my argument is that the relation between investment in
productive resources and economic performance depends on *who makes
investment decisions in corporate enterprises, what types of investments they
make, and how returns from investments are distributed.*

Who makes investment decisions?

Innovation is a creative response to external market and technological conditions because it attempts to overcome them through the generation of new
knowledge.[11] As a creative response, there are no objective guidelines for
making strategic decisions about the extent, direction and structure of the
learning process nor for resolving disputes about the strategy for learning.
Strategists thus require control of resources if they are to commit them to a
developmental process in accordance with their evaluation of the problems
and possibilities of alternative learning strategies. They also require control
to keep resources committed to the innovative strategy until the learning
process has generated the higher-quality, lower-cost products that enable the
investment strategy to reap returns.[12]

    Thus, inherent in the process of innovation, in the need to commit
resources to undertake it and the uncertainty of returns from innovative
investments, is a need for control of resources by the decision-makers who
shape the innovative process. And with that control of resources comes influence over the identity of insiders and outsiders in the enterprise and, therefore, over the scope of the work that people do in enterprises as well as their
working relationships with other employees in the enterprise.

    There are no objective bases for determining how such control should be
exercised. Because innovation is a creative response to external conditions, to
strategically shape the organization of work in an innovative way requires the
visualization of a range of potentialities that were previously hidden and that
are now believed to be accessible. Innovative strategy is thus interpretative or,
more correctly, it is a process of interpretation that takes place in an uninter-
rupted flow of learning.[13]

    What one learns as the innovative process evolves changes how one
conceives of the problem to be addressed, the possibilities for its solution and

---

[11] Joseph A. Schumpeter (1947), 'The Creative Response in Economic History', *Journal of
Economic History* (Nov.), 149–59.
    [12] Joseph A. Schumpeter (1934); Lazonick (1991), ch. 3; Lazonick and O'Sullivan (1996).
    [13] Anthony Giddens (1979), *Central Problems in Social Theory: Action, Structure and
Contradiction in Social Analysis*, Berkeley: University of California Press.

therefore the appropriate innovative strategy for continued learning. The fruits of learning may, for example, render the problem that the learning process is designed to solve unattainable and necessitate a restructuring and redirection of the learning process if failure is to be avoided. Learning may, through the discovery of new means, make possible the attainment of ends that were previously considered impossible.

Strategic decision-makers must know what the learning process is generating if, in shaping the learning process, they are to take account of the opportunities for and threats to innovative success that learning reveals. When the basis for the generation and transmission of learning is an organizational process, strategic decision-makers must become integrated into the network of relations that underlies it; they must become to some extent insiders to the learning process to allow strategy and learning to interact in the process of innovation. To the extent that strategists develop relations with the members of the learning collectivity, they can become privy to some of the knowledge that the collectivity generates, and can use it as a basis for organizing the work that members of the collectivity undertake. The integration of strategy and learning facilitates a developmental interaction of strategy and learning in which strategic decisions actively shape the direction and structure of learning and the knowledge continually generated through learning informs strategy.

In ensuring that strategists are insiders, integration enhances not only the quality of strategic decisions but also the incentives of strategists to pursue innovative investment strategies. To the extent that strategists are insiders to the learning process that sustains innovation, the value of their learning is to some extent specific to the collectivity that generates it. The innovative success of that collectivity therefore enhances the strategists' own success.

A corollary of the argument about the need for an integration of strategy and learning is that the exercise of strategic control by outsiders to the learning process, be they managers within the enterprise, financial shareholders, or other stakeholders, poses a threat to the ongoing innovative success of the enterprise because these decision-makers will have neither the abilities nor incentives to promote a sustained pattern of innovation.

What types of investments do they make?

Whether strategic decision-makers pursue investment strategies to live off the past or build for the future will have an important influence on the generation and utilization of productive resources. The problem of the adoption of adaptive strategies—that seek merely to replicate or run down existing investments—is particularly acute for enterprises and nations that have been innovative in the past and have developed and utilized resources that they can now live off. Ultimately, as competing enterprises and nations adopt innovative strategies they will render obsolete the existing productive resources of their adaptive counterparts. From a dynamic perspective, therefore, an exclusive reliance on adaptive investments is inadvisable. These investments advance neither innovation nor industrial development and in a competitive world are a recipe for 'falling behind'.

In theoretical terms the distinction between innovative and adaptive investments is stark but in practice there is no bright line between innovative and adaptive investment strategies. The most innovative strategy has adaptive elements and indeed the mix of innovation and adaptation is itself strategically influenced. To be successful, an innovative organization must decide when to rely on inputs that are readily available on the market (and hence constitute variable costs) where organizational learning is not required, and when to commit resources strategically to building integrated resources (and incurring fixed costs) to support such learning. Yet innovation cannot occur unless the business enterprise adopts a strategy that confronts the uncertainty inherent in that process.[14]

Important distinctions can also be made among different types of innovative strategies. Innovation may be based on an exclusive learning process—the strategic development of the abilities and incentives of a narrow collectivity of insiders—or an inclusive learning process—strategic investments in the abilities and incentives of a broad-based group of insiders. The collective skill bases that can be integrated to generate organizational learning vary across industries because they are characterized by different technologies that provide different opportunities for collective learning. In any given industry, moreover, the character of the integrated skill base that can generate innovation varies over time as cumulative learning transforms the possibilities for a collective skill base to develop and utilize productive resources.

How do they distribute the returns from investment?

To the extent that an enterprise successfully innovates—generates new knowledge through learning that allows it to deliver products to customers at prices that they are willing to pay—it can build and sustain a competitive advantage. The knowledge generated and transmitted through a social process is specific to that process. Existing or potential rivals cannot secure the same level of productivity from productive resources as can the dominant organization unless they replicate or surpass the organizational learning that the advantaged enterprise has created. The time-consuming need to develop the social foundations for organizational learning serves as a barrier to rapid imitation by competitors. The strategic allocation of resources to innovative investments in organizational learning can thus afford the innovative business enterprise privileged access to the new technology that organizational

[14] Lazonick (1991).

learning makes possible. That access can, in turn, serve as the basis on which profits can be appropriated and sustained by the innovative enterprise.[15]

In contrast, when the business enterprise is not engaged in innovation—when it pursues an adaptive strategy—any supernormal returns that it might generate will eventually be competed away. Learning as a basis for adaptation gives the learner access to common or standardized knowledge. The pursuit of an adaptive strategy is an attempt to compete for markets by utilizing productive capabilities or knowledge that are available elsewhere in the economy. Since other competitors have access to it, the knowledge generated on the basis of an adaptive strategy cannot yield a sustained competitive advantage. Since it does not develop a sustainable basis on which returns can be appropriated, an adaptive investment strategy cannot justify, in economic terms, a major commitment of resources to a process of learning.

How returns from innovative investments are distributed, and in particular the extent to which they are reinvested in the process of organizational learning, influences the dynamics of the enterprise's innovation process. Without continued investment, the learning collectivity's existing productive resources—the skills and knowledge of the existing insiders and the productive assets in which they are embedded—will depreciate or obsolesce as new skills, knowledge, and physical resources are developed by competing learning collectivities. As the enterprise fails to innovate through reinvestment it will lose its ability to appropriate a return and, ultimately, the capacity to set an innovative strategy for learning.

3. THE ECONOMICS OF CORPORATE GOVERNANCE

The strategic investment process that shapes an enterprise's innovative capabilities is influenced by a combination of institutionalized practices generated by the unique organizational history of an enterprise and the social and political history of the economy in which it has grown and continues to operate. At any point in time in contributing to innovation the governance system generates two conditions—*organizational integration* and *financial commitment*—that, in combination, provide the institutional support for investments in the collective development and utilization of knowledge, an integration of strategists with the insiders that generate that learning, as well as the reinvestment of earnings to finance cumulative learning by incumbent insiders. Organizational integration describes the social relations that provide certain groups of people with the incentives to integrate their capabilities and efforts within organizations so that they can develop and utilize technology. Financial commitment describes the social relations that are the basis for the

---

[15] Penrose (1995).

ongoing access of a business organization to the financial resources required to sustain the development and utilization of technology.[16]

Organizational integration leads employees to view the returns to the supply of their labour as bound up with the success of the particular enterprise in which they participate. The foundations of this expectation are the willingness of the enterprise to invest in the capabilities of particular employees, the company's practice of providing shares in the gains from innovation to employees in whom it has made such investments, and the ongoing interactions of such employees with other participants in the organization in a collective and cumulative learning process. Similarly, financial commitment means that those who control money rely on the specific enterprise to which they commit this money to generate returns. Should the same money—for example the earnings of the enterprise—come under the control of people who demand financial liquidity rather than financial commitment, then the existing financial conditions for initiating and sustaining innovative investment strategies will disappear.

Financial commitment confronts one powerful threat to the preservation and expansion of the corporation as a productive enterprise; namely, the extraction of returns from the enterprise by shareholders. As portfolio investors, and thus outsiders to organizational learning processes in the enterprises in which they hold stock, they may have little interest in, or knowledge of, the organizational requirements of innovation, and hence tend to favour financial liquidity over financial commitment. Given their quest for liquidity, of all the stakeholders in the modern industrial corporation, shareholders are the ones with the least stake in a particular company as an ongoing entity because, via the stock market, shareholders have the easiest conditions for exit of any stakeholders. They are the last group that one would expect to provide the financial commitment that long-term investments require.

Organizational integration deals with another potential threat; the extraction of returns from the enterprise by employees in the forms of higher wages and benefits that are not warranted by the ability of the corporation to generate returns. But unlike higher returns to public shareholders, which do not create incentives to develop and utilize productive resources within the corporation and which undermine financial commitment, the higher earnings of employees are often critical to achieving the organizational integration that generates the revenues that permit higher earnings to be paid. Once these higher earnings are in place, however, employees may view these levels of remuneration as their right, and indeed they may increase their consumption expenditures in line with their higher incomes. If a change in the competitive environment reduces the corporate revenues that justified these levels of remuneration, the preservation of the corporation may be threatened unless

16 Lazonick and O'Sullivan (1996).

an adjustment in either employee remuneration or revenue generation takes place.

Organizational integration and financial commitment represent social conditions that support organizational control over the critical inputs to the innovation process: knowledge and money. But in contributing to the innovation process, these inputs are not commodities. Rather they reflect the social relations to the business organization of people who supply knowledge and money. The social conditions of organizational integration and financial commitment constitute norms according to which strategic decisions are made within enterprises concerning the allocation of resources to the development and utilization of technology in these organizations and the distribution of returns from it. Without governance institutions that support organizational integration and financial commitment, or more precisely, without the organizational control over knowledge and money that these conditions support, business enterprises cannot generate innovation through strategic investment in collective learning processes.[17]

That organizational integration and financial commitment are supported by a system of governance does not imply, however, that innovation will in fact occur. To understand the relationship between the institutions of governance and the process of innovation we must understand how the conditions of organizational integration and financial commitment interact with the internal dynamics of the enterprise and the external dynamics of competition.

3.1. *The internal dynamics of the enterprise*[18]

How returns from innovative investments are distributed, and in particular the extent to which they are reinvested in the incentives and abilities of incumbent insiders influences the internal dynamics of the enterprise. The critical economic rationale for the reinvestment of returns in the further development of the knowledge of incumbent insiders is the presence of cumulation advantages in their learning process. Through the experience of innovating the learning collectivity accumulates what Veblen described as a 'common stock' of knowledge.[19] When the learning process is cumulative, through innovation—through the process of generating higher-quality and/or lower-cost products—new innovative opportunities become apparent to insiders that are not readily identifiable nor exploitable by other collectivities or individuals.

Because a successful innovation process generates both financial returns and cumulation advantages of learning, it produces the basis on which incum-

---

[17] Lazonick and O'Sullivan (1996).
[18] For an extended discussion, see Mary O'Sullivan (forthcoming), *Contests for Corporate Control: Corporate Governance in the United States and Germany*, Oxford: Oxford University Press.
[19] Veblen (1904), 328.

bent insiders can potentially retain their collective advantage in competition with other business organizations. The use of a portion of the surplus revenues generated by previous innovation to finance investment in the further exploitation and/or enhancement of the cumulation advantages of incumbent insiders permits the constant renewal and enhancement of the collective advantage of incumbent insider groups. Due to the uncertainty inherent in the innovation process, attempts to develop an extant learning process can fail in the same way that a new venture can prove unsuccessful. In contrast to a new venture, however, enterprises that have become going concerns through innovation in the past will have developed and utilized resources that they can live off, at least for a while, in the event of innovative failure.

The enterprise is, however, only one level at which the allocation of resources and returns takes place. To foster the innovative potential of an economy, when the basic unit of analysis is the business enterprise, does not imply any interest in keeping any single enterprise innovative. We should not conclude that because an organization largely creates what it exploits, to paraphrase Schumpeter, that the growth of an enterprise on the basis of the learning advantages that it has generated is necessarily in the interests of innovation and development in the economy as a whole.[20] Whether the sustained competitive advantage of previously successful collectivities of insiders within particular enterprises is synonymous with the development of the economy as a whole hinges on the relationship between cumulation advantages and strategic decision-making.

There are significant differences among governance systems in terms of their influence over the internal dynamics of the enterprise, and in particular on the degree to which strategic diseconomies are incurred in exploiting cumulation advantages. In encouraging strategists to maintain both the originating learning unit and the offspring that it spawns as elements of a unitary strategic unit, a system of corporate governance may promote a segmentation of strategy and learning in the economy. Alternatively, governance institutions may promote the continued integration of strategy and learning in the economy by giving the originating strategists incentives to devolve strategic control to decision-makers who are integrated with the offspring's learning process.

3.2. The external dynamics of competition[21]

How different systems of governance influence economic performance over time depends on their interaction not only with the internal dynamics of the

---

[20] Joseph A. Schumpeter (1975), *Capitalism, Socialism and Democracy*, New York: Harper Torchbooks.

[21] For an extended discussion, see O'Sullivan (forthcoming).

enterprise but also with the external dynamics of competition. The organizational and strategic requirements of innovative investment strategies differ across technologies and over time. For example, organizational learning in the pharmaceuticals industry relies on the integration of a very different skill base than organizational learning in the automobile industry. Moreover, even within a particular industry, the character of the integrated skill base that can generate innovation varies over time as the cumulative learning process transforms the possibilities for a collective skill base to develop and utilize productive resources. For example, compared with the skill bases within the managerial structures of the enterprise that enabled the US automobile companies to be the world's dominant mass producers from the 1920s to the 1960s, the successful challenge of the Japanese car makers has relied on broader and deeper skill bases—skill bases that include both managerial and shop-floor workers within core enterprises and organizational integration of the skill bases in these enterprises with those of their suppliers.

Because the organizational and financial requirements of innovative investment strategies vary across context, we should not expect that the social institutions that promote innovation in one era and technology will be an appropriate basis for that process in another era and industry. Given the technological characteristics of an industry and its stage of technological development, institutions of governance may, as social conditions, either promote or constrain innovative business enterprise. Certain governance systems that promote innovation in one technology may fail to advance innovative capability in another and may even retard the development of certain technologies. It is for this reason that we see substantial variations in innovative capability across industries when we hold the governance system constant.[22] Similarly, institutions of governance that promoted innovation and economic development in an earlier era may constrain them when more powerful processes of innovation emerge. To understand the relationship between economic performance and the institutions of governance over the *longue durée*, the challenge is to analyse how institutionalized practices interact with the dynamics of enterprise and competition to influence the strategies and learning of business enterprises. That interactive relationship cannot be determined in the abstract but must be studied in terms of evolving comparative and historical realities of enterprises and institutions.

4. THE LIMITS OF THE ANGLO–AMERICAN GOVERNANCE DEBATES

In contrast to the organizational-control perspective on corporate governance outlined herein, the Anglo–American debates on the subject are

[22] Lazonick and O'Sullivan (1996).

striking for their systematic neglect of the integral role that enterprises and institutions have played in the process of innovation and development in all of the advanced industrial economies. These debates have been dominated by what I call the 'shareholder-control' perspective on governance. The proponents of this perspective view shareholders as the 'owners' or 'principals' in whose interests the corporation should be run. They recognize, however, that in the actual running of the corporation, shareholders must rely on managers to perform certain functions (although they are typically vague as to what these functions are and hence why shareholders need to employ managers).

The proponents of shareholder control have argued, often with justification, that strategic managers of industrial corporations are ill-informed and self-serving in the ways in which they allocate corporate resources and returns. As a result, such managers do not adequately 'create value for shareholders'. To increase the returns to shareholders, the proponents of shareholder value advocate, first, realigning managerial incentives through the use of stock-based rewards; second, using the market for corporate control to enable shareholders to take over companies and replace managers who misallocate corporate resources; and, third, distributing more returns to shareholders so that they can directly reallocate resources in ways that 'maximize shareholder value'.[23]

But why are shareholders the 'principals' in whose interests the corporation should be run? The proponents of shareholder control assert that, as equity

[23] See, for example, Stephen A. Ross (1973), 'The Economic Theory of Agency: The Principal's Problem', *American Economic Review*, 63 (May), 134–9; Michael C. Jensen and William Meckling (1976), 'Theory of the Firm: Managerial Behavior, Agency Costs, and Ownership Structure', *Journal of Financial Economics*, 3 (Oct.); Eugene Fama and Michael Jensen (1983), 'Separation of Ownership and Control', *Journal of Law and Economics*; Michael C. Jensen (1989), 'Eclipse of the Public Corporation', *Harvard Business Review* (Sept.–Oct.); Michael C. Jensen and Richard S. Ruback (1983), 'The Market for Corporate Control: The Scientific Evidence', *Journal of Financial Economics* (Apr.); Michael C. Jensen (1986), 'Agency Cost of Free Cash Flow, Corporate Finance, and Takeovers', *American Economic Review* (May); David Scharfstein (1988), 'The Disciplinary Role of Takeovers', *Review of Economic Studies*, 55 (Apr.); Michael C. Jensen (1988), 'Takeovers: Their Causes and Consequences', *Journal of Economic Perspectives*, 2/1 (Winter); Sanford Grossman and Oliver Hart (1988), 'One Share, One Vote, and the Market for Corporate Control', *Journal of Financial Economics*, 20: 175–202; R. Morck, A. Shleifer, and R. Vishny (1989), 'Alternative Mechanisms of Corporate Control', *American Economic Review* (Sept.); Sanford Grossman and Oliver Hart (1980), 'Takeover Bids, the Free-Rider Problem and the Theory of the Corporation', *Bell Journal of Economics*, 11; Sanford Grossman and Oliver Hart (1982), 'Corporate Financial Structure and Management Incentives', in J. J. McCall (ed.), *Economics of Information and Uncertainty*, Chicago: University of Chicago Press; Kevin J. Murphy (1985), 'Corporate Performance and Managerial Remuneration: An Empirical Analysis', *Journal of Accounting and Economics*, 7 (April), 11–42; George Baker, Michael Jensen, and Kevin Murphy (1988), 'Compensation and Incentives: Practice vs Theory', *Journal of Finance*, 43: 593–616; Michael C. Jensen and Kevin J. Murphy (1990), 'Performance Pay and Top Management Incentives', *Journal of Political Economy*, 98/2: 225–64; Myron Scholes and Mark Wolfson (1991), 'Employee Stock Ownership Plans and Corporate Restructuring: Myths and Realities', Arnold W. Sametz (ed.), *The Battle for Corporate Control: Shareholder Rights, Stakeholder Interests, and Managerial Responsibilities*, Homewood, Ill.: Business One Irwin.

investors, shareholders are the only economic actors who make investments in the corporation without any contractual guarantee of a return. In so far as they secure a return on their investments, it is as 'residual claimants', and hence they alone have an interest in the size of the corporation's profit or loss. The corporation has a contractual obligation to pay fixed-income claimants a specified remuneration (the market price of their factor inputs) irrespective of the performance of the enterprise as a whole. In contrast to fixed-income claimants, it is argued, shareholders as 'residual claimants' to corporate returns have an interest in allocating corporate resources to their 'best alternative uses' to make the residual as large as possible. Since all other 'stakeholders' in the corporation will receive the returns for which they have contracted, the 'maximization of shareholder value' will result in superior economic performance for corporations and the economy as a whole.[24]

In response to the three basic questions about a system of corporate governance, therefore, the proponents of shareholder control would state that, for superior economic performance: (1) shareholders should exercise ultimate control over the allocation of resources, that (2) corporate resources should be allocated to those existing alternative investment opportunities that offer the highest expected rates of return and that, (3) as an integral element in that allocation process, shareholders should be enabled to determine the proportion of corporate returns that should be reinvested in the particular corporation and the proportion that should be distributed to them for reallocation elsewhere in the economy.

The shareholder control perspective combines traditional notions of property rights with deep-seated beliefs in the economic efficacy of the market mechanism that find expression in neoclassical economic theory and represent a distinctively 'Anglo–American' economic ideology. Yet, since the 1920s, if not before, the very existence of the corporation as a central and enduring entity in the advanced economies has prompted a number of economists to question the relevance of these beliefs.[25] As they should, for the realities of successful industrial development in the United States, as well as in Europe and Asia, during this century flatly contradict the basic assumptions of the shareholder-control perspective. Let us consider the problems with the shareholder control perspective, in dealing with the experience of the United States, in terms of each of the three critical corporate governance questions.

---

[24] Armen Alchian and Harold Demsetz (1972), 'Production, Information Costs and Economic Organization', *American Economic Review*, 69: 777–95.

[25] See Thorstein Veblen (1923), *Absentee Ownership and the Business Enterprise in Recent Times: The Case of America*, New York: B. W. Huebsch; Adolf Berle and Gardiner Means (1932), *Private Property and the Modern Corporation*, New York: Macmillan; Joseph A. Schumpeter (1975); John Kenneth Galbraith (1967), *The New Industrial State*, Boston: Houghton Mifflin.

Who should control strategic investment decisions in the corporation?

Public shareholders have not exercised strategic control in the US industrial corporation during this century. The very evolution of the corporate form in the United States entailed a separation of stock ownership from strategic control. Yet, for reasons that have been well-documented elsewhere, it was in the presence of the separation of stock ownership from strategic control that US industrial corporations made the investments in organization and technology that, by the middle decades of this century, enabled the United States to dominate the world economy.

   If, as the proponents of shareholder control argue, the problem of corporate governance is that managers have acquired too much independent power over the allocation of corporate resources and returns, the advocates of shareholder control do not explain how and why corporate managers, as so-called agents, who presumably could be hired, rewarded, and fired by shareholders, acquired such power. Historically, US corporate managers acquired power because they were the strategic decision-makers who allocated corporate resources to organizational learning processes that enabled these corporations to generate innovation and attain sustained competitive advantage in the industries in which they competed.[26] In general, the separation of stock ownership from strategic control was a precondition for placing such strategic decision-making power in the hands of managers who were integrated into the collective and cumulative learning processes that made their enterprises innovative. As the revenue-generating capabilities of these industrial corporations were sustained over the first three decades of this century, a highly liquid market in industrial stocks emerged, thus making shareholders willing to make financial investments in corporate stock without having any knowledge of, or interest in, the strategic decision-making processes that were determining corporate investments in productive resources.

   To recognize that, at some point in the evolution of a particular industrial corporation, the corporate managers who occupy positions of strategic decision-making may become ill-suited to allocate resources to innovative investment strategies in no way implies that shareholders have either the incentives or abilities to perform that function. Rather the problem is to understand why managers who currently occupy positions of strategic control lack the incentives and abilities to allocate resources to innovative strategies.

What types of investments should they make?

The proponents of shareholder control argue that shareholders allocate their financial resources to those alternative investment opportunities that offer the

---

[26] Lazonick and O'Sullivan (1996); id. (1997), 'Finance and Industrial Development: The United States and the United Kingdom', *Financial History Review*, 4/1.

highest expected rates of return. In doing so, they assume that shareholders take the alternative opportunities in which they can invest as given. There is no expectation that shareholders are engaged in making innovative investments that create new opportunities for generating returns, either directly in selecting their investment portfolios or indirectly through the activities of managers who are supposed to serve as their agents. Such a constrained view of the corporate investment process is not problematic for the proponents of shareholder control because, like the neoclassical theory of the market economy to which they link their arguments, the shareholder-control perspective ignores the process of innovation as a central phenomenon in determining the performance of the industrial enterprise or the economy in which it operates.

How far the shareholder-control perspective is from recognizing the importance of innovative investment is demonstrated in a recent presidential address to the American Finance Association by the perspective's foremost proponent, Michael Jensen. In his address, entitled 'The Modern Industrial Revolution, Exit, and the Failure of Internal Control Systems', Jensen highlights Joseph Schumpeter's concept of creative destruction as a seminal insight into the importance of 'efficient exit' from an industry.[27] Yet, of all the economists of the twentieth century, Schumpeter demonstrated the centrality of innovative investments to the process of economic development. When, in *Capitalism, Socialism, and Democracy*, Schumpeter argued (in a famous passage that Jensen quotes), 'the problem that is usually being visualized [by the economist] is how capitalism administers existing structures, whereas the relevant problem is how it creates and destroys them', his concern was with the role of corporate enterprises in generating the innovation process, not with how (as Jensen would, quite incredibly, have his followers believe) corporate managers withdraw resources from the corporate enterprise.[28] In fact, public shareholders have nothing to do with strategic allocation of resources to innovation, so it is not surprising that the proponents of shareholder control have nothing to say about Schumpeter's 'relevant problem': how, through innovation, the economy engages in 'creative destruction'.

How should they distribute the returns on these investments?

Indeed, in his subsequent writings, Schumpeter went on to stress the critical distinction between innovation that generates economic development and adaptation that simply takes existing investment opportunities as given.[29] With its focus on extracting resources from corporations through 'efficient exit'—of which 'disgorging the free cash flow' (as Jensen has so evocatively put it) is the mechanism that particularly enhances shareholder control—the

---

[27] Michael Jensen (1993), 'The Modern Industrial Revolution, Exit and the Failure of Internal Control Systems', *Journal of Finance*, 48: 833.

[28] Schumpeter (1975).   [29] Id. (1947).

shareholder-control perspective is concerned only with adaptation. The perspective has no conception, let alone a theory, of innovation.

Yet the proponents of shareholder control favour distributing returns to shareholders so that they can reallocate them to their best alternative uses. The economic rationale for the distribution of returns to shareholders, as we have seen, is that they have placed their assets at risk in the enterprise on the understanding that they can lay claim to the residual—what I shall call 'the gains to innovation'—that the enterprise generates. Deny the residual to shareholders, so the proponents of shareholder control argue, and finance for industrial investment will disappear.

But the notion that public shareholders invest in productive assets has no basis in the history of successful industrial development in the United States or any other advanced industrial economy for that matter. Public shareholders have never, as a general rule, put their financial assets at risk by investing in the productive assets of the industrial enterprise. Rather they have invested their money in the securities issued by successful enterprises on the basis of investments in productive assets that have already been made. They have been willing to place their money in these securities, not because they are 'residual claimants' to the gains from innovative enterprise but because of the liquidity of these securities on financial markets.

By the same token, in the decades prior to the 1970s, when US industrial corporations were most successful in international competition, the dividend policy of industrial corporations was to maintain the money level of dividends but not to share the gains of innovation with shareholders.[30] Successful enterprises tended to use the gains from innovation for reinvestment in productive assets, including human resources, and to increase the earnings of employees. Moreover, industrial enterprises rarely sought to boost stock prices by repurchasing stock. Yet during this period there was no shortage of capital for investment in productive resources, either in going concerns or new ventures.

Since the 1980s, however, through the transformation of Wall Street combined with the financial power of institutional investors, shareholders have been able to lay claim to a larger share of the returns of US industrial enterprises, even as these enterprises have lost market share in the product markets in which they have competed internationally. By the early 1990s the ability of shareholders to extract higher yields on the stocks that they hold in US corporations had been greatly enhanced. Under the slogan of 'creating shareholder value', these yields have been boosted by enormous increases in corporate distributions in the forms of dividends and stock repurchases.[31]

---

[30] See, for example John Lintner (1956), 'The Distribution of Incomes of Corporations among Dividends, Retained Earnings, and Taxes', *American Economic Review*, 46 (May).

[31] Lazonick and O'Sullivan (1997).

The shareholder-control perspective provides a rationale for Americans who hold corporate stock to live off the accumulations of the past; it does not provide a framework for understanding how the reform of corporate governance can help re-establish the social conditions for innovative enterprise and sustainable prosperity in the future. It is about destruction, not creation. What, then, is the alternative to the shareholder-control perspective?

One alternative that has been put forth recently in proposals to improve the competitive capabilities of American industry can be termed the 'managerial control' perspective.[32] Unlike the proponents of shareholder control, the proponents of managerial control recognize that the competitive success of the industrial corporation depends on investments in innovation that entail specialized in-house knowledge and that require time, and hence financial commitment, to achieve their developmental potential. Thus they argue that managers need discretion to allocate corporate resources which they are only assured if they have access to 'patient capital' that will enable them to see their investments in productive resources through to competitive success.

Like the proponents of shareholder control, the advocates of managerial control view strategic managers as agents of shareholders and look to large shareholders such as wealthy individuals and pension funds to become 'patient capitalists'. Hence the managerial-control perspective would profoundly disagree with the penchant of the proponents of shareholder control for 'disgorging the free cash flow', mainly because the proponents of managerial control understand the importance of what I have called financial commitment for innovative investment strategies.

In looking to public shareholders to provide financial commitment to corporations, however, the proponents of managerial control are looking to a group of people who have claims on corporations but who have never had the abilities or incentives to support innovative investment strategies. Public shareholders are, and have always been, financial investors, not industrial capitalists. In the history of successful US industrial development, some wealthy individuals have performed the role of 'patient capitalists', but they have done so as venture capitalists with a view to reaping returns by taking the new venture public once the enterprise has become a going concern.[33] The most successful venture capitalists, moreover, have had a deep knowledge of the technologies being developed and close relationships with the key developmental personnel. Once, through an initial public offering, a company that has made the transition from new venture to going concern has become

---

[32] The most vigorous proponent of the managerial control perspective in the United States has been Michael E. Porter, an economist by training and a professor of strategy at Harvard Business School. See Michael E. Porter (1990), *The Competitive Advantage of Nations*, New York: Free Press; id. (1992), *Capital Choices: Changing the Way America Invests in Industry*, Washington, DC: Council on Competitiveness.

[33] John W. Wilson (1986), *The New Venturers: Inside the High-Stake World of Venture Capital*, Lexington, Mass.: Addison-Wesley.

publicly held, the key to continued financial commitment has been the dispersion of shareholder power so that, in the quest for financial liquidity, these outsiders to the innovation process cannot reduce the corporate retentions that have been the financial basis for innovative investment.

A more fundamental problem with the managerial-control perspective, the one that has made it vulnerable to challenges from shareholder-control advocates, is that it does not connect to a theory of investment. The proponents of managerial control provide no systematic explanation of the conditions under which managers will make investments that promote innovation and generate returns and those under which such investments will not be made. Thus they provide no response to allegations that corporate managers have grown 'fat and lazy'.

The managerial-control perspective is full of words such as 'capabilities', 'knowledge', 'skills', 'learning', 'factor creation', and 'innovation' as sources of 'sustained competitive advantage' for the enterprise. This orientation alone sets it apart from the shareholder-control perspective, and brings the proponents of managerial control in much closer contact with the real world of industrial development. But, focused as it is on what existing managers think and do rather than how they are integrated into, or segmented from, the productive organizations in which they invest, the managerial-control perspective provides no analysis of the social foundations of innovation and industrial development. From the perspective of managerial control, what determines whether or not an enterprise invests in innovation is the 'mindset' of the strategic manager. But the managerial-control perspective does not see the strategic manager as an actor in a social environment that includes organizations and institutions. What determines the mindset of the manager is rarely addressed.

The dominance of the shareholder-control perspective in contemporary debates on corporate governance reflects not only the shortcomings of the managerial-control perspective but also the fact that it serves powerful interests in the economy. In the USA a substantial proportion of the population—including the 45 per cent of Americans who have pension coverage[34] and even many employees whose jobs are becoming more insecure—are sharing in a process that 'creates value for shareholders' even if it does not create sustainable prosperity for society as a whole. They share in the process of extracting value from the economy through a system of household saving that has come to rely increasingly on the prices and yields of corporate stock. By relying increasingly on the stock market to augment their incomes and savings, these relatively privileged Americans have developed a major stake in maintaining high returns on corporate stock.

---

[34] Teresa Ghilarducci (1992), *Labor's Capital: The Economics and Politics of Private Pensions*, Cambridge, Mass.: MIT Press, 3.

With the increased power of shareholders to extract returns from corporations, a small number of economists and politicians in the USA have argued that there are other corporate 'stakeholders', besides shareholders, who have a claim to corporate returns.[35] The stakeholder perspective has attracted even greater support in the UK and was one element in the electoral campaign that brought the Labour party its landslide victory in the 1997 general election.

The stakeholder perspective, as it is generally exposited, does not challenge the claims of the shareholder-control perspective that shareholders are 'principals'; it accepts that shareholders have 'residual claimant' status because they invest in the productive assets of the enterprise. Rather the stakeholder perspective argues that the physical assets in which shareholders allegedly invest are not the only assets that create value in the corporation. Human assets create value as well. According to one version of the stakeholder perspective, recently articulated by the US economist Margaret Blair, individuals invest in their own human assets, and to some extent these human assets in which they invest are 'firm-specific'.[36] Hence employees make value-creating investments in a particular firm, and therefore, alongside shareholders, should be accorded 'residual claimant' status. In allocating corporate returns, the governance of corporations should recognize the central importance of these investments in human assets to the success of the enterprise and the prosperity of the economy.

In its critique of the proponents of shareholder control and in its emphasis on investment in 'firm-specific' human assets for the success of the economy, the stakeholder perspective has a political affinity with the organizational-control perspective on corporate governance that I have put forward. Political affinity should not, however, be confused with analytical similarity. Like the shareholder-control perspective, the stakeholder perspective clings to the neoclassical theory of the market economy as its analytical framework, and makes ad hoc assumptions within this framework to stress the importance of firm-specific human assets to the economy. Specifically, the stakeholder perspective fails to analyse the process of innovation, and as a result fails to address the organizational and institutional foundations of sustainable prosperity. In response to each of the three critical corporate governance questions concerning strategic control, types of investments, and distribution of returns, let me summarize the main propositions of the organizational-

---

[35] In the academic arena, one of the most sophisticated proponents of the stakeholder perspective is Margaret Blair, an economist by training and a former journalist who is a research fellow at the Brookings Institution. See Margaret Blair (1995), *Ownership and Control: Rethinking Corporate Governance for the Twenty-First Century*, Washington, DC: The Brookings Institution. Another leading advocate of the stakeholder perspective in the USA is Robert B. Reich, a lawyer by training and, until recently, the US Secretary of Labor.

[36] See also John Kay and Aubrey Silberston (1995), 'Corporate Governance', *National Institute Economic Review* (Aug.); Gavin Kelly, Dominic Kelly, and Andrew Gamble (1997) (eds.), *Stakeholder Capitalism*, London: Macmillan.

control perspective, and indicate how the stakeholder perspective on corporate governance falls short of understanding the foundations of sustainable prosperity.

Who should control strategic investment decisions in the corporation?

The organizational-control perspective argues that strategic investment decisions should be made by participants in the corporation who are integrated into the organizational learning processes that can generate products that are higher quality and lower cost than those previously produced. Such strategic integration provides the only basis for making investment decisions in the face of inherent uncertainty with any prospect, other than pure luck, of success. Whatever the hierarchical structure of authority and responsibility within the corporation for committing financial resources to innovative investment strategies, those who wield this authority and responsibility must be integrated into the relevant learning collectivities if they are to have the abilities and incentives to transform inherent uncertainty into sustained competitive advantage.

The stakeholder perspective has no conception of strategic control primarily because it has no theory of the firm other than as a combination of physical and human assets that for some reason—labelled 'firm-specificity'—happen to be gathered together in a particular company. As in neoclassical economic theory, actual investment decisions are made by individual actors with shareholders investing in physical assets and employees investing in human assets. The role of corporate governance is to get factor returns 'right', so that these individual actors are induced to make the 'firm-specific' investments that the enterprise requires. Such a perspective focuses only on the relation between types of investment (physical or human, general or specific) and returns, and hence cannot address how strategic control over the allocation of resources may or may not result in innovative investments.

What types of investments should they make?

For the enterprise to remain innovative, investments must be made in organizational learning processes that can generate higher-quality, lower-cost products than currently exist. It is inherent in the innovation process that the breadth and depth of the skills that must be integrated to produce a particular product will change over time as technology develops. To participate effectively in this dynamic process, business enterprise must be capable of transforming its social organization. To promote sustainable prosperity, corporate governance must be concerned with investments in social organization that can generate innovation and competitive advantage.

The stakeholder perspective refers to 'firm-specific' assets but makes no attempt to understand the investments in organizational learning that make assets specific to a particular collectivity. In *Ownership and Control: Rethinking Corporate Governance for the Twenty-First Century*, Margaret Blair recognizes the need for an analysis of what she calls 'wealth creation'[37] in order to make the case for a corporate governance process that allocates returns to 'firm-specific' human assets. But she provides no analysis of the process that generates higher quality, lower-cost products. She merely asserts that investment in 'firm-specific' assets can generate 'quasi-rents' for the investor, but does not specify under what conditions (technological, organizational, and competitive) such increased returns are generated, or why they should be specific to a particular company.

How should they distribute the returns on these investments?

The organizational-control perspective argues that, to promote sustainable prosperity, returns must be reinvested in learning collectivities that can generate sustained competitive advantage. The need for financial commitment means that returns under the control of the organization are foundations for ensuring investment in learning processes that are collective and cumulative. But the changing character of the organizational-learning processes that can generate competitive advantage means that cumulation disadvantages will eventually arise if the units of strategic control do not change accordingly. To promote sustainable prosperity, corporate governance must be concerned not only with allocating returns to those participants in the enterprise who are engaged in cumulative learning but also with ensuring that, in the form of committed finance, control over returns devolves to strategic decision makers who are and remain integrated into the processes of organizational learning. At the same time, to promote sustainable prosperity, corporate governance must be concerned with limiting the allocation of returns to those interests— such as public shareholders—who can exercise claims on corporate returns but who make no contribution to the processes of collective and cumulative learning.

Lacking a concept of strategic decision-making and an analysis of the innovation process, the stakeholder perspective sees returns as attaching to specific human and physical assets, and views the claims to these assets as being based on the investments that individual shareholders and employees make. The assumptions that both investment in and returns from productive investments attach to individuals, even when these factors of production are combined in firms, preclude an analysis of the collective character of corporate investment and corporate returns. Hence the stakeholder perspective has no analytical basis for understanding a system of corporate governance that can allocate returns from existing productive investments to new productive investments that are collective. To promote sustainable prosperity, a system

---

[37] Blair (1995), 232–4, 240 ff., 327–8.

of corporate governance must facilitate collective decision-making concerning the allocation of resources and returns.

The problem of corporate governance and industrial development is not resolved by simply advocating that industrial corporations be run for other 'stakeholders'—especially employees—besides shareholders. The danger is that different groups who can lay claim to shares of corporate revenues will, as has increasingly been the case with shareholders, extract corporate revenues whether or not their contributions to the generation of these revenues make these returns possible on a sustainable basis. The result of the creation of a 'stakeholder society' might be to increase the propensity for major industrial enterprises and the economy in which they operate to live off the past rather than invest for the future.

If sustainable prosperity is the objective, proposals to reform the corporate governance system must be based on a theory of the innovative enterprise. Without such a theory, stakeholder arguments run the risk of encouraging other groups, besides shareholders, to become claimants to a given, and even diminishing pool of returns. To avoid such an economic stalemate requires a conception of how investments in people working together in organizations can generate the returns in international competition that make sustainable prosperity possible. Only if we understand how the institutional foundations of organizational control in corporate enterprises have evolved in comparative-historical perspective do we have any hope of generating the social foundations on which organizational control in corporate economies can be democratized.

11. Organizational Learning and International Competition*

William Lazonick

THE SKILL-BASE HYPOTHESIS

Since the 1970s a persistent feature of the US economy has been increasing income inequality, to the point where the United States now has the most unequal distribution of income among the advanced industrial economies. Sustainable prosperity—the spreading of the benefits of economic growth to more and more people over a prolonged period of time—appears to have become an elusive objective. At the same time, in the late 1990s, after more than two decades of intense competitive challenges, the United States retains international leadership in a range of science-based industries such as computer electronics and pharmaceuticals as well as in service sectors related to such things as finance and food. The US economy appears capable of innovation, but incapable of sustainable prosperity.

Are innovation and equality inherently in opposition to one another? In previous work with Mary O'Sullivan, we hypothesized that the coexistence of innovation and inequality in the US economy in the 1980s and 1990s reflects a systematic bias of major US corporations against making innovative investments in broad and deep skill bases.[1] Rather, these corporations, which exercise inordinate control over the allocation of resources and returns in the economy, are choosing to invest, and are best able to innovate, in the production of goods and services that use narrow and concentrated skill bases to develop and utilize technology.

Why are 'skill bases' important to the economy? They form the foundation on which people engage in collective and cumulative—or organizational—learning, which is in turn central to the process of economic development. Case-study evidence suggests that the manufacturing industries in which the US economy has been most severely challenged by high-wage foreign competition—industries such as automobiles, consumer electronics,

* I gratefully acknowledge the contributions of Mary O'Sullivan to the form and substance of this chapter. Funding for this research was provided by the Jerome Levy Economics Institute and the Center for Global Partnership.

[1] William Lazonick and Mary O'Sullivan (1996), 'Corporate Governance and Corporate Employment: Is Prosperity Sustainable in the United States?', Report to the Jerome Levy Economics Institute (Dec.).

machine tools, and commodity semiconductors—are those in which innovation and sustained competitive advantage demand investments in broader and deeper skill bases. If the 'skill-base hypothesis' is valid, then it may well be that innovation and equality can go hand in hand.[2] From a policy perspective, the relevant issue is how business enterprises can be induced to make innovative investments in broad and deep skill bases.

The skill-base hypothesis adds an important dimension to American debates on the relation between investments in 'technology' and sustainable prosperity. On one side have been those who stress the weakened innovative capabilities of the US economy in international competition.[3] They have called for the US government and businesses to allocate more resources to education, training, research, and co-operative investment projects that can support the United States in making a competitive response. These arguments assume, often more implicitly than explicitly, that these innovative responses will promote sustainable prosperity in the United States.

On the other side have been those who argue that income inequality cannot be blamed on international competition. Rather they attribute growing inequality to the employment impacts of 'new technology'.[4] The volume of world trade, they argue, is not large enough to have a significant impact on the distribution of income in the United States. If the United States has problems keeping people employed at high wages, it is because, for a given level of investment, technologies of the computer age do not create the same quantity and quality of employment opportunities for Americans as did the technologies of the past. Income inequality has grown, they argue, because new technologies displace employment opportunities that used to be well-paid. Pay attention to raising the levels of both investment and relevant skill in the US economy, and the income distribution will improve.

The skill-base hypothesis argues that both international competition and technological change are important determinants of the distribution of income. But the hypothesis is embedded in a theory of innovation and economic development in which the impacts of international competition and technology on income distribution are not independent of either corporate investment strategy or the national institutions that influence corporate strategy. If valid, the skill-base hypothesis implies that, by investing in broad and deep skill bases, corporations can generate innovation and contribute to sustainable prosperity. The key supply-side policy issue then is how to influence

[2] Ibid.

[3] Stephen Cohen and John Zysman (1987), *Manufacturing Matters*, New York: Basic Books; Michael L. Dertouzos, Richard K. Lester, and Robert M. Solow, and the MIT Commission on Industrial Productivity (1989), *Made in America: Regaining the Productive Edge*, Cambridge, Mass.: MIT Press; Laura D'Andrea Tyson (1992), *Who's Bashing Whom?: Trade Conflict in High-Technology Industries*, Washington, DC: Institute for International Economics.

[4] See Paul Krugman and Robert Lawrence (1994), 'Trade, Jobs, and Wages', *Scientific American* (Apr.); Paul Krugman (1997), *Pop Internationalism*, Cambridge, Mass.: MIT Press.

corporate strategy to innovate in technologies that demand investments in broad and deep skill bases.

Powerful support for this hypothesis can be found in the experience of Japanese–US industrial competition over the past few decades. Japan has taken on and surpassed the United States in many industries in which it was the previous world leader. The foundations of Japanese success in international competition, I shall argue, were investments in broad and deep skill bases to generate organizational learning. The problems related to innovation and equality in the United States in the 1980s and 1990s have not been inherent in technology. Rather the problems derive from corporate strategies to develop and utilize technology. These strategies, and the investment in skill bases that they entail, are in turn influenced by American institutions of corporate governance and corporate employment. These institutions, we have contended, have encouraged corporations to invest in narrow and concentrated skill bases in a world of international competition in which innovation comes increasingly from investing in broad and deep skill bases.[5] If we are correct, reversing the trend toward income inequality in the United States must go much deeper than growth policies or industrial policies. It will require transformation of the way industrial corporations are governed and the way people are employed

ORGANIZATIONAL INTEGRATION

Almost all of the major industrial corporations in the US economy in the post-World War II era made investments in managerial learning from the early decades of the twentieth century, if not before. Many of the productive and competitive advantages of these investments in managerial organization still accrued to these corporations decades after the particular individuals involved in these collective learning processes had left the corporate scene.

In comparative international perspective, US industrial corporations were not unique in building their managerial organizations into formidable sources of sustained competitive advantage. What made US industrial corporations unique among their counterparts in the advanced economies was their dedication to a strategy of taking skills, and hence the possibilities for craft learning—much less corporate learning—off the shop floor.[6] This process of transforming skilled craft work into 'semi-skilled' operative work was a prolonged one, constrained as it was by the development of new tech-

[5] Lazonick and O'Sullivan, 'Corporate Governance and Corporate Employment'.

[6] William Lazonick and Mary O'Sullivan (1997), 'Big Business and Skill Formation in the Wealthiest Nations: The Organizational Revolution in the Twentieth Century,' in Alfred D. Chandler, Jr., Franco Amatori and Takashi Hikino (eds.), *Big Business and the Wealth of Nations*, Cambridge: Cambridge University Press; William Lazonick (1990), *Competitive Advantage on the Shop Floor*, Cambridge, Mass.: Harvard University Press.

nology through managerial learning. But, as reflected in the distinction between 'salaried' and 'hourly' personnel, the strategy of relying exclusively on the managerial organization for the development of new productive capabilities has been, throughout the twentieth century, a distinctive characteristic of US industrial development.

The American corporate strategy of confining organizational learning to those employed within the managerial structure enabled the United States to become the world's leading industrial power during the first half of the twentieth century.[7] On the basis of this leadership, US industrial corporations were able to provide high pay and stable employment to not only managerial employees but also shop-floor workers, whether they be skilled or semiskilled.

Over the past few decades, however, powerful international competitors have arisen who have developed productive capabilities by integrating managers and workers into their organizational learning processes. The *hierarchical segmentation* between managers and workers that the American 'managerial revolution' entailed became a major institutional barrier to making the types of investments in organizational learning required to sustain prosperity in the US economy. In an era of intense international competition in which sustained competitive advantage went to those enterprises and nations that made investments in, and integrated, the organizational learning of both managerial and shop-floor personnel, the investment strategies of most US industrial corporations that focused only on managerial learning fell short.

The competitive problem that has faced US industrial corporations is that, over time for a particular product, the innovation process, of which the organizational learning process is its social substance, has become increasingly *collective* and *cumulative*. Organizational learning has become increasingly collective because innovation—the generation of higher quality, lower cost products—depends on the integration of an ever-increasing array of specific productive capabilities based on intimate knowledge of particular organizations, technologies, and markets. Organizational learning has become increasingly cumulative because the collective learning that an organization has accumulated in the past increasingly forms an indispensable foundation for the augmentation of organizational learning in the present and future.

The increasingly collective and cumulative character of organizational learning means that, for a particular product, an innovative investment strategy is one that entails investments in *broader and deeper skill bases*—divisions of labour that extend further down the organizational hierarchy and involve more functional specialties. The investments in skill bases are not simply investments in the learning of large numbers of individuals performing a wide

---

[7] Lazonick and O'Sullivan, 'Big Business and Skill Formation'.

variety of functions. For these investments in broader and deeper skill bases to generate higher quality, lower cost products requires *organizational integration*, a set of social relations that provides participants in a complex division of labour with the incentives to cooperate in contributing their skills and efforts toward the achievement of common goals.

At any point in time, the technological possibilities and organizational requirements of the innovation process vary markedly across industries in terms of the extent of the skill base in which the innovating enterprise must invest. In industries, such as pharmaceuticals, in which value-added comes mainly from research, design, and marketing, *narrow and concentrated skill bases* of scientists, engineers, and patent lawyers remain sufficient for generating higher quality, lower cost products. In such industries, US industrial enterprises have been able to remain world leaders. But in industries, such as automobiles, where value-added comes mainly from manufacturing processes that combine a complex array of physically distinct components, international competitive challenges have been based on investments in broader and deeper skill bases. The investments in organizational learning occur not only within corporate management structures but also on the shop floor and in the vertical supply chain. In those industries in which international competition demands investments in such broad and deep skill bases, once-dominant US industrial enterprises have lost substantial competitive advantage.

In the US automobile industry, American-based companies have regained some of the markets they have lost—or at least have stemmed the loss of market share. The skill-base hypothesis posits that they have done so by investing in broader and deeper skill bases than was previously the case.[8] In responding to these competitive challenges, moreover, the organizational problem that has faced US industrial enterprises over the past few decades has gone beyond the hierarchical segmentation between managers and workers. Even within the managerial organization—the traditional locus of organizational learning in US enterprises—organizational integration appears to have given way to two types of segmentation which we call *functional* and *strategic*.

Compared with both the integrated organizational structures of foreign competitors and the integrated managerial structures that characterized the most successful US companies in the past, organizational learning within the managerial structures of US enterprises has been limited by the *functional segmentation* of different groups of technical specialists from one another. Specialists in marketing, development, production, and purchasing may be highly skilled in their particular functions, but relative to their counterparts abroad, in US enterprises they tend to respond to incentives that lead them to

---

[8] I am currently engaged in a comparative study of organizational integration and competitive advantage in the automobile industry, supported by the Center for Global Partnership, in collaboration with the International Motor Vehicle Program.

learn in isolation from one another. Functional segmentation makes it difficult if not impossible for such isolated specialists to solve complex manufacturing problems that require collective and cumulative learning.

In addition, in comparative and historical perspective, a distinctive characteristic of US industrial enterprises since the 1960s has been the *strategic segmentation* of those top managers who control enterprise resources from those lower down the managerial hierarchy on whom the enterprise has relied for organizational learning. In allocating vast amounts of resources, top managers of major US industrial corporations have increasingly lost the incentive to remain cognizant of the problems and possibilities for organizational learning within the enterprises over which they exercise control. Within a particular enterprise, tendencies toward hierarchical, functional, and strategic segmentation may be mutually reinforcing, thus making it all the more difficult for an enterprise, or group of enterprises, to invest in organizational learning once they have embarked on the organizational-segmentation path.

The skill-base hypothesis seeks to test these propositions concerning the growing importance of hierarchical, functional, and strategic integration for attaining and sustaining competitive advantage, and the increasing tendency toward organizational segmentation along these three dimensions in US industrial corporations in historical and comparative perspective. The skill-base hypothesis, and the theoretical perspective on innovation and economic development in which it is embedded, derives from our historical and comparative analyses of the role of organizational integration in shifts in international competitive advantage.[9] The empirical evidence required to test the hypothesis must be derived from in-depth analyses of the investment strategies, organizational structures, and competitive performance of particular companies based in different nations that have engaged in head-to-head competition in particular industries.

The purpose of this chapter is to motivate such a research agenda by drawing on some of the findings of a now vast range of literature on the interaction of organization and technology in US-Japanese industrial competition. This evidence, much of it deriving from the experiences of management consultants and case-studies by business academics, provides substance to the skill-base hypothesis. In this chapter, I shall focus on differences in hierarchical integration and organizational learning in Japanese and American enterprises. I shall argue that understanding hierarchical integration of technical specialists and production operatives forms an indispensable foundation for

[9] William Lazonick (1991), *Business Organization and the Myth of the Market Economy*, Cambridge: Cambridge University Press; Mary O'Sullivan (1996), 'Innovation, Industrial Development and Corporate Governance', Ph.D. dissertation, Harvard University, June; Lazonick and O'Sullivan, 'Big Business and Skill Formation'; William Lazonick and Mary O'Sullivan (1996), 'Organization, Finance, and International Competition', *Industrial and Corporate Change*, 5, 1; Lazonick and O'Sullivan, 'Corporate Governance and Corporate Employment'; Mary O'Sullivan, 'Sustainable Prosperity, Corporate Governance, and Innovation in Europe' (this volume).

understanding the functional integration of technical specialists themselves—
a subject that now dominates much of the management literature on technological competition. Absent from this chapter will be a discussion of strategic
integration and segmentation, a subject that, in relation to the skill-base
hypothesis, has been treated at length elsewhere, and that provides the analytical interface between issues of corporate governance and organizational
learning.[10] In what follows, therefore, I shall be concerned with the social
structures that generate organizational learning rather than with the social
structures that allocate resources to building different types of skill bases.

ORGANIZATIONAL LEARNING

If there is one nation that has challenged the United States for international
industrial leadership in the last half of the twentieth century, that nation is
Japan. In 1950 Japan's GDP per capita was only 20 per cent of that of the
United States; in 1992 90 per cent.[11] The Japanese challenge had come, moreover, not in those industries in which American companies were weak or that
they had neglected. On the contrary, the challenge came in industries such as
automobiles, electronics, and machine tools in which the United States had
attained a seemingly invincible position as the world's leading mass-
producer.

Since the 1980s much has been written about the institutional and organizational sources of Japanese competitive advantage. Social institutions such
as lifetime employment and cross-shareholding and organizational practices
such as total-quality management and consensus decision-making have been
critical elements of Japan's phenomenal rise from the ashes of defeat after the
Second World War. But these institutions and organizations would not have
generated the so-called Japanese economic miracle in the 1950s and 1960s had
Japan not already possessed in the immediate aftermath of the war an accumulation of technological capabilities.

Japan had been accumulating capabilities in mechanical, electrical, and
chemical technologies since the late nineteenth century when the Japanese
'managerial revolution' had begun. At the time of the Meiji Restoration in

[10] O'Sullivan, 'Innovation, Industrial Development and Corporate Governance'; ead. (forth-
coming), *Contests for Corporate Control*, Oxford: Oxford University Press; Lazonick and
O'Sullivan, 'Corporate Employment and Corporate Governance'; eid. (1997), 'Finance and
Industrial Development: Pt. I, The United States and the United Kingdom', *Financial History
Review*, 5/1; and eid. (1997), 'Finance and Industrial Development: Pt. II, Japan and Germany',
Financial History Review, 5/1.

[11] Angus Maddison (1994), 'Explaining the Economic Performance of Nations, 1820–1989',
in William J. Baumol, Richard R. Nelson, and Edward N. Wolff (eds.), *Convergence of
Productivity: Cross-National Studies and Historical Evidence*, New York: Oxford University
Press, 22.

1868, Japan had little in the way of modern industrial capabilities.[12] Under the slogan 'Rich Nation, Strong Army', the Restoration government implemented a strategy for industrial development that was heavily dependent on borrowing knowledge, technologies, and even institutions from abroad.[13] In the first half of the 1870s, private and public interests set up institutions of higher education—most notably Keio University, the Institute of Technology (later part of Tokyo Imperial University), and the Commercial Law School (which became Hitotsubashi University)—to supply key personnel to an innovative industrial economy.[14] By the 1880s Japan had a steady supply of both indigenous graduates and teachers.[15]

Large numbers of university graduates were lured into industry, with the *zaibatsu* (including their affiliated industrial enterprises) taking the lead.[16] From 1900 to 1920, the employment of graduate engineers increased from 54 to 835 at Mitsui and from 52 to 818 at Mitsubishi.[17] These highly educated personnel were not only eagerly recruited but also well paid by the companies that employed them. In addition, companies often incurred the considerable expense of sending these employees abroad for varying lengths of time to acquire more industrial experience.[18]

During the inter-war period the overall development strategy of the Japanese economy became increasingly dominated by the investment requirements of militarization and imperial expansion. Relying heavily on the *zaibatsu*, Japan devoted considerable resources to building technological capabilities in mechanical, electrical, and chemical science and engineering. In the immediate aftermath of the Second World War, as the Allied Occupation engaged in the dissolution of the once-powerful *zaibatsu*,[19]

[12] See Tessa Morris-Suzuki (1994), *The Technological Transformation of Japan*, Cambridge: Cambridge University Press.

[13] Richard Samuels (1994), *'Rich Nation, Strong Army': National Security and the Technological Transformation of Japan*, Ithaca, NY: Cornell University Press; D. Eleanor Westney (1987), *Imitation and Innovation*, Cambridge, Mass.: Harvard University Press. On the development of a financial system for industrial development, see Lazonick and O'Sullivan, 'Finance and Industrial Development: Pt. II.

[14] Johannes Hirschmeier and Tsunehiko Yui (1981), *The Development of Japanese Business*, 2nd edn., London, Allen & Unwin, 166; Janet Hunter (1984), *A Concise Dictionary of Modern Japan*, Berkeley: University of California Press, 47; Etsuo Abe (1996), 'Shibusawa, Eiichi (1840–1931)', in Malcolm Warner (ed.), *International Encyclopedia of Business and Management*, London: Routledge, 4451.

[15] Shin'ichi Yonekawa (1984), 'University Graduates in Japanese Enterprises before the Second World War', *Business History*, 26 July, 193–218; Ryoichi Iwauchi (1989), 'The Growth of White-Collar Employment in Relation to the Educational System', and H. Uchida (1989), 'Comment', in T. Yui and K-. Nakagawa (eds.), *Japanese Management in Historical Perspective*, Tokyo: University of Tokyo Press, 83–108.

[16] Yonekawa, 'University Graduates in Japanese Enterprises'.

[17] Uchida, 'Comment', 108.

[18] Iwauchi, 'Growth of White-Collar Employment', 99; Hirschmeier and Yui, *Development of Japanese Business*, 154.

[19] T. Adams and I. Hoshii (1972), *A Financial History of the New Japan*, Tokyo: Kodansha International, 23–5. See also T. A. Bisson (1954), *Zaibatsu Dissolution in Japan*, Berkeley:

Japanese scientists and engineers organized to seek new ways to develop and utilize their capabilities.

In 1946 they formed the Japanese Union of Scientists and Engineers (JUSE), an association devoted to promoting the nation's technological development through education, standard-setting, and the diffusion of information. Influenced by US occupation officials versed in statistical quality control (SQC) techniques that the United States had used for military production during the war, JUSE focused on the application of quality control in an economy based on production for commercial markets. In 1949 JUSE established the Quality Control Research Group (QCRG), which included participants from academia, industry, and government.

The following year JUSE sponsored an eight-day seminar on SQC by Dr W. Edwards Deming, a physicist who had been working for the US government developing the sampling methods for SQC.[20] These techniques were used to monitor mass-produced output for systematic deviations from 'quality' standards as a prelude to controlling (identifying and correcting) quality problems. Deming's lectures were well received as was the volume of these lectures that JUSE promptly published. The author donated the royalties from the book to JUSE, which in turn used the funds to establish the now-famous Deming Application Prize, awarded annually since 1951 to an industrial company for its achievements in the application of quality control (QC) methods.[21]

One of the key figures in applying QC methods to Japanese industry was Kaoru Ishikawa, an engineering professor at the University of Tokyo. Starting in 1949, under the auspices of QCRG, Ishikawa began teaching the QC Basic Course to industrial engineers, using translated British and American texts. 'After conducting the first course', Ishikawa recalled,

it became clear to us that physics, chemistry, and mathematics are universal and are applicable anywhere in the world. However, in the case of quality control, or in anything that has the term 'control' attached to it, human and social factors are strongly at work. No matter how good the American and British methods may be, they cannot be imported to Japan as they stand. To succeed, we had to create a Japanese method.[22]

University of California Press; Eleanor Hadley, *Antitrust in Japan*, Princeton: Princeton University Press,, 1970.

[20] Kaoru Ishikawa (1985), *What is Total Quality Control? The Japanese Way*, Englewood Cliffs, NY: Prentice-Hall, 16.

[21] Izumi Nonaka (1995), 'The Development of Company-Wide Quality Control and Quality Circles at Toyota Motor Corporation and Nissan Motor Co. Ltd.', in Haruhito Shiomi and Kazuo Wada (eds.), *Fordism Transformed: The Development of Production Methods in the Automobile Industry*, Oxford: Oxford University Press.

[22] Ishikawa, *What is Total Quality Control?*, 16–17.

Ishikawa, along with others, developed the Japanese method in the 1950s through their direct involvement with Japanese manufacturing companies, particularly in the fledgeling automobile industry.[23]

What was different about Japanese conditions that made it necessary to 'create a Japanese method'? And how by the 1970s and 1980s did the Japanese method that was created become the world's most powerful manufacturing approach for setting new standards of high quality and low cost? In particular, how did Japanese manufacturing for mass markets differ from the system that Americans had previously developed in the first half of the twentieth century when US industry established itself as the world's leading mass-producer?

The fundamental difference between the Japanese and American organization of mass production was on the shop-floor. The American system of mass production that dominated the world economy by the mid-twentieth century was based on the production of long runs of identical units by expensive special-purpose machines tended by 'semi-skilled' operatives.[24] The transformation of the high fixed costs of these mass-production technologies into low unit costs of final products required the co-operation of these shop-floor workers in the repetitive performance of narrow manual functions needed to maintain the flow of work-in-progress through the interlinked mechanical system.

The American machine operatives themselves were not involved in either the monitoring of the quality of work-in-progress or the search for a solution to quality problems in the manufacturing process. By design, they were excluded from the process of organizational learning that generated the American system of mass production.[25] Reflecting the American practice of confining organizational learning to the managerial structure, and developing technologies that displaced the need for skill on the shop-floor, in the United States quality control had evolved as a strictly managerial function. Leading American mass-producers were willing to provide, and indeed the most successful companies did provide, greater employment security and higher wages to shop-floor workers to ensure their co-operation in keeping pace with the expensive high-speed, special-purpose machinery. These companies, that is, established incentives to gain the co-operation of operatives in the *utilization* of technology. The managers of these companies were unwilling to grant these operatives any role in the *development* of technology but rather confined such organizational learning to the managerial structure. Indeed in the

---

[23] Nonaka, 'Development of Company-Wide Quality Control', 143. See also Shigeru Mizuno (1984), *Company-Wide Total Quality Control*, Tokyo: Asian Productivity Organization.

[24] On the emergence of American mass production, see David Hounshell (1984), *From the American System to Mass Production, 1800–1932*, Baltimore: Johns Hopkins University Press.

[25] On the historical origins of this hierarchical segmentation, see Lazonick, *Competitive Advantage on the Shop Floor*, chs. 7–9.

American companies considerable managerial learning was devoted to organizing work and developing mass-production technologies.[26]

In the post-Second World War Japanese automobile industry, companies
like Toyota and Nissan did not have the luxury of long runs. Reflecting
Japan's low level of GDP per capita, in 1950 the entire Japanese automobile
industry produced 31,597 vehicles, which was about the volume that US companies produced in one and a-half days.[27] In that year, Nissan accounted for
39 per cent of production and Toyota 37 per cent, while for the industry as a
whole 84 per cent of the vehicles produced were trucks.[28] As production
increased over the course of the 1950s, with cars becoming a larger proportion of the total, Nissan or Toyota had to produce an increasing variety of
vehicles to survive. In responding to these demand-side conditions, therefore,
these companies had no possibility of achieving low unit costs by simply
adopting American mass-production methods.

On the supply-side, over the course of the twentieth century Japanese
industry had developed capabilities that could now enable companies like
Toyota and Nissan to develop and utilize technology in a profoundly different way. These companies could draw on a sizeable supply of highly educated
and experienced engineers. Many Toyota employees, for example, had accumulated relevant technological experience over the previous decades working
for the enterprise group when it was Japan's leading producer of textile
machinery.[29] In addition, the automobile industry was able to attract many
engineers who had gained experience in Japan's aircraft industry before and
during the war.[30]

Before the war, moreover, many Japanese companies had integrated foremen into the structure of managerial learning so that they could not only
supervise but also train workers on the shop-floor. Whereas in the United
States, the foreman, as 'the man in the middle', served as a buffer between the
managerial organization and the shop-floor, in Japan the foreman was an
integrator of managerial and shop-floor learning. From the late nineteenth
century, a prime objective of US managerial learning had been to develop
machine technologies that could dispense with the skills of craft workers on
the shop-floor. In contrast, with an accumulation of such craft skills lacking
in Japan, the problem that had confronted technology-oriented managers

---

[26] *Competitive Advantage on the Shop Floor*, chs. 7–9; William Lazonick (1997), 'Rethinking
"Taylorism": Organization of Innovation for the Twenty-First Century', INSEAD, photocopy,
June.

[27] Michael Cusumano (1985), *The Japanese Automobile Industry: Technology and
Management at Nissan and Toyota*, Cambridge, Mass.: Harvard University Press, 75, 266,

[28] Ibid. 75.

[29] William Mass and Andrew Robertson (1996), 'From Textiles to Automobiles: Mechanical
and Organizational Innovation in the Toyoda Enterprises, 1895–1933', *Business and Economic
History*, 25/2.

[30] See Kazuo Wada (1995), 'The Emergence of the "Flow Production" Method in Japan', in
Shiomi and Wada, *Fordism Transformed*.

from the Meiji era had been to develop skills on the shop-floor as part of a co-ordinated strategy of organizational learning.

The rise of enterprise unions in the early 1950s both reflected and enhanced the social foundations for this hierarchical integration. During the last half of the 1940s, the transformation of corporate control threatened to go much further as dire economic conditions and democratization initiatives gave rise to a militant labour movement of white-collar (technical and administrative) and blue-collar (operative) employees. The goal of the new industrial unions was to implement 'production control': the takeover of idle factories so that workers could put them into operation and earn a living.[31] As an alternative to the 'production control' strategy of militant unions, leading companies created enterprise unions of white-collar and blue-collar employees. In 1950 under economic conditions deliberately rendered more severe by the Occupation's anti-inflationary 'Dodge line', companies such as Toyota, Toshiba, and Hitachi fired militant workers and offered enterprise unionism to the remaining employees. The post-Korean War recession of 1953 created another opportunity for more companies to expel the militants and introduce enterprise unionism. The continued and rapid expansion of the Japanese economy in the 'high-growth era' ensured that enterprise unionism would become an entrenched Japanese institution.[32]

The prime achievement of enterprise unionism was 'lifetime employment', a system that gave white-collar and blue-collar workers employment security to the retirement age of 55 or 60. Foremen and supervisors were members of the union, as were all university-educated personnel for at least the first ten years of employment before they made the official transition into 'management'. Union officials, who were company employees, held regularly scheduled conferences with management at different levels of the enterprise to resolve issues concerning remuneration, work conditions, work organization, transfers, and production.[33]

These institutional conditions supported the integration of shop-floor workers into a company-wide process of organizational learning. Top managers had ultimate control over strategic investments, and technical

[31] Joe Moore (1983), *Japanese Workers and the Struggle for Power, 1945–1947*, Madison: University of Wisconsin Press; Andrew Gordon (1985), *The Evolution of Labor Relations in Japan: Heavy Industry, 1853–1955*, Cambridge, Mass.: Harvard University Press, 343; N. Hiwatari (1996), 'Japanese Corporate Governance Reexamined: The Origins and Institutional Foundations of Enterprise Unionism', paper prepared for the Conference on Employees and Corporate Governance, Columbia University Law School, 22 Nov.

[32] Gordon, *Evolution of Labor Relations in Japan*, ch. 10; Cusumano, *The Japanese Automobile Industry*; David Halberstam (1986), *The Reckoning*, New York: Morrow, 1986, pt. 3; Hiwatari, 'Japanese Corporate Governance'.

[33] See K. Shimokawa (1994), *The Japanese Automobile Industry: A Business History*, London: Athlone, ch. 3; K. Nakamura, 'Worker Participation: Collective Bargaining and Joint Consultation', in M. Sako and H. Sato (eds.), *Japanese Labour and Management in Transition*, London: Routledge.

specialists designed products and processes, typically on the basis of technology borrowed from abroad. But, given these managerial capabilities, the unique ability of Japanese companies to transform borrowed technology to generate new standards of quality and cost depended on the integration of shop-floor workers into the process of organizational learning.

Through their engagement in processes of cost-reduction, Japanese shop-floor workers were continuously involved in a more general process of improvement of products and processes that, by the 1970s, enabled Japanese companies to emerge as the world leader in factory automation. This productive transformation became particularly important in international competition in the 1980s and 1990s as Japanese wages approached the levels of the advanced industrial economies of North America and Western Europe. During the 1980s and 1990s, influenced as well by the impact of Japanese direct investment in North America and Western Europe, many Western companies have been trying, with varying degrees of success, to implement Japanese high-quality, low-cost mass-production methods.

Especially since the 1980s a huge English-language literature has emerged on Japanese manufacturing methods, much of it written by industrial engineers with considerable experience as employees of and consultants to manufacturing companies in Japan and the West. In addition, there is a growing body of academic research on the subject, although it tends to focus more on functional integration than on hierarchical integration. My purpose here is to summarize this body of evidence to make the case that, in comparison with the once-dominant American mass-producers, a fundamental source of Japanese manufacturing success has been the hierarchical integration of shop-floor workers in the process of organizational learning. Then, in the following sections, I shall summarize how, within Japanese companies, hierarchical integration contributed to the generation of higher-quality, lower-cost products as part of a process of organizational learning that included functional integration and strategic integration as well.

In a comprehensive account of Japan's manufacturing challenge, Kiyoshi Suzaki, a former engineer at Toshiba who then turned to consulting in the United States, contrasts the operational and organizational characteristics of a 'conventional' (traditional American) company and a 'progressive' (innovative Japanese) company in the use of men, materials, and machines in the production process (see Table 11.1).[34] In the generation of higher-quality, lower-cost products, the integration of Japanese shop-floor workers into the process of organizational learning contributed to (1) the more complete *utilization of machines*; (2) superior *utilization of materials*; (3) improvements in *product quality*; and (4) *factory automation*. In summarizing the ways in which hierarchical integration contributed to these innovative outcomes in

[34] Kiyoshi Suzaki (1987), *The New Manufacturing Challenge*, New York: Free Press.

Table 11.1. Operational and organizational characteristics of American and Japanese manufacturing

	American company	Japanese company
Operational characteristic:		
Lot size	Large	Small
Set-up time	Long	Short
Machine trouble	High	Low
Inventory	Large	Small
Floor space	Large	Small
Transportation	Long	Short
Lead time	Long	Short
Defect Rate	High	Low
Organizational characteristic:		
Structure	Rigid	Flexible
Orientation	Local optimization	Total optimization
Communication	Long chain of command	Open
Agreement	Contract-based	Institution-based
Union focus	Job-based	Company-based
Skill base	Narrow	Broad
Education/training	Low quality	High quality
Training	Insignificant	Significant
Supplier relations	Short-term/many competitors	Long-term/selected few

Source: Adapted from Kiyoshi Suzaki, *The New Manufacturing Challenge*, 233.

Japan, I shall indicate how and why Japanese practice differed from the hierarchical segmentation of shop-floor workers that was, and still largely remains, the norm in American manufacturing.

Utilization of machines

In the decade after the war, the Japanese pioneered in cellular manufacturing—the placement of a series of vertically related machines in a U-shape so that a worker, or team of workers, can operate different kinds of machines to produce a completed unit of output. Used particularly for the production of components, cellular manufacturing requires that workers perform a variety of tasks, and hence that they be multi-skilled.

The Japanese system differed from the linear production system used in the United States in which shop-floor workers specialized in particular tasks, passing the semi-finished unit from one specialized worker to the next. Historically, this fragmented division of labour resulted from the successful strategy of American managers in the late nineteenth century to develop and utilize mechanized technologies that could overcome their dependence on craft contractors who had previously controlled the organization of work.[35] To better supervise the 'semi-skilled' workers who operated the new mechanized technologies, American managers then sought to confine adversarial shop-floor workers to narrow tasks. After the rise of industrial unionism in the 1930s, shop-floor workers used these narrow job definitions as a foundation for wage-setting, thus institutionalizing this form of job control in collective bargaining arrangements.

The prevalence of adversarial bargaining and job control only served to increase the resolve of most US corporate managers to keep skill and initiative off the shop-floor in the decades after the Second World War. Meanwhile, developing and utilizing the capabilities of the multi-skilled shop-floor worker in a myriad of ways, Japanese companies created new standards of quality and cost. This continuous improvement, which the Japanese called *kaizen*,[36] enabled Japanese companies to out-compete the Americans, even in their own home markets, even as Japanese wages rose and the yen strengthened in the 1980s and 1990s.

With the need to use mass-production equipment to produce a variety of products in the 1950s, Japanese companies placed considerable emphasis on reducing set-up times. Long set-ups meant excessive downtime, which means lost output. Once set in motion, the search for improvements often continued over years and even decades. For example, in 1945 the set-up time for a 1000-ton press at Toyota was four hours; by 1971 it was down to three minutes. A ring-gear cutter at Mazda that took more than six hours to set up in 1976 could be set up in ten minutes four years later.[37]

By the 1980s the extent of the market that Japanese manufacturers had captured meant that small-batch production was no longer the necessity it had been 30 years earlier. But the ability of these companies to do what the Japanese call 'single-digit' (under ten minutes) set-ups enabled them to use the same production facilities to produce a wide variety of customized products. Single-digit set-ups had become a powerful source of international competitive advantage.

The reduction of set-up times involves the redesign of fixtures, the standardization of components, and the reorganization of work. Shop-floor workers must be willing and able to perform as much of the set-up operations as possible for the next product batch while machines are producing the current product batch. The reorganization of work needed to reduce set-ups represented another productive activity that could take advantage of the

---

[35] David Montgomery (1987), *The Fall of the House of Labor*, Cambridge: Cambridge University Press.
[36] Masaaki Imai (1986), *Kaizen: The Key to Japan's Competitive Success*, New York: Random House.
[37] Suzaki, *New Manufacturing Challenge*, 43.

incentive and ability of Japanese shop-floor workers to engage in a variety of tasks. The broader knowledge of the production process that these workers possessed was in turn used to find new ways to reduce set-up times.

In the United States, in contrast, the problem of reducing set-up times was neglected in part because of long runs and in part because of the unwillingness of American management to invest in shop-floor skills. In Japan a dynamic learning process was set in motion in which the learning of shop-floor workers was critical. In the United States, hierarchical segmentation meant that when long runs of identical products were no longer a viable competitive strategy, corporations had not yet developed the skill bases for reducing set-up times.

If shop-floor skills can prevent down time through quick set-ups, they can do so as well through machine maintenance. Keeping machines trouble-free requires the involvement of shop-floor workers for continuous inspection and daily maintenance as well as specialized maintenance engineers to solve chronic problems and to train the shop-floor operatives. As Suzaki has put it,

zero machine troubles can be achieved more effectively by involving operators in maintaining normal machine operating conditions, detecting abnormal machine conditions as early as possible, and developing countermeasures to regain normal machine conditions. This requires development of a close working relationship among operators, maintenance crews, and other support people as well as skill development and training to increase the abilities of those involved.[38]

In American mass production, shop-floor workers have not only lacked the skills to maintain machines. They have also been denied the right to maintain machines by managers who fear that, far from reducing down time by keeping machines trouble-free, such shop-floor intervention will be used to slow the pace of work. Indeed one role of first-line supervisors employed on American mass-production lines has typically been to ensure that production workers do not interfere with machine operations on the assumption that such intervention will make the machines more trouble-prone.

Cellular manufacturing, quick set-ups, and machine maintenance all contribute to higher levels of machine utilization and lower unit costs. But ultimately unit costs are dependent on how quickly products can be transformed from purchased inputs into saleable outputs. That is, unit costs depend on cycle-time.

For example, at Mitsubishi Electric Corporation between 1985 and 1989, cycle-time for semiconductor chips was reduced from seventy-two days to thirty-three days, even as the number of chip styles more than doubled to 700 and the number of package types assembled increased from twenty to seventy.[39] As Jeffrey Funk (who worked at Mitsubishi Electric for a year)

---

[38] Ibid. 123.

[39] Jeffrey L. Funk (1992), *The Teamwork Advantage: An Inside Look at Japanese Product and Technology Development*, Cambridge, Mass.: Productivity Press, 197.

described it: 'The reductions in cycle time were achieved through numerous engineer and operator activities.' The engineers were primarily responsible for making system-wide improvements concerned with identifying and resolving production bottlenecks, and with developing 'product families' of different types of chips that undergo the same processes, thus reducing set-up times and eliminating mistakes. The operators were primarily responsible for identifying possibilities for localized improvements on the wafer and assembly lines. Each operator was in a working group that met once or twice a month, through which they made numerous suggestions for improvements, a high proportion of which were acted upon by engineers. Operators responsible for wafer furnaces contributed, for example, to improvements in the delivery, queuing, and loading system, all of which reduced cycle-time.

A comparison of the Mitsubishi wafer department with a US factory using similar equipment found that the Japanese factory produced four times the number of wafers per direct worker, employed fewer support workers per direct worker, had a higher ratio of output to input in the wafer process, and had a cycle-time that was one-fourth of that achieved by the US factory. 'These improvements', according to Funk,

lead to shorter cycle time, higher yields, less wafer breakage, and higher production of wafers per direct worker. The multifunctional workers enable Mitsubishi to have fewer support staff. Since the direct workers perform many of the activities typically performed by support staff in a U.S. factory, the direct workers can determine which activities are most important and how to improve the efficiency of these activities.[40]

Utilization of materials

Perhaps the most famous Japanese management practice to emerge out of the 'high growth era' was the just-in-time inventory system, (JIT). By delivering components to be assembled as they are needed, the carrying costs and storage costs of work-in-progress can be dramatically reduced. But JIT only works if the parts that are delivered just in time are of consistently high quality. JIT only yields lower unit costs when component suppliers, be they in-house or external subcontractors, have the incentive and ability to deliver such high-quality parts. It was to ensure the timely delivery of such high-quality components, for example, that in 1949 and 1950 the first step taken by Taichi Ohno in developing JIT at Toyota was to reorganize the machine-shop into manufacturing cells that required multi-skilled operatives.[41]

In the Japanese assembly process, JIT demands high levels of initiative and skill from production workers. Using the *kanban* system, it is up to assembly

[40] Funk, *The Teamwork Advantage*, 198–204.
[41] Wada, 'The "Flow Production" Method in Japan', 22.

workers to send empty containers with the order cards—or *kanban*—to the upstream component supplier to generate a flow of parts. The assembly worker, therefore, exercises considerable minute-to-minute control over the flow of work—a delegation of authority that American factory managers deemed to be out of the question in the post-Second World War decades on the assumption that shop-floor workers would use such control to slow the speed of the line. To prevent a purported shortage of components from 'creating' a bottleneck in the production process, American managers kept large buffers of in-process inventory along the line.

The Japanese assembly worker also has the right to stop the line when because of part defects, machine breakdowns, or human incapacity, the flow of work cannot be maintained without a sacrifice of product quality. A light goes on to indicate the location of the problem so that others in the plant can join the worker who stopped the line in finding a solution to the problem as quickly as possible. To participate in this process, therefore, shop-floor workers must develop the skills to identify problems that warrant a line stoppage and to contribute to fixing the problem. Without hierarchical integration, JIT and *kanban* cannot work.[42]

Product quality

The willingness of Japanese companies to develop the skills of shop-floor workers led to a very different mode of implementing quality control in Japan than in the United States. Statistical quality control (SQC) was, as already mentioned, originated in the United States. In American manufacturing, however, SQC remained solely a function of management, with quality-control specialists inspecting finished products after they came off the line. Defective products had to be scrapped or reworked, often at considerable expense. Defects that could not be detected because they were built into the product would ultimately reveal themselves to customers in the form of unreliable performance, again at considerable expense to the manufacturing company, especially when higher-quality producers came on the market.

For American companies, from the 1970s the higher-quality producers were typically the Japanese. In Japan, the integration of shop-floor workers into the process of organizational learning meant that product quality could be monitored while work was in progress in the production process, and thus that defects could be detected and corrected before they became built into the finished product. The result was less scrap, less rework, and more revenues from satisfied customers.

---

[42] Kuniyoshi Urabe (1988), 'Innovation and the Japanese Management System', in Kuniyoshi Urabe, John Child, and Tadao Kagono (eds.), *Innovation and Management: International Comparisons*, Berlin: Walter de Gruyter.

In the 1950s, American managers could justify the exclusion of shop-floor workers from participation in quality control on the grounds that the SQC methods in use were too complicated for the blue-collar worker. Only more highly educated employees were deemed capable of applying these tools. Given the quality of education received by young Americans destined to be 'semi-skilled' factory operatives, the managers of US companies had a point. Under a system of mass education that could vary markedly across some 15,000 school districts, the generally low quality of working-class schooling was consistent with the minimal intellectual requirements of repetitive and monotonous factory jobs. This correspondence between schooling and prospective skill requirements in hierarchically segmented workplaces helps to explain why to this day the United States ranks among the lowest of the advanced economies in terms of the quality of mass education and among the highest in terms of the quality of higher education.

In Japan, even in the 1950s, blue-collar workers with manufacturing companies were high-school graduates. But as part of a national system of education of uniformly high standards, they received much the same quality education as those who would go on to university. Even then, the involvement of Japanese shop-floor workers in SQC was accomplished by making the methods more easily accessible and usable by blue-collar workers. As Kaoru Ishikawa, the pioneer in the implementation of SQC in Japan, put it: 'We overeducated people by giving them sophisticated methods where, at that stage, simple methods would have sufficed.'[43]

The reliance of Japanese companies on the skill and initiative of shop-floor workers for superior machine utilization and reductions in materials costs made these employees ideal monitors of product quality. Relying on this skill base, SQC became integral to the Japanese practice of building quality into the product rather than, as in the United States, using SQC to inspect completed products that had defects built in.

In the 1960s the involvement of shop-floor workers in improving machine utilization, materials costs, and product quality became institutionalized in quality control (QC) circles. In addition to initiatives undertaken by individual companies to apply QC methods in particular factories, a series of radio broadcasts by JUSE in the late 1950s had broadcast the potential of quality control. Then, in 1960, JUSE put out a publication, *A Text on Quality Control for the Foreman*, that became widely used by first-line supervisors in the workplace.[44] The success of this publication led to a monthly magazine, *Quality Control for the Foreman* (*FQC*). In the process of gathering information for the magazine, JUSE found that, in many factories, foremen and workers had formed themselves into small groups to discuss quality control and its application to specific problems. The editorial board of *FQC* (of which

---

[43] Ishikawa, *What Is Total Quality Control?*, 18.   [44] Ibid. 21.

Ishikawa was the chairman), in issuing the following statement, effectively launched the QC circle movement:

1. Make the content [of FQC] easy for everyone to understand. Our task is to educate, train, and promote QC among supervisors and workers in the forefront of our work force. We want to help them enhance their ability to manage and to improve.
2. Set the price low to ensure that the journal will be within the reach of everyone. We want as many foremen and line workers as possible to read it and benefit from it.
3. At shops and other workplaces, groups are to be organized with foremen as their leaders and include other workers as their members. These groups are to be named QC circles. QC circles are to use this journal as the text in their study and must endeavour to solve problems that they have at their place of work. QC circles are to become the core of quality control activities in their respective shops and workplaces.[45]

QC circles could be registered with *FQC* (which published lists of new registrants). Beginning in 1963 a national QC circle organization was created, complete with central headquarters, nine regional chapters, conferences, seminars, and overseas study teams. Twenty years later there were almost 175,000 QC circles registered with nearly 1.5 million members.[46]

QC circles became extremely effective in generating continuous improvements in the quality and cost of Japanese manufactured products because in the early 1960s when the QC circle movement took off so many Japanese companies had already developed production systems that relied on the skill and initiative of shop-floor workers. In participating in the continuous improvement of these production systems, moreover, shop-floor workers did not solve problems in isolation from the rest of the organization but rather as part of a broader and deeper process of organizational learning that integrated the work of engineers and operatives. The foreman as team leader served as the conduit of information up and down the hierarchical structure.

The QC circle movement, led by JUSE, helped to diffuse throughout Japanese industry the organizational and technological advances made at the leading companies. For example, in the mid-1960s there were frequent breakdowns of a newly installed automatic metal-plating machine in the assembly division of Toyota's Motomachi Plant. The relevant QC circle systematically considered possible causes, and through testing came up with solutions. In reporting the work of this QC circle, *FQC* stated: 'The supervisor may understand the design of the machine and how to run it, but is probably unaware of its detailed tendencies or weaknesses. The people who know best about the condition of the machine are the workers, and quality circles provide an opportunity to get important information from them.'[47]

In solving problems in machine utilization, QC circles found that the solutions invariably entailed improvements in product quality as well. As Izumi

[45] Ibid. 138.
[46] Ibid. 138–9. See also Nonaka, 'Development of Company-Wide Quality Control'.
[47] Ibid. 154.

Nonaka has put it in his account of the history of quality control at Toyota and Nissan:

Toyota production methods, such as just-in-time, kanban, and jidoka (automation) are well known, but it should be stressed that, in relation to quality control, if 100 per cent of the parts reaching a given process are not defect free, Toyota methods will not work smoothly. In other words, quality is the foundation of Toyota production methods. From about 1963, just-in-time and jidoka were adopted in all Toyota factories, and a close relationship between these methods and quality was immediately established.[48]

The QC circle movement focused Japanese workers on the goal of achieving 'zero defects'—detecting and eliminating defects as the product was being built rather than permit defects to be built into the product. In recounting why an incipient zero defect (ZD) movement (initiated by the US Department of Defense for its contractors) failed in the United States in the mid-1960s, Ishikawa put the blame squarely on the failure of American companies to integrate shop-floor workers into the process, as was being done in Japan. 'The ZD movement became a mere movement of will', Ishikawa observed, 'a movement without tools. . . . It decreed that good products would follow if operation standards were closely followed.' In the Japanese quality control movement, however, it was recognized that 'operation standards are never perfect'.

What operations standards lack, experience covers. In our QC circles we insist that the circle examine all operation standards, observe how they work, and amend them. The circle follows the new standards, examines them again, and repeats the process of amendment, observance, etc. As this process is repeated there will be an improvement in technology itself.

Not so, however, in the United States, where management practice 'has been strongly influenced by the so-called Taylor method'. In the United States, according to Ishikawa,

engineers create work standards and specifications. Workers merely follow. The trouble with this approach is that the workers are regarded as machines. Their humanity is ignored. [Yet] all responsibilities for mistakes and defects were borne by the workers. . . . No wonder the [ZD] movement went astray.[49]

In the late 1960s and early 1970s, on the eve of the Japanese challenge to US manufacturing, many American industrial managers began to worry not so much about the quality of the products they were generating as about the quality of shop-floor work itself. The alienated worker was fingered as the source of lagging productivity.[50] During the first half of the 1960s, the annual

---

[48] Ishikawa, *What Is Total Quality Control?*, 151.
[49] Ishikawa, *New Manufacturing Challenge*, 151–2.
[50] See US Department of Health, Education, and Welfare (1972), *Work in America*, Cambridge, Mass.: MIT Press; Richard E. Walton (1979), 'Work Innovations in the United States', *Harvard Business Review*, 57 (July–Aug.).

average rate of increase of manufacturing productivity in the United States had been 5.1 per cent while that of manufacturing wages had been 3.9 per cent. But in the second half of the 1960s, when the annual rate of increase of manufacturing productivity averaged a mere 0.6 per cent, manufacturing wages rose at a rate of 5.9 per cent. Amidst an escalation of absenteeism and unauthorized work stoppages, the productivity problem sparked a search among US manufacturing companies for new structures of work organization that would secure the co-operation of shop-floor workers in realigning the relation between work and pay.[51]

Within the automobile industry, the United Auto Workers joined corporate management on a National Joint Committee to Improve the Quality of Worklife, that then had to convince workers that programmes of 'job enrichment' and 'job enlargement' were not merely new ways to speed up production and reduce employment. Unfortunately, during the 1970s, even many promising experiments at work reorganization that had already yielded significant productivity gains were cut short when middle managers and first-line supervisors realized that the ultimate success of the programmes entailed a loss of their power in the traditional hierarchically segmented organization.[52] Indeed, in general, the more pervasive response to the productivity problem in American manufacturing in the 1970s was an increase in shop-floor supervision rather than the transformation of work organization. From 1950 to 1970, the number of foremen per 100 workers in American manufacturing increased from 3.4 to 4.8; by 1980 this ratio had shot up to 8.0.[53]

Perhaps the most important implication of hierarchical segmentation in the United States was that it fostered functional segmentation. Distant from the realities of problem-solving in the actual production process, US technical specialists sought to solve problems by using the tools of their own particular disciplines, putting up barriers to communicating even with other specialists within the managerial organization, and throwing partially solved problems 'over the wall' into the domains of other functional specialists.[54] In Japan, by

[51] See Lazonick, *Competitive Advantage on the Shop Floor*, 280–4.

[52] See Richard E. Walton (1975), 'The Diffusion of New Work Structures: Why Success Didn't Take', *Organizational Dynamics*, 3 (Winter); Andrew Zimbalist (1975), 'The Limits of Work Humanization', *Review of Radical Political Economics*, 7 (Summer); Stephen A. Marglin (1979), 'Catching Flies With Honey: An Inquiry into Management Initiatives to Humanize Work', *Economic Analysis and Workers' Management*, 13.

[53] Nelson Lichtenstein (1989), ' "The Man in the Middle". A Social History of Automobile Industry Foremen', in Nelson Lichtenstein and Stephen Meyer (eds.), *On the Line: Essays in the History of Auto Work*, Urbana, Ill.: University of Illinois Press.

[54] The problem of functional segmentation in US–Japanese competition has in recent years become a prime focus of comparative studies carried out in American business schools. See for example Kim B. Clark and Takahiro Fujimoto (1991), *Product Development Performance*, Boston: Harvard Business School Press; Funk, *Teamwork Advantage*; D. Eleanor Westney (1994), 'The Evolution of Japan's Industrial Research and Development', in Masahiko Aoki and Ronald Dore (eds.), *The Japanese Firm: The Sources of Competitive Strength*, Oxford: Oxford University Press.

contrast, the hierarchical integration of technical specialists in a learning process with production workers created lines of communication and incentives to solve problems in concert with other specialists. Relative to their competitors in the United States, the result of functional integration for Japanese manufacturers has been not only superior product quality but also more rapid new-product development.[55]

The different way in which quality control was implemented in Japan and the United States is a case in point. In Japan, QC was embedded in the whole structure of organizational learning. Izumi has argued that in Japan quality control is 'the responsibility of all employees, including top and middle management as well as lower-level workers, from planning and design, to production, marketing, and sales . . . [in] contrast with the American reliance on specialist quality control inspectors.'[56] Ishikawa has emphasized the functional segmentation of American QC inspectors:

In the United States and Western Europe, great emphasis is placed on professionalism and specialization. Matters relating to QC therefore become the exclusive preserve of QC specialists. When questions are raised concerning QC, people belonging to other divisions will not answer, they will simply refer the questions to those who handle QC.

In Western countries, when a QC specialist enters a company, he is immediately put in the QC division. Eventually he becomes head of a subsection, a section, then of the QC division. This system is effective in nurturing a specialist, but from the point of view of the entire business organization, is more likely to produce a person of very limited vision.

For better or for worse, in Japan little emphasis is placed on professionalism. When an engineer enters a company, he is rotated among different divisions, such as design, manufacturing, and QC. At times, some engineers are even placed in the marketing division.[57]

Factory automation

In the late 1970s, American manufacturers continued to attribute the mounting Japanese challenge to low wages and the persistent productivity problem at home to worker alienation. By the 1980s and 1990s, however, the innovative reality of the Japanese challenge became difficult to ignore, as the Japanese increased their shares of US markets across a range of key industries, even as Japanese wage rates rapidly rose and the yen steadily strengthened.

Yet, even then, there appeared to be a way out for US manufacturers that did not require imitation of the Japanese by building broader and deeper skill

[55] Clark and Fujimoto, *Product Development Performance*; Funk, *Teamwork Advantage*; Daniel I. Okimoto and Yoshio Nishi (1994), 'R&D Organization in Japanese and American Semiconductor Firms', in Aoki and Dore, *The Japanese Firm*.
[56] Nonaka, 'Development of Company-Wide Quality Control'.
[57] Ishikawa, *New Manufacturing Challenge*, 23.

bases. Since the 1950s American management had dreamed of building 'the Factory of the Future'—a completely automated production facility that would do away with the need to employ production workers altogether.[58] Yet, notwithstanding massive investments by US corporations and the US government in factory automation, attempts by American companies to create the 'factory of the future' failed.[59]

In sharp contrast, building on their investments in broad and deep skill bases, and decades of continuous improvement of production processes, Japanese companies succeeded. At the end of 1992, the Japanese had installed about 349,500 robots compared to 47,000 in the United States and 39,400 in Germany.[60] The Japanese also developed and utilized flexible manufacturing systems (FMS)—computer-controlled configurations of semi-independent work stations connected by automated material handling systems—in advance of, and on a scale that surpassed, other nations.[61] Japan's success in machine tools and factory automation reflected their leadership in the integration of mechanical and electronics technologies, or what since the mid-1970s the Japanese have called 'mechatronics'.[62]

For example, in his case-study of the introduction of FMS at Hitachi Seiki, Ramchandran Jaikumar found that the first two attempts, undertaken between 1972 and 1980, had failed because of insufficient co-ordination across functions. In 1980, therefore, the company set up the Engineering Administration Department that 'brought together a variety of different functions from machine design, software engineering, and tool design'.[63] The new structure of organizational learning, which built on the lessons of the previous failures, led to success. The development teams on the two failed attempts had, according to Jaikumar,

integrated the different components of their systems through machinery design rather than through general systems engineering concepts. They had viewed flexible manufacturing systems as technical problems to be solved with technical expertise. The difficulty of evaluating trade-offs whenever conflicts arose over design specifications or procedures convinced Hitachi Seiki that it was problems of coordination among people that was stymying systems development. The company realized that what was

[58] See David F. Noble (1984), *Forces of Production: A Social History of Industrial Automation*, Oxford: Oxford University Press, ch. 4.

[59] For an excellent case-study, see Noble, *Forces of Production*; see also Robert J. Thomas (1984), *What Machines Can't Do: Politics and Technology in the Industrial Enterprise*, Berkeley: University of California Press.

[60] Tsuneta Yano Memorial Society (1993) (ed.), *Nippon: A Charted Survey of Japan, 1993/94*, Tokyo: Kokusei-sha, 191.

[61] Ramchandran Jaikumar (1989), 'Japanese Flexible Manufacturing Systems: Impact on the United States', *Japan and the World Economy*, 1.

[62] See Fumio Kodama (1995), *Emerging Patterns of Innovation: Sources of Japan's Technological Edge*, Boston: Harvard Business School Press, 193; also V. Daniel Hunt (1988), *Mechatronics: Japan's Newest Threat*, New York: Chapman and Hall.

[63] Jaikumar, 'Japanese Flexible Manufacturing Systems', 126.

needed was to view FMS as a manufacturing problem to be solved with both manufacturing and technical expertise. Consequently the third phase of FMS development
at Hitchi Seiki was a radical departure from the previous two.[64]

In his comparisons of Japanese and US FMS in the first half of the 1980s,
Jaikumar found that, even though the FMS installations in both countries
contained similar machines doing similar kinds of work, the Japanese developed the systems in half the time, produced over nine times as many parts per
system in average annual volumes that were about one-seventh of American
practice, with much greater automation, and utilization rates.[65] 'Differences
in results', said Jaikumar, 'derive mainly from the extent of the installed base
of machinery, the technical literacy of the workforce, and the competence of
management. In each of these areas, Japan is far ahead of the United
States.'[66]

More specifically, he described how the Japanese developed the reliability
of FMS to achieve untended (automated) operations and system uptime
levels of over 90 per cent, in the process transforming not only shop-floor
technology but also the job of a 'shop-floor operator'.

The entire project team remains with the system long after installation, continually
making changes. Learning occurs throughout and is translated into on-going process
mastery and productivity enhancement. . . . Operators on the shop floor, highly skilled
engineers with multifunctional responsibilities, make continual programming changes
and are responsible for writing new programs for both parts and systems as a whole.
Like designers, they work best in small teams. Most important, Japanese managers see
FMS technology for what it is—flexible—and create operating objectives and proto-
cols that capitalize on this special capability. Not bound by outdated mass-production
assumptions, they view the challenge of flexible manufacturing as automating a job
shop, not simply making a transfer line flexible. The difference in results is enormous.[67]

Central to factory automation have been teams of highly educated and
highly trained engineers who had mastered their technical specialties but who
were also able and willing to integrate across electronic, mechanical, and
chemical specialties. As stated earlier, that the Japanese could even consider
entry into complex manufacturing industries such as automobiles and consumer electronics after the Second World War was because of the learning
that their scientists and engineers had accumulated in the decades before as
well as during the war. But the Japanese history of the hierarchical integration of traditional blue-collar workers into the development and utilization of
manufacturing technology laid the basis for functional integration as technology became more and more complex.

[64] Jaikumar, 'Japanese Flexible Manufacturing Systems', 126.
[65] Ibid. 129.   [66] Ibid.   [67] Ibid. 130.

The accumulated learning of Japan's scientists and engineers after the war was in and of itself no match for that which the American's possessed. Yet, during the post-war decades Japanese scientists and engineers developed and utilized their collective capabilities in manufacturing as part of an organizational learning process that integrated the capabilities of shop-floor workers in making continuous improvements to the manufacturing process. In the 1980s and 1990s this history of hierarchical integration played a significant role in fostering the functional integration that has been key to Japan's success relative to the United States in factory automation.

The importance of taking organizational learning to the shop floor also applies in the semiconductor industry, the most complex and automated of manufacturing processes. As Okimoto and Nishi argue in their excellent comparative study of Japanese and US semiconductor manufacturing:

Perhaps the most striking feature of Japanese R&D in the semiconductor industry is the extraordinary degree of communication and 'body contact' that takes place at the various juncture and intersection points in the R&D processes—from basic research to advanced development, from advanced development to new product design, from new product design to new process technology, from new process technology to factory-site manufacturing, from manufacturing to marketing, and from marketing to servicing. Owing to pragmatic organizational innovations, Japanese semiconductor manufacturers have excelled—where many American and European manufacturers have faltered—at the seemingly simple but extremely difficult task of making smooth 'hand-offs' at each juncture along the long-interconnected R&D pipeline.[68]

The key links in this pipeline in Japanese semiconductor R&D are between divisional labs and factory engineering labs. Engineers from these labs, according to Okimoto and Nishi, 'continually meet and interact in seeking to iron out problems that inevitably arise in mass-manufacturing new products.'[69] Okimoto and Nishi continue, stressing the importance of the integration of R&D with manufacturing:

The largest concentration [of engineers] is usually found at the FELs [factory engineering laboratories], located at factory sites where the messy problems of mass production have to be worked out. The majority of Japanese engineers have at least some exposure to manufacturing engineering as part of their job rotation and career training. Not only is there no stigma attached to manufacturing assignments; the ladder of promotion leading up to higher reaches of executive management—and beyond (including *amakudari*, or post-career executive entry into new companies)—pass through jobs that involve hands-on manufacturing experience. It is almost a requirement for upward career and post-career mobility.

In the United States, by contrast, manufacturing engineers carry the stigma of being second-class citizens. To the manufacturing engineers falls the 'grubby' work of

[68] Okimoto and Nishi, 'R&D Organization in Japanese and American Semiconductor Firms', 193.
[69] Ibid. 195.

production—for which they receive lower pay and lower prestige compared with the 'glamorous' design jobs. In how many US semiconductor companies can it be said that the majority of engineers are engaged in manufacturing? Few, if any. And, looking at the large number of merchant semiconductor houses in Silicon Valley, we see that only a minority even possess manufacturing facilities, much less factory engineering laboratories.[70]

It would appear more generally that, by focusing the skills and efforts of engineers on continuous improvements in quality and cost in the production process, hierarchical integration provided a foundation for functional integration in Japanese manufacturing. If, in the first half of the 1980s, most Western analyses of the sources of Japanese competitive advantage focused on the integration of the shop-floor worker into the organizational learning process, over the last decade or so the emphasis has shifted to the role of 'cross-functional management', 'company-wide quality control', or 'concurrent engineering' in generating higher-quality, lower-cost products. Much of the discussion of functional integration has been focused on its role in 'new product development' in international comparative perspective.[71] But, I would argue, the key to understanding the influence of functional integration on innovation and international competitive advantage is the integration of product and process development, and the skill-base strategy that such integration entails. Such an understanding of organizational integration requires an analysis of functional integration in relation to the legacy of hierarchical integration or segmentation.

INTERNATIONAL COMPETITION

If valid, the skill-base hypothesis can reconcile the fact that many US industrial enterprises still remain innovators in international competition with the evidence on the increase in income inequality in the United States. A systematic bias of US industrial corporations to compete for product markets by increasingly investing in narrow and concentrated skill bases could provide a significant explanation for the income inequality trends over the last two decades or so. Testing the skill-base hypothesis may help provide answers to a number of related questions concerning the ways in which, in particular industries and activities, US industrial corporations have responded to international competitive challenges:

---

[70] Okimoto and Nishi, 'R&D Organization in Japanese and American Semiconductor Firms', 193.

[71] See for example Clark and Fujimoto, *Product Development Performance*. See also Ikujiro Nonaka and Hirotaka Takeuchi (1995), *The Knowledge-Creating Company*, Oxford: Oxford University Press.

• To what extent have US companies exited from particular industries, and particular activities within a particular industry, in which they have been challenged by enterprises that have invested in broader and deeper skill bases as an alternative to transforming their strategies and structures to make the requisite investments in organizational learning?

• To what extent have the attempts of US companies to respond to these competitive challenges been hampered by their failure to confront and transform sufficiently the strategic, functional, and hierarchical segmentation that they have inherited from the past?

• What can we learn about the incentive and ability of US companies to make investments in broader and deeper skill bases by comparing strategy, organization, and performance of different companies in the same industry—for example, Ford, GM, and Chrysler in automobiles—that have sought to respond to the same international competitive challenges?

• What has been the importance of foreign direct investment—for example, Japanese 'transplants' in the United States—as distinct from international trade in shaping the responses of US companies to international competitive challenges?

• What has been distinctive about the investment strategies and organizational structures of US companies that have become or remained leaders in international competition in the 1980s and 1990s? Did an historical legacy of investments in broader and deeper skill bases, and a relative absence of organizational segmentation, enable an older company like Motorola or 3M to continue to make such investments in the 1980s and 1990s, thus representing the exceptions that prove the rule in US industry? Have newer companies such as Intel and Microsoft become world leaders through the organizational integration of narrow and concentrated skill bases?

Such questions indicate that testing the skill-base hypothesis and its immediate implications requires in-depth research of particular companies that compete in particular industries in different national economies in different, and typically over prolonged, periods of time. The more limited objective of this chapter has been to elaborate the analytical framework for testing the skill-base hypothesis by synthesizing available evidence on differences in organizational learning in industries in which the United States and Japan compete head-to-head.

What are those industries, and how has competitive advantage been shifting between the United States and Japan? These questions are difficult to answer without in-depth case studies of particular industries. The importance of foreign direct investment, cross-border outsourcing, and third-country exports means that trade data provide only a partial picture of shifts in head-to-head competitive advantage. Moreover, even within narrowly defined industrial classifications of traded goods such as 'jet engines and parts', the skill-base hypothesis may be able to explain the specialization of the United

States in certain activities (e.g. engine design) and the specialization of Japan in other activities (e.g. precision-engineered components), and how that international specialization is changing over time.[72]

Nevertheless, again with a view toward motivating such industry-specific research, I shall conclude this chapter with an overview and brief discussion of the major shifts in US–Japanese trade from the late 1970s to the mid-1990s (see Tables 11.2–11.4). In 1995 Japan exported $120.9bn. of goods to the United States (27.3 per cent of all Japanese exports) and imported $75.4bn. from the United States (22.4 per cent of all Japanese imports) for a merchandise trade surplus of $45.5bn.[73] The United States is by far Japan's foremost trade partner for both exports and imports. Japan's next largest trade partners in 1995 were, for exports, South Korea (7.1 per cent of Japan's total) and, for imports, China (10.7 per cent of the total).[74]

Table 11.2. Japan–USA bilateral merchandise trade, 1979, 1987, and 1995 (millions of US dollars (current))

	1979		1987		1995	
	Exports	Imports	Exports	Imports	Exports	Imports
TOTAL	26,402.5	20,430.8	83,579.9	31,490.5	120,858.9	75,408.1
Foodstuffs	189.0	4,422.9	404.1	6,778.9	303.4	15,951.4
Raw materials	136.5	6,927.3	167.3	7,039.8	380.9	9,329.1
Light goods	2,200.6	1,660.7	6,465.5	3,037.6	7,979.4	8,745.8
Chemical goods	653.1	2,053.3	2,080.8	4,035.3	4,826.2	7,072.7
Metal goods	3,939.6	481.1	4,101.8	901.0	4,045.1	2,190.4
Machinery:	19,008.3	4,310.2	69,493.9	9,075.4	100,182.5	30,515.6
Office machines	679.9	530.1	7,373.7	1,589.9	14,183.7	4,862.5
Electrical machinery	4,393.3	1,349.9	17,050.1	3,008.9	29,384.8	12,746.4
Transportation equip.	10,106.4	985.5	32,050.3	1,854.7	32,023.9	5,987.7
Precision instruments	1,515.9	357.9	4,325.0	620.1	6,545.7	1,844.5
Re-exports, unclassified	275.4	575.3	866.5	622.5	3,141.0	1,603.0

Of Japan's exports to the United States in 1995, 82.9 per cent fell under the broad category of 'machinery'. This category included, among the major classifications, office machines (11.7 per cent of all goods exports), electrical machinery (24.3 per cent), transportation equipment (26.5 per cent, of which automobiles were 18.3 per cent and automobile parts 6.5 per cent), and precision instruments (5.4 per cent) (see Table 11.4). The remainder of Japanese exports to the United States consisted largely of chemical goods (4.0 per cent), metal goods (3.3 per cent), and light industrial products (6.6 per cent).

[72] See Beth Almeida (1997), 'Are Good Jobs Flying Away?: Aircraft Engine Manufacturing and Sustainable Prosperity', Report to the Jerome Levy Economic Institute.
[73] *Japan Economic Almanac, 1977*, Tokyo: *Japan Economic Journal*, 107.   [74] Ibid.

Table 11.3. Japan–USA trade growth, 1979–1995 (1979=100)

	Japanese exports to USA			US exports to Japan		
	1979	1987	1995	1979	1987	1995
TOTAL	100	317	458	100	154	369
Foodstuffs	100	214	161	100	153	361
Raw materials	100	123	279	100	102	135
Light goods	100	294	363	100	183	527
Chemical goods	100	319	739	100	197	344
Metal goods	100	104	103	100	187	455
Machinery:	100	366	527	100	211	708
Office machines	100	1,085	2,086	100	300	917
Electrical machinery	100	388	669	100	223	944
Transportation equip.	100	317	317	100	188	608
Precision instruments	100	285	432	100	173	515
Re-exports, unclassified	100	315	1,141	100	108	279

Table 11.4. Proportionate shares of Japan–USA bilateral merchandise trade, 1979, 1987, and 1995 (percentage of annual bilateral exports)

	Japanese exports to USA			US exports to Japan		
	1979	1987	1995	1979	1987	1995
TOTAL	100.0	100.0	100.0	100.0	100.0	100.0
Foodstuffs	0.7	0.5	0.3	21.6	21.5	21.2
Raw materials	0.5	0.2	0.3	33.9	22.4	12.4
Light goods	8.3	7.7	6.6	8.1	9.6	11.6
Chemical goods	2.5	2.5	4.0	10.1	12.8	9.4
Metal goods	14.9	4.9	3.3	2.4	2.9	2.9
Machinery:	72.0	83.1	82.9	21.1	28.8	40.5
Office machines	2.6	8.8	11.7	2.6	5.0	6.4
Electrical machinery	16.6	20.4	24.3	6.6	9.6	16.9
Transportation equip.	38.3	38.3	26.5	4.8	5.9	7.9
Precision instruments	5.7	5.2	5.4	1.8	2.0	2.4
Re-exports, unclassified	1.0	1.0	2.6	2.8	2.0	2.1

Source: Ministry of International Trade and Industry, *White Papers on International Trade*, 1980, 1988, 1996, Tokyo.

What did the United States export to Japan? Machinery accounted for 40.5 per cent of US exports, consisting mainly of office machines (6.5 per cent), electrical machinery (16.9 per cent, of which semiconductors and integrated circuits were 7.1 per cent), and transportation equipment (7.9 per cent). The remainder of US *manufactured* exports to Japan consisted mainly of an assortment of light products (11.6 per cent, including textiles, paper products, records and tapes, and sporting goods) and chemical goods (9.4 per cent). But all manufactured goods only accounted for less than two-thirds of US exports to Japan. Over one-third of US exports to Japan in 1995 were either foodstuffs (21.2 per cent) or raw materials (10.6 per cent). For Japan, its foodstuffs and raw materials exports were only 0.6 per cent of its total exports to the United States.

Note that, in the 1970s, as the Japanese challenge mounted, the United States was even more reliant, in relative terms at least, on exports of foodstuffs and raw materials to Japan. In 1979, 55.5 per cent of US exports to Japan took the form of these basic materials. In that year 65 per cent of Japan's raw materials imports from the United States were soybeans (5.7 per cent of total imports), wood (11.2 per cent), and coal (5.0 per cent). By 1995 Japan imported a somewhat larger quantity of soybeans (but the proportion of total imports fell to 1.5 per cent), and absolutely smaller quantities of wood (4.2 per cent) and coal (0.9 per cent). Hence over the 16-year period, the relative importance of foodstuffs for US exports to Japan was maintained, while the relative, and in some cases absolute, importance of raw materials declined.

The case of US agriculture is a case in point of the need for in-depth industry-specific analyses of the sources of sustainable competitive advantage. Looking at the trade data, an economist might conclude that the importance of raw materials, and particularly foodstuffs, in US exports to Japan is simply a matter of very different land–labour ratios in the two nations' factor endowments. To draw such a conclusion, as valid as it might appear on the surface, would, however, miss the critical importance of collective and cumulative learning on a national scale over the past century in making agriculture the one industrial sector in which the international competitive advantage of the United States is most sustainable. It would neglect a century-long history of organizational learning, akin to the managerial revolution that occurred within major US industrial corporations, in which the US Department of Agriculture created a national system of research and development that diffused new technology to millions of farmers through the state-based activities of land-grant colleges, experiment stations, and county agents. Indeed, the legacy of this massive investment in organizational learning is not only productive supremacy in agriculture but also the world's foremost structure of industrial research institutions embedded in the US system of higher education.[75]

[75] Louis Ferleger and William Lazonick (1993), 'The Managerial Revolution and the Developmental State: The Case of U.S. Agriculture', *Business and Economic History*, 22/2; eid. (1994), 'Higher Education for Industrial Innovation', *Business and Economic History*, 23/1.

Note also that the relative importance of machinery exports from Japan increased substantially in the first 8-year period, while the relative importance of US machinery exports increased from 1979 to 1995, with the major gains being made in the late 1980s and early 1990s. The United States made these gains despite the continued decline of its machine-tool industry in the face of relentless Japanese competition.[76] By 1991, compared with the US machine-tool industry, the value of Japanese machine-tool production was 356 per cent and machine-tool exports 443 per cent.[77] In the 1990s, the Japanese have also successfully challenged the German machine-tool manufacturers, surpassing them for the first time in 1992 in the value of production, and in 1993 in the value of exports. Capturing larger and larger shares of export markets through 1996, Japanese companies now completely dominate the mid-range and high-range markets for CNC (computer numerically controlled) machine tools. The low-end markets have been left mainly to Taiwanese companies, and the high-end niches in non-CNC machine tools remain in the hands of the Swiss, Germans, and, to a more limited extent, the Americans.[78]

Between 1987 and 1995 the US gains in machinery were mainly in integrated circuits (up 4.6 per cent) and automobiles (up to 3.9 per cent), these two categories accounting for almost 75 per cent of the increase in US machinery exports as a proportion of total exports. Within the category of Japanese transportation equipment exports, in 1985 30.2 per cent were automobiles (3,278,724 vehicles) and another 6.2 per cent were auto parts; in 1995 these figures were 18.2 per cent (2,066,255 vehicles) and 6.6 per cent respectively. The decline in Japanese exports reflected the Japanese strategy of foreign direct investment in automobiles, either directly in the United States or in Southeast Asian countries such as Thailand and Indonesia that then exported automobiles or parts to the United States. In 1985 Japanese automobile companies produced 254,000 cars and 107,000 trucks in the United States; in 1995 1,942,000 cars and 414,000 trucks.[79] In 1987, the leading US industry within the transportation equipment category was aircraft, which represented 5.0 per cent of all exports. In 1995 aircraft had declined to 2.6 per cent of US exports to Japan, and had been surpassed by automobiles, which were 4.2 per cent of US exports (294,874 vehicles), up from only 0.3 per cent (88,395 vehicles) in 1987.

It was mainly Japanese companies operating in the United States that were doing the exporting. Of just over 100,000 automobiles exported from the United States to Japan in 1994, 53,500 were from Honda, USA and another 11,300 from Toyota USA, leaving about 35 per cent of the exports to be

[76] Robert Forrant (1997), 'Good Jobs and the Cutting Edge: The U.S. Machine Tool Industry and Sustainable Prosperity', Report to the Jerome Levy Economics Institute.
[77] Yano Memorial Society, *Nippon*, 199.
[78] Forrant, 'Good Jobs and the Cutting Edge'.
[79] *Japan Economic Almanac, 1996*, Tokyo: *Japan Economic Journal*, 151.

shared between GM, Ford, and Chrysler (some of whose cars were produced through joint ventures with Japanese companies). The total number of cars exported to Japan by the three US automakers was less than the number exported by Volkswagen/Audi and only about 60 per cent of the combined sales of BMW and Mercedes Benz in Japan. Each of the US companies was also outsold in Japan by Rover, Opel (owned by GM), and Volvo.[80]

The United States and Japan almost balance trade within the classification 'aircraft engines and parts'.[81] Increasingly parts dominate the trade in aircraft engines, especially from Japan to the United States. The ability to integrate innovation in advanced materials with precision engineering has been the key to Japan's growing success. Building on pioneering investments in the development of polyacryonitric carbon fibre by Toray Industries in the 1970s, three Japanese synthetic fibre producers now dominate 60 per cent of the world market.[82] Finding a market at first as a light and durable material for sports equipment such as tennis rackets and golf clubs, in the 1980s Japanese-made carbon fibre became a primary composite material used in both aircraft and engines. For example, Ishikawajima-Harima Heavy Industries—one of the three major Japanese companies involved in jet-engine manufacture—currently produces carbon fibre blades for jet engines made by General Electric.[83] Japan's competitive advantage in producing such parts that combine advances in chemical and mechanical engineering would seem to derive from its investments in broad and deep skill bases.

Organizational integration also appears important in explaining trade in semiconductors. In 1995, Japanese exports of integrated circuits accounted for 6.2 per cent of all Japanese exports to the United States (up from 1.4 per cent in 1987), and hence represented one-quarter of 1995 electrical machinery exports. This bilateral trade in integrated circuits reflects US specialization in microprocessors and Japanese specialization in dynamic random access memories (DRAMs)—an international division of labour built on investments in different skill bases in the two nations. Describing the 'lagged parallel model' of new product development, pioneered at Toshiba and subsequently diffused to other Japanese enterprises as well as US-based Texas Instruments, Okimoto and Nishi have pointed out that:

the lagged parallel project model is effective for work on only certain types of technology. It works for DRAMS, SRAM [sic], and other commodity chips, which share highly predictable linear trajectories of technological advancement. The model is not particularly well suited for products based on nonlinear, highly volatile technological

[80] *Japan Economic Almanac, 1996*, Tokyo: *Japan Economic Journal*, 101, 103.

[81] Almeida (1997), 'Are Good Jobs Flying Away?'.

[82] *Japan Economic Almanac, 1997*, 210: Kodama, *Emerging Patterns of Innovation*, 59–60. See also Tsuneo Suzuki (1994), 'Toray Corporation: Seeking First-Mover Advantage', in Takeshi Yuzawa (ed.), *Japanese Business Success: The Evolution of a Strategy*, London: Routledge.

[83] See Steve Glain (1997), 'IHI Keeps Japan in the Jet-Engine Race', *Wall Street Journal*, June 17, 1997.

trajectories, where the parameters of research for the next and successive product generations cannot be understood ahead of time. Thus it is not accidental that Japanese companies have dominated in commodity chips but have lagged behind U.S. companies in logic chips, microprocessors, and software for applications and operating systems. The latter may require a different, perhaps less structured, organizational approach.[84]

As for computers, American success in PCs and packaged, standardized software does not mean that the Japanese have not been successful competitors. US government agencies, including the military, have been buying supercomputers from the Japanese. The success of a company like Toshiba in laptop computers reflects Japan's long-standing success at miniaturization, a technological advance that requires the integration of design and manufacturing. Japan also dominates international competition in liquid crystal displays (LCDs), a technology invented by RCA in 1967, but developed from the early 1970s most successfully by Sharp in a growing number of applications. By 1992, Sharp controlled 38 per cent of the world's rapidly growing market for LCDs.[85]

In the United States, there is growing evidence that even in industries such as jet engines and medical equipment, the trend in the United States is out of manufacturing and even design, and into the low fixed-cost and highly lucrative business of servicing high-technology equipment.[86] A recent hostile takeover attempt of Giddings & Lewis, the largest machine-tool maker in the United States, by another American company, Harnischfeger, had as its objective the shedding of the target's business of manufacturing machine tools for the automotive industry so that the company could focus on servicing installed machinery.[87] In the end, a 'white knight', the German company, Thyssen, acquired Giddings, promising to maintain its manufacturing business. But the fact is that considerable money can be made by taking a reputable manufacturing company and turning it into a servicing company.

Precisely because the United States has been a leader in industries such as jet engines, medical equipment, and machine tools, the nation has a huge accumulation of experienced technical specialists, many of whom no longer have as secure employment with equipment producers as they had in the past. Some of these people are finding continued employment servicing the equipment that the companies for which they worked used to both produce and service. In the past, they acquired these skills through organizational learning.

---

[84] Okimoto and Nishi, 'R&D Organization in Japanese and American Semiconductor Firms', 197–8.

[85] Kodama, *Emerging Patterns of Innovation*, 56–8.

[86] Almeida, 'Are Good Jobs Flying Away?'; Chris Tilly (1997), 'The Diagnostic Medical Equipment Industry: What Prognosis for Good Jobs?', Report to the Jerome Levy Economics Institute.

[87] 'Giddings Accepts Buyout Offer From Thyssen of $675 Million', *Wall Street Journal*, 9 June 1997.

But their utilization of these skills today confines them to narrow and concentrated functions that removes them even further from the processes of organizational learning that will drive innovation in the future.

In the absence of indigenous manufacturing capability and organizational learning in these industries, where will the next generation of American high-technology service specialists accumulate new state-of-the-art skills? The US economy has a vast accumulation of high-technology skills that derives from the organizational learning that took place in managerial structures over the past century, and off of which it can live, and even innovate, for some time into the future. But, if instead of using this organizational learning to build broader and deeper skill bases, American businesses move toward relying on even narrower and more concentrated skill bases, the trends toward income inequality of the last two decades will continue. If I am right, addressing the problem of income inequality in the United States means paying serious attention to the comparative research agenda and the issues of corporate employment and corporate governance that the skill-base hypothesis implies.

12. Technology Policy: Strategic Failures and the Need for a New Direction*

Keith Cowling and Roger Sugden

There are a number of straws in the wind suggesting that something is amiss with the process of technological development within the industrial economy. Partly it is a sense of underperformance within the market economy relative to what might be seen as the technological potential, for example the recorded productivity growth slowdown within the advanced industrial countries relative to their performance in the earlier period of the Golden Age. Partly also a sense that where government has intervened in the process the results have often been disappointing, for example the poor returns from the subsidization of private R&D. Concerns like this lead some to suggest incremental reforms within the market and within public technology policy to correct market failure and government failure. We are not of this persuasion. We believe that these straws in the wind are indicative of a deeper malaise of the market economy as it exists today and of a public policy which remains supportive of its present structure. A new direction in technology policy is required to sustain a new direction for the economy.

The chapter begins by exploring a new approach to general issues of welfare and policy-making which appears more appropriate to the market economy as it exists today. The focus is on strategic failure rather than market failure *per se*. This strategic failure can be traced back to the concentration of decision-making within the market economy as it has evolved in the twentieth century under the dominance of the modern corporation. This concentration of decision-making, we shall argue, of necessity, means that people's talents are in many respects stifled and constrained. Thus it is suggested that the key to successful development is a move away from the present structure of decision-making towards more diffuse and deconcentrated economies. Rather than being largely supportive of present structures, we suggest that to be successful, in terms of enhancing the general level of welfare or wellbeing, technology policy must support, guide, and encourage the evolution of the

* We wish to acknowledge the helpful comments of Akira Goto, John Grieve Smith, Michael Waterson, and participants at a seminar at the National Institute of Science and Technology Policy, Tokyo and at the Conference on Innovation, Cooperation, and Growth, Robinson College, Cambridge.

market system into one which releases the talent of more people. Following the general welfare and policy analysis the chapter draws out specific aspects of strategic failure linked to technological decisions at the level of both theory and observation, within both the economy and public policy, before examining and drawing lessons from some of the successful cases of technological development and policy. Finally, we will seek to identify a way forward for technology policy, conforming with our guiding principles as developed and informed by our observations and analysis of both the failures and successes of past and present policies.

AN ALTERNATIVE VIEW OF WELFARE AND POLICY[1]

Rather than start our analysis with the market, we choose to start with the firm, specifically the modern corporation. This is in line with Simon's view that the so-called market economy is more accurately described as an organizational economy (Simon, 1991). Further, the analysis of the firm is located in planning, as did Coase in his seminal contribution (Coase, 1937). This is a point that has been neglected. Coase in fact sees firms as islands of economic planning. From there he jumps to the market/non-market dichotomy. But if instead we stay with planning and build our analysis from an acceptance of its presence, an alternative path can be developed. This may be seen as starting the analysis with the modern corporation, therefore with planning rather than markets.[2]

The large modern corporation may be seen as a hierarchical organization (see e.g. Coase, 1937; Radner, 1992), in which different types of decision are being made. We may therefore conceive of a corporate hierarchy comprising various tiers of decision-making, each tier constraining the choices made in all of the lower tiers. At the pinnacle of this hierarchy is strategic decision-making. Explaining precisely what is meant by a strategic decision is not easy, but the general concept is straightforward: the power to make a strategic decision is the ability to determine a firm's broad direction, for example, the direction of its technological development.

If it is agreed that firms have the scope to make strategic decisions and if it is agreed that such decisions are the pinnacle of a hierarchy then a firm may be seen as a means of co-ordinating production from one centre of strategic decision-making (Cowling and Sugden, 1998). This has important implications. It is a key feature of large firms' activities to subcontract part of their production to *legally* distinct, small firms. However, if the subcontract leaves the large firm making the strategic decisions concerning the entire production process, including those parts carried out by the small enterprises, then our

---

[1] A fuller, but earlier, statement of our views is contained within Cowling and Sugden (1994).
[2] Loasby (1995) suggests that to start with planning is in fact an Austrian assumption.

analysis suggests these are not various firms engaged in production; for the purposes of economic analysis there is simply one firm.

The focus on strategic decision-making has important implications for social efficiency. In economics a widely used, fundamental assumption is that decisions are made in the interests of the decision-makers. Thus we would expect corporate strategy to be formulated in the interests of those making strategic decisions. In an economy which is dominated by a few large producers there is no reason to assume that this will not leave others worse off, at least on some occasions. Thus the outcome may be inefficient, in so far as a change may benefit the decision-makers to the detriment of others.

Crucial to this argument is the idea that strategic decision-making in large corporations is concentrated in the hands of an elite. Quite who does or who does not control a firm has been the subject of debate in the literature. Some argue control is with managers, particularly senior managers. Others focus on a subset of shareholders. Yet others suggest that senior managers and important shareholders are essentially the same set of people. But a consensus across all of these views is that control rests with a subset of those 'connected' with the firm's activities, and certainly does not rest with the firm's workforce.[3] Strategic decision-making is concentrated in the hands of an elite.

Because free-market systems concentrate strategic decisions in the hands of an elite, they are posed with inevitable difficulties. This can be illustrated most dramatically by focusing on the current impact of transnational corporations which today in many ways play a dominant role in the free-market system (United Nations, 1993). Transnationals can use their global flexibility to play-off both people (as workers) and government in different countries: they are able to 'divide and rule'. Moreover they may, as a consequence of their strategic decisions promote a world of uneven development (Hymer, 1972). Hymer argues that a world dominated by transnationals would be characterized by such a tendency because the structure of the world's economies, the distribution of wealth and the pattern of development would reflect the hierarchical structure of transnational corporations. It is those strategic decision-makers who determine the firm's broad corporate objectives whereby strategic-planning remains the prerogative of the 'major centres' and whereby 'lower level activities' are spread to lesser areas in which labour is especially cheap. People in the 'lesser' areas are excluded from strategic decision-making otherwise they might be able to realize some of their ambitions.

We are faced with fundamental deficiencies at the heart of free-market systems. These deficiencies have important welfare consequences for the people who live under such systems. Strategic failure—strategic decision-making

---

[3] Aoki (1991) appears to dispute this in the case of the Japanese firm, but his analysis and observations would seem to concur with the consensus. Although participation in decision-making by the workforce in the Japanese corporation is more extensive than the case of the US corporation this does not extend to *strategic* decisions.

concentrated in the hands of an elite, thereby preventing the attainment of socially desired outcomes—is the core explanation of these deficiencies.

The obvious possibility for alleviating these deficiencies is to tackle their source head-on: to look for ways of appropriately involving more and more people affected by strategic decisions in the process of making these decisions. Indeed failure to succeed in this respect will condemn an economy to be guided by the dictates of whichever elite is formulating strategy. This clearly suggests that the very essence of industrial policy should be to design ways of democratizing strategic decision-making in production, and the very essence of technology policy should be to design ways of democratizing strategic decision-making in the area of technology, for example with an emphasis on smaller firms, as against national champions, particularly smaller firms organized in mutually supportive groups (Cowling and Sugden, 1993).

STRATEGIC FAILURE IN TECHNOLOGICAL DEVELOPMENT

Consonant with the concentration of decision-making within the economy as it exists today we should expect to observe constraints on technological change: the innovation path a firm pursues will be that best suiting the subset of the population involved in its strategic decision-making, not that serving the interests of communities in which the firm operates. For instance firms will resist the introduction of new forms of work organization that undermine the power of strategic decision-makers. We might also expect large dominant corporations to withhold innovations so as not to disrupt monopoly positions, but at the same time to engage in the strategic use of defensive R&D to deter entry in order to achieve similar ends. In line with this view there has been some documentation of the suppression of technical progress by major corporations, including cases involving Standard Oil with new lubricants and synthetic rubber; Monsanto, also with new lubricants; both General Electric and Westinghouse with fluorescent lighting, and also with radio alongside AT&T (Scherer, 1980). We turn now to a number of theoretical contributions which bolster our views about strategic failure with regard to technology before assessing the quantitative evidence.

The theoretical contributions we shall highlight relate to principal–agent problems within hierarchical systems which imply strategic failure in the area of innovation, and short-termism with regard to investment, which could be interpreted as investment in R&D. The former contribution argues that hierarchical organizations often perform poorly in inducing the adoption of innovations and this is due to the large incentive costs they face (Dearden, Ickes, and Samuelson, 1990). The motivation for their analysis was provided by the Soviet Union, but we see no reason why the results are not applicable to hierarchical systems in general. The authors contrast a decentralized *or what they see as a market system* with a hierarchical system. We see the more relevant comparison as differentiating between on the one hand market systems which are characterized by hierarchical decision-making and on the other non-hierarchical, diffused, and decentralized, structures of decision-making. For us, Dearden *et al.* appear to be contrasting an actual hierarchical system which (formerly) existed with an idealized decentralized economy which does not appear to exist. This is not to deny that the former Soviet Union was hierarchical, but rather to point out that the dominant institutions of the free-market system are themselves strongly hierarchical. Within the context we choose to work, we suggest their results are supportive of our implication of strategic failure in technological development in hierarchical systems. The marginal cost of adopting innovations in a decentralized system is simply the technical cost of innovation, incentive cost externalities are eliminated, therefore private and social costs and benefits coincide and efficient levels of adoption prevail. Within hierarchical systems, the technical cost of adoption is augmented by increasingly large incentive costs, therefore the rate of adoption is lower than in decentralized economies and inefficiently low rates of adoption prevail.[4] Dearden *et al.* conclude: 'it appears as if this difficulty is inherent in the hierarchical nature of the system. Mere adjustments in incentive schemes within the hierarchical system are unlikely to counter the problem' (p. 1120). We would agree with them about the former Soviet Union. We would simply add that the same conclusion could be drawn about the former Soviet Union's capitalist adversaries, if with less force.

A related principal–agent problem which has been recently analysed is that between management and shareholders over retentions and the rate of investment (Dickerson, Gibson, and Tsakalotos, 1995). Their paper shows that when these groups act independently the firm will invest suboptimally: for our purposes the suboptimal investment could be in the innovation process. Co-operation would imply greater investment and higher joint income. The result relates back to the interaction between the principal–agent problem, the characteristics of the financial system and the market for corporate control. The agency problem prevents shareholders from adopting the co-operative solution—they are not sure what management will do with the retained earnings. The managers' problem is that they 'have no incentive to commit themselves to a co-operative agreement since they have no guarantee that they will receive the rewards for abstaining from consumption . . . they could be vulnerable to takeover' (Dickerson *et al.*, 363). The authors see the German system of a supervisory board in each company representing stakeholders, 'not only shareholders and management, but all those who have an interest in the continuing success of the firm, including suppliers, customers, employees,

---

[4] The principal–agent problem they choose to focus on is the ratchet effect which appears in repeated principal–agent relationships. The benefits from adoption (for the principal) are in effect 'ratcheted' away in the process.

etc.' (p. 364), as a way out of these dilemmas. They see this sort of insider control as encouraging 'the building and maintenance of long-term, high-trust relationships which tend to be co-operative in nature'. The Japanese system seems to offer similar characteristics. Both systems are considerably removed from the dominant Anglo-US system of governance and control underpinning much of the 'free market' economy.

It is interesting to note at this point that the Dickerson *et al.* model relates back to a much earlier paper (Lancaster, 1973), in which capitalists make strategic decisions subject to the constraint of workers bargaining for wage share. The Lancaster results reveal a socially suboptimal level of investment and again this can be interpreted as a socially suboptimal level of technological progress. The growing importance of transnational production can be seen as both a response to the problem by capitalists, in the sense of weakening the bargaining constraint on their strategic decisions, and as adding a further element to the workers' dilemma, since accumulation may take place without contributing to their welfare. Thus investment and accumulation at the location at which the bargain is struck is even lower. This analysis will pertain eventually to all locations. Transnationality has complicated and widened the disjunction between saving and investment decision. Fully resolving the problem requires joint (co-operative) strategy-making.

But these are merely theoretical speculations about the functioning of the capitalist market economy. Other than referring to cases of the actual suppression of technical progress we have as yet provided no actual evidence of the malfunctioning of the free-market economy in this regard. However, we would maintain that substantial evidence exists although at this time it must be regarded as straws in the wind rather than a systematic documentation of a cast-iron case. In this area of analysis there are major measurement problems and existing research does not allow definitive conclusions (Griliches, 1994).

The first piece of evidence we offer is the low rate of productivity growth in the United States over the last quarter of the twentieth century. At first sight it might appear remarkable that at a time of seemingly enormous scientific and technological advance the most technologically advanced country in the world has failed to maintain a rate of labour-productivity growth in advance of 1 per cent per annum (OECD, 1991, 1995), little more than a third of that sustained over two centuries of English pin manufacturing (Pratten, 1980). Given that we are dealing with the largest economy in the world, and the major source of technology, this lack of performance constitutes one of the most significant economic features of the last quarter of the twentieth century. Furthermore, given that decompositions of US labour productivity growth (1929–82) ascribe more than two-thirds to the growth of scientific and technological knowledge (Denison, 1985), it is natural to seek explanations for the slowdown in productivity in terms of a slowdown in the growth of this knowledge or a decline in its effectiveness.

It seems clear that there has been a coincident dramatic slowdown in the growth rate of R&D in real terms in the United States since the Golden Age; between the period 1953–70 and 1970–87 the growth rate fell from 6.6 to 3.4 per cent per annum (US National Science Board, 1988). In turn this slowdown may be connected to a slowdown in the rate of capital accumulation which embodied technical change (Wolff, 1991), although this has been questioned by Hulten (1992). Whether a given amount of R&D is as effective as it was in the past is a matter of some dispute. In a recent study, Scherer (1993) reports interindustry results for the United States from which he concludes 'technological innovation does not appear to have lost its power in driving productivity growth forward' (p. 22). However, there is a problem of interpretation: relatively dynamic industries with high rates of productivity growth are likely to fund high R&D expenditures. No attempt is made to separate out these effects. Griliches's (1994) survey of earlier studies reveals a mixed picture—some results point to the declining impact of R&D whilst others show no such effect. Griliches provides some new results comparing the periods 1958–73, 1973–89, and 1978–89 for the United States. The results are highly conditional on the presence of the computer industry in the regressions; it is an extreme outlier. Including the computer industry there is no evidence of diminishing 'potency', but excluding it, reducing the industry observations from 143 to 142, shows the potency of R&D after the Golden Age to be much reduced. The earlier problem of interpretation remains.

Jones (1995) looks at the aggregate picture since 1950. The United States has recorded a five-fold increase in scientists and engineers engaged in R&D over the period 1950–90 (from 200,000 to 1 million) but total-factor productivity growth reveals no trend over the same period! He points out that an R&D effect on productivity growth can be salvaged by appeal to a continual exogenous decline in productivity growth, but he offers no insight into this. His results imply no long-run growth effects from a policy of subsidizing R&D. He reports similar results for Germany, France, and Japan (in the case of France and Japan there is evidence of total-factor productivity decline). Earlier studies aimed at evaluating the contribution of R&D to the time series evolution of the growth of productivity, rather than focusing on long-run trend, appear to extend these results. On the basis of his survey, Griliches (1994) is able to conclude that 'the magnitude of the estimated effects was modest, not enough to account for the bulk of the observed residual or the fluctuations in it' (p. 4).

These conclusions, and those of Jones, are consistent with a variety of observations suggesting a limited impact of R&D on technology and thus on production. First, there is the widespread evidence on the long-term decline in the number of patents in relation to the number of engineers and scientists employed in R&D, or the expenditure on R&D, a feature of much of the twentieth century (Griliches, 1994; Evenson, 1991). It is unclear whether the fact that the resulting 'rate of growth of domestic patents in the US was close to zero during the last three decades' (Griliches, 1994) is significant in terms of production and growth because it is obviously an imperfect measure of invention. Second, there has been much talk of black holes within the economy. Bailey and Gordon (1988) report the inefficiency in the use of huge increases in computing power in the US non-manufacturing sector—'the US has been throwing its computers down a big black hole, and presumably other countries are doing the same' (Gordon, 1992). Given that the computer industry plays such a critical role in the R&D/productivity growth nexus this is a worrying observation. Third, is the evidence for R&D expenditures being concentrated within firms which seem unproductive in its use. Using a unique, and very rich source of data on innovations in the UK, Pavitt, Robson, and Townsend (1987) found that the largest firms (at least 10,000 employees), whilst accounting for 80 per cent of recorded R&D in 1975, only managed to generate 47 per cent of significant innovations over the period 1970–9. The system appears to be concentrating research effort where it is least effective in terms of its contribution to raising the rate of innovation and thus technological dynamism. This particularly significant finding, given the quality of the data, is echoed in recent surveys of innovation research. For example Scherer and Ross (1990) conclude, 'very high concentration has a positive effect only in rare cases, and more often it is apt to retard progress by restricting the number of independent sources of initiative and by dampening firms' incentive to gain market position through accelerated R&D' (p. 660). In a similar vein, Cohen (1995) concludes his own survey with the following statement:

the most robust finding from the empirical research . . . is that there is a close, positive monotonic relationship between size and R&D which appears to be roughly proportioned among R&D performers in the majority of industries or when controlling for industry effects. In addition, innovative output appears to increase less than proportionately with firm size and R&D productivity appears to decline with firm size. (p. 196)

The above pieces of evidence, consistent with the presence of strategic failure in the process of technological development within the free-market economy, are only fragmentary. Other interpretations are possible, other evidence may point in different directions, and there are major problems with the data on which we must rely. But having made these qualifications we are left nevertheless with a body of analysis and evidence which points to possible deficiencies in the functioning of the free market in the allocation of resources to technological development. The next section extends this analysis of a malfunctioning economy in the direction of public policy on technology in the quite general case where policy has merely sought to support the allocation of resources to technological development whilst leaving the market as the final arbiter of the *direction* of such investment.

WRONG DIRECTIONS: SOME FAILURES IN PUBLIC POLICY ON TECHNOLOGY

There is wide acceptance of the case for government involvement in the development of technology, given the many and obvious reasons for market failure, with appropriability being a central one (Stoneman and Vickers, 1988). Simply, the market does not offer the appropriate incentives for the generation and diffusion of new knowledge because of the nature of information itself. Whilst it is possible to demonstrate that the market will yield too much research and development—for example, firms may get locked into a socially unproductive product rivalry involving minimum product differentiation but substantial industry-wide investment—nevertheless the usual presumption is that, left to its own devices, too little will be done, so that government needs to step in to raise the level beyond that which the market would choose to deliver. But this leaves the market as the final arbiter of the *direction* of investment in new technology, with government simply raising the overall momentum of investment by favouring research and development with a variety of stimulatory policies. Thus the technology policy of government becomes transmuted into simply subsidizing corporate decisions concerning research and development expenditures. As Geroski (1990) argues, such subsidies tend disproportionately to benefit large firms because they formally account for most measured research and development expenditure, whereas much activity which could accurately be described as research and development goes unrecorded in smaller organizations. We have already reported results which would imply that subsidizing the large corporation in the area of R&D would not be appropriate—it would accentuate the market's tendency to locate R&D in its least socially productive organizations. According to Geroski (1990) there is a tendency for the public sector to end up financing second-best projects, especially those seen to be of national prestige. This may be reflected in the results of empirical research on the returns to R&D: in his survey of this research Griliches (1994) concludes 'the other important and consistent finding is a significant positive premium on company financed R&D relative to the government supported R&D in industry'. More directly there is the question whether or not public subsidy to private firms actually stimulates a higher level of R&D.

In a recent paper Fölster and Trofimov (1996) identify the theoretical possibility that in a world of oligopolistic rivalry subsidy could actually reduce R&D activity and, using a unique data base, demonstrate that the theoretical possibility may have real-world validity. They use a quality ladder model to demonstrate that the strategic use of R&D can become less profitable in the presence of subsidy: there is a balance of effects with the strategy becoming less effective (each firm realizes that subsidy to the other firm decreases the effectiveness of R&D in limiting the rivals' quality improvement), but also less costly. The authors test the model using data from two surveys of Swedish industrial firms in 1988 and 1990. These surveys mapped forty-five technologies over the period 1982 to 1990 and reports on the R&D investment of the group of rival firms operating in the area of each technology. Subsidies are found to have a significant, positive, but not large, effect on the R&D of the firm receiving it: one dollar in subsidy increases the firm's total R&D by 0.2 dollars. However, a dollar of subsidy given to competing firms *decreases* the observed firm's R&D by 0.3 dollars.

This is only one study of the effect of dynamic rivalry on the impact of R&D subsidy, but it is based on a rich and unique data source. The authors suggest their findings are consistent with patterns at the aggregate level: countries with high R&D expenditures in relation to GDP, like the United States, Japan, and Sweden, tend to subsidize R&D less than many other countries, and public subsidy to private firms tends to exhibit low returns, as reported earlier. The question arises about the potential effectiveness of *publicly conducted* R&D, where the results are freely available to all users. It will not be faced with the same strategic effects, but the precise effects will depend on the relation between public and private R&D. These are issues we raise in the next section.

MORE HOPEFUL APPROACHES: SOME PUBLIC POLICY SUCCESSES

As argued earlier there is a general presumption within economics in favour of government support for the innovative process: social returns are expected to exceed private returns. And yet we have presented evidence which questions whether the ultimate impact of R&D is socially beneficial in terms of its contribution to productivity growth: despite an enormous growth in this activity there appears to be no long-term positive trends in total factor productivity growth in the advanced industrial countries; black holes appear in the most unlikely quarters (i.e. where there is the most intensive innovatory activity) and some indices of invention seem to be in decline. Yet a wide array of research findings demonstrate high private and social returns to R&D (Griliches, 1994). How can these observations be reconciled? In a world where R&D is an instrument of corporate strategy *vis-à-vis* consumers and rivals the reconciliation is fairly straightforward. The returns to R&D can be expected to be particularly high because of the considerable retaliatory lag to such policies. It is also possible to argue that consumers are sensitive to minimal product differentiation which itself attracts substantial research activity. For these sort of reasons the private returns to R&D at the firm level can be high without having any perceptible effect on aggregate welfare. At the industry level some of these private returns will wash out—but some will remain. By raising R&D expenditures an industry can raise barriers to the entry of potential rivals, and entry deterring strategic investment of this sort is apparently commonplace, Singh, Utton and Waterson (1997). An industry can also increase the share of the consumer's budget allocated to the output of the industry by using product innovation to expand industry demand, see Pagoulatos and Sorenson (1986).

What about the observed high social returns to R&D? There have been lots of studies of agriculture, going back to the original (Griliches, 1958), innovatory study of hybrid corn and recently surveyed by Huffman and Evenson (1993). There is every reason to maintain that in this case the high observed social returns represent real gains in aggregate social welfare, provided they pass the green test, and we shall reserve further comment on that for later. In the case of oligopolistic industry we have to be more circumspect.

In any industry where output is restricted below the social optimum, for example because of monopoly or oligopolistic power, measures to raise output will be seen as socially productive, at least in partial equilibrium terms, witness the discussions on advertising and welfare, for example in Dixit and Norman (1978). R&D can play this role. Whether its general equilibrium social welfare properties are similar remains dubious, at least within the oligopolistic free-market system. Just as with advertising, R&D can be seen to be an important element of a process by which positions of market power may be created, enhanced and protected. Whilst there is a possible positive side to this process, Pavitt, Robson, and Townsend's rich and unique data base (1987) has been subject to econometric examination and has revealed that innovation is retarded by concentration and restrictions on entry (Geroski and Stewart, 1991). We have reported earlier the commonplace use of R&D as a major element of a strategy of entry deterrence. Thus the circle is closed; corporate R&D is widely used to create the conditions which retard industrial dynamism. These linkages may underpin the generally observed result, previously reported, that the dominant corporations are effectively cornering the market for R&D talent (scientific and engineering) whilst depressing the innovative output of such talent or at least its use. It may serve its function to deter by simply lying on the shelf, so long as the credible threat remains that it can be brought into use should a potential entrant ever threaten to become an actual entrant or should an actual rival ever threaten to bring a similar product off the shelf.

Nevertheless given the malfunctioning of the free-market system it remains the case that, if appropriately directed, public intervention should be capable of securing welfare gains. Surely it is not difficult to imagine that the enormous growth in scientific and engineering talent engaged in R&D over recent history might possibly be organized to achieve some increase in the constant long-term productivity growth achieved in the United States over the twentieth century. Public investment in R&D in agriculture might be an appropriate place to begin to identify more hopeful approaches to public intervention in technology.

Agriculture is an industry whose technological development depends on co-operation between its units of production over R&D, on R&D by its supplying industries, or on the organization of its R&D by government, or on some combination of the three. Its diffuse structure of production renders one of these solutions necessary. Co-operation is an attractive solution but may be difficult to organize without outside help. R&D by supplying industries, which are typically oligopolistic, is problematic given the asymmetry of power between the two sides which is likely to lead to a biased trajectory in R&D investment favouring the supplying industries (chemicals, engineering, etc.). Government R&D, plus public extension policy aimed at the diffusion of innovation across the substantial numbers of farmers involved in production, would seem an attractive organization for R&D activity in this sector, particularly if it can be married to the co-operative solution by say pump-priming co-operative initiatives. It is not surprising therefore that estimates of rates of return to public R&D have been found to be very considerable, Huffman and Evenson (1993). This is R&D conducted by government in agricultural research stations or in the universities. The returns to this form of organization of research contrast sharply with the poor or non-existent returns to public investment in industrial R&D which consists primarily of subsidized R&D in the dominant corporations. We do not have many examples for oligopolistic industries of government funding research directed at the industry but conducted by some form of public agency outside the industry. There are cases, and the universities are obviously one form of organization used, but outside agriculture publicly funded research institutions seem to be engaged in basic research rather than research directed at the particular research needs of specific industries. The social returns to such research will be difficult to pinpoint and we know of only few attempts to do so: as Swann (1996) concludes, 'There is relatively little econometric research which attempts to quantify directly the effects of basic research on productivity growth at an aggregate level' (p. 8).

Nevertheless, there are cases of public agencies conducting research aimed at the particular needs of specific industries and we feel there is much to be learned from them. From our perspective the Third Italy provides many examples of the successful non-hierarchical provision of R&D to systems of integrated small-firm production by local and regional government agencies acting in concert with co-operative institutions set up by these firms. During the turmoil of the 1970s these agglomerations of small production units forming industrial districts or networks emerged as efficient competitors to other forms of production organization, such as the dominant large-scale, vertically integrated corporation (Piore and Sabel, 1984; Best, 1990). This emergence of the 'new competition' depended on many things, but a crucial factor was the willingness of local and regional government to join with other public agencies in the provision of technological knowledge to such networks; the crucial point is that government alone is not the actor, and that what matters is public agencies/actors more generally: 'technological knowledge (had) to be provided as a "club good" for the network' (Bianchi and Bellini, 1991). The most famous example is the textile district in Emilia Romagna. An information centre, CITER, was established as a consortium involving regional government and small firms' associations. 'The centre became the catalyst for the emerging group of innovators, because it has made explicit an existing innovation problem, and it has induced the individual firms to accelerate the pace of innovation' (Bianchi and Bellini, 1991). Subsequently computer-aided design facilities were introduced.

Similar experiences have been reported elsewhere in the region of Emilia Romagna, for example in ceramics, shoes, and agricultural machinery; and in other regions, for example, a university consortium in Puglia providing services related to information technology, a regional agency promoting technology transfer from universities in Genova, a centre for the provision of digital technologies in Ancona (Bianchi and Bellini, 1991). These policies appear to have been especially successful, (see for example Best, 1990), and seem to have created a 'remarkable resilience' in the face of adversity, for example the rapid growth of low-cost production in and around the Pacific Rim (Dei Ottati, 1996). And there are other examples scattered throughout Western Europe, in places such as Baden–Württemberg (Germany), West Jutland (Denmark), the Southern Regions of France, and Catalunya. The existence of industrial districts supported by local and regional research agencies appears to have achieved an extraordinary dynamism. Furthermore, Japan also appears to provide an organizational infrastructure for the modernization of the small-firm sector as an entire system through public agencies (Best, 1990). By the provision of research facilities, and the fostering of co-operation within the small-firm sector, government, in these various cases, has helped to ensure the dynamic efficiency of small-scale production and precluded the necessity to move to larger-firm structures and hierarchical organizations. Within our perspective, this represents a move towards a socially optimal structure of production, allowing a diffuseness of production required by the search for a more democratic structure of decision-making.

These various examples would seem to suggest a complementarity between public and private R&D, an issue we raised earlier. This suggestion receives econometric support in a broader context in a recent paper explaining R&D intensity differences across countries (Chou, Kimura, and Talmain, 1995). After correcting for domestic and international scale effects, they discover that non-commercial basic research (public) appears to induce higher levels of business-enterprise research expenditure (private). This gives further support to the idea that public intervention in the area of R&D should be organized as publicly conducted R&D allowing free access by all interested parties to the results, rather than concentrating on subsidizing the private activities of dominant business corporations, the results of which will be broadly inaccessible to other interested parties. This is in line with the results of earlier studies (see the review by Hall, 1995).

There has been much interest over recent years in identifying the roots of Japanese industrial success. It has been noted that the Japanese government has been following a more proactive developmental strategy than either the USA or Europe and a different sort of technology policy has been embedded within it (Mowery, 1995). Whilst Japan sustains high levels of R&D intensity, the government share of national R&D is low (20 per cent) and its share of R&D performed in industry is almost non-existent (2 per cent) (Odagiri and Goto, 1993), certainly much lower than the case for the USA, respectively 48 and 35 per cent (Mowery, 1995). At the same time Japanese government priorities, within their budget, are quite different. More than half (50.8 per cent in 1987) of government budget appropriations in Japan go to education, and nearly a quarter (23.2 per cent) go to energy, whereas only 4.5 per cent go to defence (Cohen and Noll, 1992). This contrasts with the USA, where only 3.6 per cent go to education and the same to energy, whereas defence takes 68.6 per cent. Since defence R&D is not primarily directed at economic development, the impact on economic performance of public R&D on economic performance in the USA is likely to be diminished relative to Japanese public R&D. (This does not, of course, deny that spillovers from defence R&D may have a significant positive effect on economic development and indeed that defence itself constitutes a major part of the economy and thus its own dynamism is an element in overall economic dynamism.)

These data suggest that Japan has sustained high levels of R&D intensity without major government financing and that the impact of public expenditure may have been greater because little was diverted to the ends of military strategy as opposed to a strategy of economic development. The emphasis of Japanese policy has been to create co-operative research programmes within industry and to use public funding as a catalyst for such development. Also,

the research agenda of successful programmes generally was established by industry or with significant input from private managers, rather than being determined primarily by government managers. Many of the most effective programmes of co-operative research, particularly in Japan, have focused less on advancing the scientific or technological frontier than on diffusing advanced technologies among participants and narrowing the gap between average–best practice. (Mowery, 1995: 527)

In so far as Japan has established an unrivalled industrial dynamism among the advanced industrial countries this policy would appear to have paid off, although whether it can be sustained in the future is widely debated:

it may be a policy more suited to moving to the international frontier rather than penetrating it. Nevertheless, given the perspective on welfare and policy advanced in this chapter, there are questions to be raised about the policy on its own terms.

Whilst the fostering of co-operation among agglomerations of small firms in the development and use of innovations appears generally unproblematic and is to be encouraged by appropriate public investment aimed at a system of production, we should generally be more circumspect about encouraging co-operation among dominant corporations and providing public investment support for research agendas proposed by such groupings. Rather than simply augmenting the power of such groups, public agencies should generally seek to open up their agenda and strategy-making to a broader array of interests. It is notable that recent public concerns expressed in Japan with regard to the so-called 'hollowing-out' of the Japanese manufacturing economy have been voiced with particular anxiety by the small-firms community who have helplessly watched the major corporations move their production and demand for the output of Japanese small firms offshore. The private success of co-operative strategies within the large-firm sector does not represent unambiguous success for the Japanese economy and community. We shall develop this point further in the last section.

A WAY FORWARD

As mentioned above, there is a wide acceptance of the case for government involvement in the development of technology but the conventional view is that, essentially, the market should remain the final arbiter of the direction of innovation with government simply raising the overall momentum by favouring R&D with a variety of stimulatory policies. In contrast we would put the policy emphasis much more on the qualitative dimension. Whether the total magnitude of research and development, and related expenditures on extension services aimed at promoting the diffusion of technology, should be raised or not within a particular area of economic activity would be derivative of the community's (local, regional, national, or supranational) overall industrial strategy. The socially incomplete nature of the decision structure, reflecting the concentration of strategic decision-making in a few hands, within the modern free-market economy, dominated as it is by hierarchically organized, large corporations, means that the pattern of research and development cannot be expected to be socially optimal.

Given that the development of new technology is so fundamental to the pace, direction and form of industrial development it is necessary to consider the question of government within a much broader perspective. Otherwise it is all too easy for the technology policy of government to become transmuted into simply subsidizing corporate decisions concerning R&D expenditures rather than aiming to raise the basic dynamism of the industrial economy. Following research by Nelson (1993) it may be concluded that 'from the viewpoint of an entire economy, improving the ability of mature industries to absorb and exploit the products of R&D intensive industries may be more important than nurturing strength in these so-called "sun-rise" industries' (Mowery, 1995: 543).

We would argue, following our earlier presentation of an alternative view of welfare and policy, that it is necessary to design future government initiatives as part of a wider concern to develop a diffuse, deconcentrated economy consistent with a move away from a concentrated structure of decision-making. Thus in the area of technological change we need to be circumspect about a policy favouring scale. Following our earlier discussions automatic grants and subsidies would therefore be inappropriate as would a policy favouring national champions. This focus away from large organizations may well have a positive impact on innovation, crucially the output of the R&D process, given their low recorded productivity in this regard (Cohen, 1995). The considerable evidence on the inefficiency of the R&D process within the large, dominant corporations which control the vast majority of industrial R&D resources is supportive of the view that the hierarchical large firm is, by its very nature, an essentially stifling organization where individual talent is all too often constrained by institutional straight-jackets. IBM's current dramatic difficulties, despite its former enormous economic power, may be illustrative of the general problem. We have considered certain theoretical insights into this phenomenon earlier in the chapter. Also, following Sah and Stiglitz (1986, 1988), Delmastro (1997) demonstrates that a polyarchy (for example, an industrial district) selects a larger proportion of available projects than does a hierarchy. Within the terms of his model, serial structures (hierarchies) are more conservative than parallel structures (polyarchies) in taking a particular type of decision, say as regards an innovation. More generally, it seems likely that promoting an economy of smaller firms will free more and more individuals to pursue their own and their firm's development, and thus encourage innovative activity. Smaller firms can operate in ways that encourage individuals to contribute ideas about development. They can also operate in ways that better facilitate human development, again feeding the innovation process.

Nevertheless a successful system for encouraging technological progress requires far more than shifting research resources away from large hierarchical firms; especially important is the design of mutually supportive organizations and arrangements to meet the collective needs of smaller firms; that is, public investment in a wider infrastructure rather than state aid in the traditional sense. These needs may focus on, for instance, the availability of sophisticated techniques for designing new products, and access to long-run finance and hands-on managerial advice, identified by Geroski (1990) as important for supporting risky research and development projects (see also Minns and Rogers, 1990). To meet these needs we have already reviewed evidence of a number of regional cases within Europe with experience of the successful design and operation of supportive structures. Consider the case of CITER (Centro Informazione Tessile dell'Emilia Romagna), a textile and clothing industry support centre for the region which we described earlier. In the context of the alternative approach to welfare and policy we have proposed, the significance of this initiative is that it appears to be a successful example of a non-hierarchical, co-operative institution supporting small producers by efficiently providing services they collectively require. There are economies of scale associated with the development and use of new techniques and CITER appears to have obtained such scale economies without the need for large, hierarchical organizations. Small producers using the computer-aided design system have access to the sort of techniques usually associated with large-scale production, yet they apparently maintain their independence, including their independence in design capability. This is precisely the sort of initiative that our theoretical analysis suggests is essential to successful economic development—and we have many variegated examples of this sort of successful institution scattered throughout Europe, not dominating national technology but important elements of successful regional development.[5]

When advocating a diffuse and deconcentrated economy it is natural to look at Third Italy where the small-firms sector has received so much attention by policy-makers and has been so successful, but lessons can be drawn from the other European experiences and indeed beyond. The Baden-Württemburg model of technology transfer, linking the universities and technical institutes in the region to the system of small and medium-sized enterprises (Löhn and Stadelmeier, 1990); the provision of forty-five technical training centres in West Jutland, Denmark, which appears to have stimulated the dramatic development of a highly diffused engineering industry within an essentially rural community (Kristensen, 1990); the high technology industrial districts of the United States developed in close association with local universities (Piore and Sabel, 1984); the 'indispensable infrastructure' of innovation within US agriculture provided by the federal government in the USA (Piore and Sabel, 1984); the establishment of public corporations (the Japan Electronic Computer Company in 1961; the Japan Robot Leasing Company in 1980) to purchase domestically produced computer equipment and robotics and lease them to (small) Japanese firms (Anchordoguy, 1989).

All represent successful, variegated examples of the non-hierarchical provision of technology to systems of small and medium-sized enterprises. In so

[5] In the UK the ceramics industry has created a similar type of co-operative institution.

far as the *production* of technology involves scale economies and the *use* of the technology does not, at least beyond a size of firm consistent with a diffuse industrial district, the provision of technology by public agency and/or co-operation ensures an effective, non-hierarchical system. Where current technologies necessitate large-scale production, policy should be augmented to include efforts aimed at discovering ways of changing these technologies to suit small-scale users of the technology. Lest some see this as a wasteful diversion of scarce resources it should be added that the process of selection of technologies within the free-market system is not without bias. The bias will be introduced by those making strategic decisions over technology. Whilst greater efficiency may be sought, more fundamentally the technology must suit their interests. This can be expected to imply a technology which allows them to effectively control the process of production and also be consistent with the objective of market control. Thus a technology incorporating economies of scale and scope will generally be preferred, as will one favouring the hierarchical organization of production. There can be no presumption that existing technologies are either optimal or invariant. If we are serious about wanting to extend the ambit of a diffuse system of production, for reasons of social efficiency, then we need to investigate the possibilities of new technologies consistent with the efficient operation of such systems.

Thus our approach to technology policy again implies the need to view government initiatives in a broad context: initiatives to foster and stimulate technological change should be designed as part of a wider concern with developing a democratic economy, necessitated by the strategic failure associated with the concentrated decision structures embedded within the free-market system. But different regions and different countries have very different starting positions, witness the stark contrast between the established advanced capitalist economies, the transition economies and the various groups of developing economies. Building diffuse, deconcentrated economies from this contrasting patchwork implies the need for a bottom-up and varied approach rooted in local communities, with these communities encouraged to pursue their common interests at national and indeed multinational level. A system for fostering technological progress that builds from local communities, to national communities and thence to the possibility of multinational communities—multinational webs as envisaged in Sugden (1996).

A web is seen to be a large group of production units which taken individually are relatively small but which taken as a group constitutes a production process on a large scale, with units co-operating with each other by providing mutual support in a process which also promotes the emergence of new and rival production units, without which the web would be likely to wither and stagnate.[6] There would be obvious tensions but the web would provide a con-

---

[6] Government could support such development by providing start-up capital which is often seen as problematic in the case of small, new enterprises.

text in which tensions could be faced and resolved. (It is notable that similar tensions, in the use of common resources, have been resolved by community institutions (see for example, Ostrom and Gardner 1993). The industrial districts discussed earlier are examples of webs geographically confined. A source of great strength for Italian industrial districts has been their interlinked development as societies and economies.

In order to achieve a capacity for invention and innovation, . . . it is essential that many people understand the technology with which they work. This in turn requires continual informal interaction in cafés and bars and in the street. In this way new ideas are formed and transmitted.   (Brusco, 1990: 16)

This is clearly problematic at a multinational level, although multinational educational institutions dedicated to serving particular webs may seem an appropriate institutional structure which might act as a partial replacement of café society (Sugden, 1996).

It would be the function of public policy to provide the educational, scientific, and technological infrastructure which would allow these webs to flourish and grow. Many countries are coming round to the view that small business policy has to be taken seriously, and Japan has taken this more seriously than most over an extended period (Best, 1990). The recent White Paper on Small and Medium Enterprises (1996) states that 'any revitalization of the Japanese economy cannot realistically be anticipated in the absence of a vibrant and dynamic small business sector', but the shift of manufacturing offshore by the large enterprises is causing huge problems for the sector. Various possible transformations of the small-business sector are being discussed, including the possibility of learning from the experiences of Third Italy in terms of developing local networks (Japan Small Business Research Institute, 1996). We agree with the sentiment expressed in the report that 'the small business sector has become the perfect environment for persons to realise their full potential as individuals' (p. 252). We would simply add that in order to 'make themselves more attractive as places of employment for an altogether larger section of the population than they are managing to attract at present' (JSBRI, 1996: 252) they need to build supportive networks of production which are both multinational and open to the entry of new firms and new ideas within the context of a supportive public infrastructure. We suggest that only in this way will a new structure emerge capable of supplanting the existing dominance of the hierarchically organized transnational corporations which we see as primarily responsible for the strategic failure of the free-market system. In terms of technology policy, we strongly concur with the view expressed by Metcalfe (1993) that an adequate innovation system 'is likely to be a pluralist system supporting many different sources of innovation with an emphasis on the diversity of micro level activity rather than a centrally-driven conception of the innovation process' (p. 232).

REFERENCES

Anchordoguy, M. (1989), *Computer Inc.: Japan's Challenge to IBM*, Cambridge, Mass.: Harvard University Press.

Aoki, M. (1990), 'Towards an Economic Model of the Japanese Firm', *Journal of Economic Literature*, 28/1: 1–27.

Baily, M. N. and Gordon, R. J. (1988) 'Measurement Issues, The Productivity Slowdown, and the Explosion of Computer Power', *Brookings Papers on Economic Activity*, 19/2: 347–420.

Best, M. (1990), *The New Competition: Institutions of Industrial Restructuring*, Cambridge: Polity Press.

Bianchi, P. and Bellini, N. (1991), 'Public Policies for Local Networks of Innovators', *Research Policy*, 4.

Brusco, S. (1990), 'The Idea of the Industrial District: Its Genesis', in F. Pyke, G. Becattini, and W. Sengenberger (eds.), *Industrial Districts and Inter-Firm Cooperation in Italy*, Geneva: International Institute for Labour Studies.

Coase, R. H. (1937), 'The Nature of the Firm', *Economica*, 4: 386–405.

Chou, C., Kimura, F., and Talmain, G. (1995), 'R&D Effort, Domestic and International Scale Effects', Second World Congress of the Econometric Society, Tokyo.

Cohen, W. (1995), 'Empirical Studies of Innovative Activities', in P. Stoneman (ed.), *Handbook of the Economics of Innovation and Technological Change*, Oxford: Blackwell.

Cohen, L. R. and Noll, R. (1992), 'Research and Development', in H. J. Aaron and C. L. Schultze (eds.), *Setting Domestic Priorities: What Can Government Do?*, Washington DC, The Brookings Institution.

Cowling, K. and Sugden, R. (1993), 'Industrial Development, Markets and Democratic Processes: Fostering Technological Change', *Occasional Papers in Industrial Strategy*, 12, Research Centre for Industrial Strategy, University of Birmingham (Feb.).

———— (1994), *Beyond Capitalism: Towards a New World Economic Order*, London: Pinter.

———— (1998), 'The Essence of the Modern Corporation: Markets, Strategic Decision-Making and the Theory of the Firm', *Manchester School*, 66/1 (Jan.), 59–86.

Dearden, J., Ickes, B., and Samuelson, L. (1990), 'To Innovate or not to Innovate: Incentives and Innovation in Hierarchies', *American Economic Review*, 80/5 (Dec.), 1105–24.

Dei Ottati, G. (1996), 'The Remarkable Resilience of the Industrial Districts of Tuscany', ESRC Centre for Business Research, Cambridge, Working paper, 28.

Delmastro, M. (1997), 'A Critical Review of Hierarchical Models of the Firm', mimeo, Department of Economics, University of Warwick.

Denison, E. F. (1985), *Trends in American Economic Growth 1929–1982*, Washington, DC: The Brookings Institution.

Dickerson, A. P., Gibson, H. D., and Tsakalotos, E. (1995), 'Short-termism and Underinvestment: The Influence of Financial Systems', *Manchester School*, 63/4 (Dec.), 351–67.

Dixit, A. and Norman, V. (1978), 'Advertising and Welfare', *Bell Journal of Economics* (June).

Evenson, R. E. (1991), 'Patent Data by Industry: Evidence for Invention Potential Exhaustion?', in *Technology and Productivity: The Challenge for Economic Policy*, Paris: OECD, 238–48.

Fölster, S. and Trofimov, G. (1996), 'Do Subsidies to R&D Actually Stimulate R&D Investment?', Industrial Institute of Economic and Social Research, Stockholm.

Geroski, P. (1990), 'Encouraging Investment in Science and Technology, in K. Cowling and R. Sugden (eds.), *A New Economic Policy for Britain: Essays on the Development of Industry*, Manchester: Manchester University Press.

—— and Stewart, G. (1991), 'Competitive Rivalry and the Response of Markets to Innovative Opportunities', in S. Arndt and G. W. McKenzie (eds.), *The Competitiveness of the UK Economy*, London: Macmillan.

Gordon, R. J. (1992), 'Discussion of N. Crafts, "Productivity Growth Reconsidered"', *Economic Policy* (Oct.), 387–426.

Griliches, Z. (1958), 'Hybrid Corn: An Exploration in the Economics of Technological Change', *Econometrica*, 25/4 (Oct.), 501–22.

—— (1994), 'Productivity, R&D and the Data Constraint', *American Economic Review*, 84/1 (Mar.), 1–23.

Hall, B. H. (1993), 'New Evidence on the Impacts of R&D', *Brookings Papers on Economic Activity: Microeconomics*.

—— (1995), 'The Private and Social Returns to Research and Development: What Have we Learned', unpub. paper (June).

Huffman, W. E. and R. E. Evenson (1993), *Science for Agriculture*, Ames, Ia.: Iowa State University Press.

Hulten, C. R. (1992), 'Growth Accounting when Technical Change is Embodied in Capital', *American Economic Review*, 82/4 (Sept.), 964–80.

Hymer, S. H. (1972), 'The Multinational Corporation and the Law of Uneven Development', in J. N. Bhagwati (ed.), *Economics and World Order*, London: Macmillan.

Japan Small Business Research Institute (JSBRI) (1996), *The Age of Small Business: the Foundation of the Japanese Economy*, Tokyo.

Jones, C. I. (1995), 'Time Series Tests of Endogenous Growth Models, *Quarterly Journal of Economics*, 110/2 (May), 495–526.

Kristensen, P. (1990), 'Education, Technical Culture and Regional Prosperity in Denmark', in G. Sweeney, T. Casey, P. Kristensen, and N. R. Prujai (eds.), *Education, Technical Culture and Regional Prosperity*, Dublin: SICA.

Loasby, B. (1995), 'Understanding Markets', Discussion and Working Papers 2:95, Turku School of Economics and Business Administration, Turku, Finland.

Lancaster, K. (1973), 'The Dynamic Inefficiency of Capitalism', *Journal of Political Economy*, 85/5 (Sept./Oct.), 1092–1109.

Löhn, J. and Stadelmeier, M. (1990), 'The Baden-Württemberg Model of Technology Transfer', in K. Cowling and H. Tomann (eds.), *Industrial Policy After 1992: An Anglo-German Perspective*, London: Anglo-German Foundation.

Metcalfe, J. S. (1993), 'Technology Policy and Innovation Systems from an Evolutionary Perspective', in K. Hughes (ed.), *The Future of UK Competitiveness and the Role of Industrial Policy*, London: Policy Studies Institute.

260   KEITH COWLING AND ROGER SUGDEN

Minns, R. and Rogers, M. (1990), 'The State as Public Entrepreneur', in Cowling and Sugden (eds.), *A New Economic Policy for Britain*.
Mowery, D. (1995), 'The Practice of Technology Policy', in Stoneman (ed.), *Handbook of the Economics of Innovation and Technological Change*.
Nelson, R. R. (1993), 'A Retrospective', in R. R. Nelson (ed.), *National Innovation Systems: A Comparative Study*, Oxford: Oxford University Press.
Odagiri, H. and Goto, A. (1993), 'The Japanese System of Innovation: Past, Present, and Future', in Nelson (ed.), *National Innovation Systems*.
OECD (1995), *Historical Statistics*, Paris: OECD.
Ostrom, E. and Gardner, R. (1993), 'Coping with Asymmeries in the Commons: Self-Governing Irrigation Systems Can Work', *Journal of Economic Perspectives*, 7/4: 93–112.
Pagoulatos, E. and Sorenson, R. (1986), 'What Determines the Industry Elasticity of Demand?', *International Journal of Industrial Organization*, 4/3: 237–50.
Pavitt, K., Robson, M., and Townsend, J. (1987), 'Size Distribution of Innovating Firms in the UK: 1945–83', *Journal of Industrial Economics*, 35: 297–316.
Piore, M. and Sabel, C. (1984), *The Second Industrial Divide: Possibilities for Prosperity*, New York: Basic Books.
Pratten, C. (1980), 'The Manufacture of Pins', *Journal of Economic Literature*, 18/1: 93–6.
Radner, R. (1992), 'Hierarchy: The Economics of Managing', *Journal of Economic Literature*, 30/3: 1382–415.
Scherer, F. M. (1980), *Industrial Market Structure and Economic Performance*, 2nd edn., Chicago: Rand McNally, 431–3.
—— (1993), 'Lagging Productivity Growth: Measurement, Technology and Shock Effects', *Empirica*, 20/1: 5–24.
—— and Ross, D. (1990), *Industrial Market Structure and Economic Performance*, 3rd edn., Boston: Houghton Mifflin.
Sah, R. K. and Stiglitz, J. E. (1986), 'The Architecture of Economic Systems: Hierarchies and Polyarchies', *American Economic Review*, 76: 716–27.
—— —— (1988), 'Committees, Hierarchies and Polyarchies', *Economic Journal*, 98: 451–70.
Simon, H. A. (1991), 'Organizations and Markets', *Journal of Economic Perspectives*, 5/2: 25–44.
Singh, S., Utton, M., and Waterson, M. (forthcoming), 'Strategic Behaviour of Incumbent Firms in the UK', *International Journal of Industrial Organization*.
Small and Medium Enterprise Agency, MITI (1996), *Small Business in Japan*, White Paper on Small and Medium Enterprises in Japan, Tokyo.
Stoneman, P. and Vickers, J. (1988), 'The Assessment: The Economics of Technology Policy', *Oxford Review of Economic Policy*, 4, pp. i–xvi.
Sugden, R. (1996), 'Multinational Economies and the Law of Uneven Development', *Occasional Papers in Industrial Strategy*, 37 (May), Research Centre for Industrial Strategy, University of Birmingham.
Swann, P. (1996), 'The Economic Value of Publicly Funded Basic Research: A Framework for Assessing the Evidence', mimeo, University of Manchester.
United Nations (1993), *World Investment Report 1993: Transnational Corporations and Integrated International Production*, New York: United Nations.

US National Science Board (1988), *Science and Engineering Indicators*, Washington, DC, 294.

Wolff, E. (1991), 'Capital Formation and Productivity Convergence over the Long Term', *American Economic Review*, 81/3 (June), 565–79.

INDEX